Alexander Alexandrovitch Zin a small village some 180 miles north east of Moscow. After serving with the Soviet armed forces as a pilot during the Second World War he studied philosophy at Moscow University and held a series of academic posts both at that university and in the Institute of Philosophy of the Soviet Academy of Sciences. As an outspoken anti-Stalinist Zinoviev came under increasing harassment and was finally expelled from the Soviet Union in 1978. Professor Zinoviev today lives in Munich. He has written a number of books on the subject of Communism, including *The Yawning Heights*, *Notes of a Nightwatchman* and *The Radiant Future*.

ALEXANDER ZINOVIEV

The Reality of Communism

Translated by Charles Janson

PALADIN
Granada Publishing

Paladin Books
Granada Publishing Ltd
8 Grafton Street, London W1X 3LA

Published by Paladin Books 1985

First published in Great Britain by
Victor Gollancz Ltd 1984

TRANSLATOR'S NOTE
I am most grateful to Mr Michael Kirkwood, Senior Lecturer,
School of Slavonic and East European Studies, University of
London, for his revision of my translation of this sometimes very
difficult text. He has made a good number of outright corrections
and introduced many improvements that will bring home to the
reader the significance of the author's more subtle arguments and
paradoxes.

ISBN 0-586-08500-9

Printed and bound in Great Britain by
Collins, Glasgow

Set in Baskerville

CONTENTS

vi

THE REASON

In our time Communism no longer appears as a system of abstract ideas and starry-eyed promises. It is no longer an event somewhere on the periphery of civilization. For some it is the standard way of life; for others the threat of invasion by powerful Communist states; for yet others it seems the likely next stage in their country's internal development. And yet the West's notions of the actual forms of life in a Communist country are still such as to provoke an ironic smile, angry indignation or dumb bewilderment. For instance, some Westerners were chatting about the picture of Communist society which I drew in *The Yawning Heights*. One said: 'As regards queuing you've obviously exaggerated. What would someone want to stand for hours in a queue for, if he can come back a few hours later and get what he wants, without queuing?' The Soviet émigrés present laughed until they cried when they heard my interlocutor's remark. For them it was a well-known axiom that, according to the rules of life under Communism, the ordinary citizen without special privileges must, on a specific number of occasions and in one way or another, waste a certain amount of time in order to satisfy some simple need.

Let me give another example. I was talking about one of the laws of Communism as it actually exists, of its eagerness to penetrate every possible nook and cranny, of its efforts to control its environment and make it identical to itself. One of my audience made this comment, 'All right, let's suppose Soviet soldiers arrive here in Western Europe. They'll see that the standard of living is higher here than in the Soviet Union, that there are democratic freedoms and other blessings of civilization. When they've seen all this and understood that the Soviet leaders had been deceiving them, they'll go back home, turn things upside down and live like we do in the West.'

This time I and my former compatriots were in no mood for laughter. If the soldiers of Communist countries invade Western Europe, there won't be much left of the Western form of life for the purpose of comparison and moralistic conclusions. Besides, if people from Communist countries come here, it won't be to learn anything, but to teach, and to foist on the West their own system and standard of living. And they will have a good chance of doing this, because there are more than enough Communists and fellow-travellers in the West.

And again I hear this reply: 'So what?' 'There's nothing terrible about that,' said another conversationalist, 'the Western countries will become convinced through experience that the Communist way of life is repulsive and then they will reject it.' What can I say to that?! Alas, that there won't be any 'then'. 'Then' will already be too late. A country isn't an individual person; a social system isn't a wife one has grown tired of. A victory for the Communist social system in a country entails a fundamental and far-reaching restructuring of society. In a short space of time a large number of people will occupy a privileged position and set themselves up in comparative comfort. The majority of the population will be relieved of many worries and will receive a minimum living standard. The sort of man who will come out on top is the one whom the new system suits more than the old. Social selection will so influence the conduct of future generations that people will no longer be fitted for, or interested in, a reversal of history. A mighty apparatus of power and ideological indoctrination will be installed in short order. It will suppress all attempts to turn back the clock. The sacrificial victims will soon be forgotten. The authorities will begin a frenetic acclimatization of the mass of the population to the new conditions of existence. There will no longer be a way back. In order to 'return' to the blessings of the Western civilization, they will have to begin the battle all over again, from within the new social system. To do that society will have to complete a new historical cycle of many centuries at the cost of hitherto unheard-of sacrifices. And it is still doubtful whether such a 'return' would succeed. 'You exaggerate the stability and the power of the Communist regime' was the answer I got to that.

Quite often I bump into people who regard the Communist regime as unstable because it is founded on deception and coercion, exercised by a handful of Communist rulers. However, most commentators no longer believe this contention. But even those in politics and political science, if one is to judge by their speeches and books, have a very confused idea of the Communist regime and the sources of its power and stability. They use a conceptual system which is appropriate for the analysis of Western societies, but which loses all sense when applied to Communist society; and they apply to it criteria which are so alien that any reliable results are only achieved by accident.

A striking example of this was the reaction in the West to the incursion of Soviet troops into Afghanistan. It took the West unawares and caused dismay, although from the viewpoint of predictive possibility the event was a trivial one. Not long before the invasion the USSR withdrew a part of its forces from Eastern Germany. Many in the West interpreted that as a gesture in the interests of peace. In the middle of December I gave a lecture to the German-American Society of Munich and said that there was nothing peace-loving whatever about this action and that the Soviet tanks which had been withdrawn would soon appear elsewhere where they were more needed, for example in Afghanistan. I'm afraid that my audience regarded this prediction rather as a rhetorical device. I do not claim that it had much value within a theory of knowledge. On the contrary, I stress its banality. But it is only banal if and when ratiocinations about Communism make disciplined use of a conceptual system which is in fact applicable to a study of Communism.

Then there are the quite normal hopes of the West that Western Communism would be quite different from Soviet Communism. At times even opponents of Communism attribute many of the negative features of the Communist way of life to purely Russian conditions. They think that what exists in the USSR isn't real Communism (or Socialism). They hope for 'Communism with a human face' or 'Democratic Communism' in the West. This kind of judgement, which seems so monstrously inept to anyone who has experienced real-life Communism, is as frequent here in the West as are the views about the absence of civil rights and about repression in the Soviet camp which have become habitual. It is these very views which have prompted me to write this book.

MY PURPOSE

The conception of Communism as an actual type of society which I set out here took shape in my mind many years ago. But it was only fairly recently that I found it possible to state it publicly. This I did in my books *The Yawning Heights* (written in 1974), *Notes of a Nightwatchman* (1975), *The Radiant Future* (1976), *In the Ante-Chamber of Paradise* (1977) and *The Yellow House* (1978); and also in speeches here in the West, some of which are put in the book *Without Illusions* published in 1979. These books and speeches taken together give a description of actual Communist society, beginning with its deep abstract laws and ending with the details of real life and the psychology of its citizens. This was done in literary, not scientific, form. But I see no shortcoming in this because I am consciously not addressing a small circle of specialists and hoping for their approval, but a large circle of ordinary people who may derive some benefit from my observations. But in this book I shall chart the most fundamental points of my understanding of Communism outside the literary context. In the course of it I shall try to give a more or less generalized description of that particular type of life and to reveal the method of thought which enabled me to make my judgements.

It is inevitable that the problem of method in reasoning, interpretation, and investigation should come to the fore. The facts about life in Communist societies have already been accumulated in abundance. They are widely known. But knowledge of facts does not of itself necessarily lead to understanding. There is still a need for orientation. Somehow we have to order and process the facts, and on the basis of these facts invent a system of ideas and judgements which we can use to orientate ourselves and see ahead in the ever-changing and unusually confusing flux of life. But this is impossible without a special technique and methodology. I investigated this technique professionally over many years. My results were published in many works on logic and scientific method; and perhaps I may refer those of my readers who are interested to them. In this book I will expound from time to time a minimum of the methodology of scientific thought appropriate to the problems discussed. I will try to do this in a generally accessible form and within the context of judgements about Communism. Moreover, these methodological parts of the book will constitute an essential part of the picture of society itself; so that everything that I have said and will say in the so-called 'preliminary' sections of the book is not a preparation for the social picture which is to be exhibited later but already fragments of the picture itself.

I have lived the greater part of my life in the Soviet Union. Obviously, then, the concrete facts of the Soviet social life have given me and still give me the substance of my reflections. But this book is not about the peculiarities of the Soviet Union. It is a description of every Communist society, the Soviet Union included. However, the Soviet Union does not appear exceptional in one sense. It was there that the type of society, in which Communist relationships between people are dominant, first entered history. There it was not imposed from outside as in the Eastern European countries; it was established immanently according to social laws and in certain historical conditions. It was in the Soviet Union that Communism quickly grew to classical maturity and clearly revealed its merits and its defects. It was there that it became an infectious example for other countries, the purveyor of Communist ideas and of the means of their fulfilment. Victorious and secure in the

Soviet Union, Communism became the strong-point and the stimulus for the Communist attack on the world in general. In one way or another it attracted the other parts of the planet into its sphere of influence. Thus real-life Communism is not simply an aggregate of independent Communist countries similar to each other, but a specific phenomenon whose defined core is the Soviet Union.

However, if I extrapolate from the particularities of the Soviet Union, I do so in order to highlight something which is true of Communism per se, irrespective of however many individual examples there might be of societies of that type. Indeed if the Soviet Union were the only Communist country, this extrapolation would be just as possible, and in fact indispensable for a scientific understanding of its social system. In this book I shall not pay attention to China and its pretensions to a historical role in order to avoid complicating the exposition. The general picture of Communist society is independent of the presence of empires vying with each other for the title.

From a cognitive viewpoint the Soviet Union does have advantages. Just as in its day England was the country of classical capitalism for those interested in studying the mechanics of the latter, so the Soviet Union became and still remains the country of classical Communism. It is here that one could and still can study the phenomena and laws of the Communist form of life of the last decades in their purest form. Much more than in the other Communist countries one can study them almost under 'laboratory conditions'. In the Soviet Union the phenomena of Communism have developed their clearest forms. That goes also for those phenomena whose social features are amorphous and dim in actuality: in the Soviet Union the very indistinctness of social manifestation is, so to speak, most clearly delineated. The reader must get used to the fact that this type of apparent paradox is characteristic of the Communist version of life. In the books which I have mentioned scores of such 'paradoxes' came to light. Critics regarded them as a literary device, although I was aiming at as literal a representation of reality as possible and not at all at verbal conjuring tricks.

Of course, if one constantly has before one the example of life in Soviet society it is difficult to detach oneself entirely from its individual characteristics which may not exist in other countries. However there is no need to jump to conclusions about that. Because something doesn't exist today it doesn't follow that it won't happen tomorrow. Besides, different countries invent their own solutions for common tasks, creating the illusion that there are no general models of social life. For instance, natural conditions in the Soviet Union have always been favourable to mass repressions, in the *taiga*, in the Arctic region and in the northern seas one can hide millions of corpses without trace. It would be harder to repeat anything similar in Italian or French conditions or elsewhere in the West. But the same tendency which, in the USSR, was embodied in mass repression could take a different form in the West. Moreover, the Soviet Union could lend the West a fraternal hand and put at its disposal its own immeasurable potential in this connection. Finally, if the reader is still not convinced that the picture of Communism presented to him is not just a picture of the peculiarities of the Soviet Union, the author can still find consolation in the following thought: the Soviet Union in itself is a serious enough phenomenon in the history of humanity; and an understanding of its stable nature is of value in itself. I also hope that there will be people in the Soviet Union who will be able to read this work and extract from it some lessons for themselves.

In this book I shall aim at the most popular type of exposition. But it does not follow that it can be understood without effort. The true grasp of anything is not gained without effort: only error and delusion are reached without it. Understanding is, in fact, resisting the onslaught of errors masquerading as self-evident truths. Most people who have an interest in social problems are not inclined to make a great effort. They imagine that every man can take a look at the social phenomena surrounding him, pass judgement on them and at once become a specialist in the field. In the USSR many millions incessantly observe the facts of Communist life and many thousands make judgements about them. But can we say that there are many who understand that society?

And a final warning: understanding a society is not the same as unmasking its defects. Unmasking is negative: understanding positive. Unmasking affects the emotions; understanding is exclusively in the realm of reason.

The enemy of the unmasker is the apologist; the enemy of understanding is error. Unmasking may be the enemy of understanding no less than apologetics. That is why there will be no unmasking passages in this book. And if apparent cases of unmasking should be found I would ask the reader to add them to the category of specific instances exemplifying general points. But the absence of unmasking does not always indicate apologetics. The effort to understand the essence of the Communist social system does it much more harm than any sensational unmasking of its ulcers.

The apologist seeks to highlight the virtues of a particular society and to exaggerate them, while playing down its defects or keeping silent about them altogether. Conversely, unmasking means concentrating attention on the defects and exaggerating them while the virtues are diminished or ignored. Understanding does not at all mean the adoption of some middle line or some just proportion between positive and negative, good and evil. In the exercise of understanding there is no positive or negative. For understanding there are only objective facts, objective laws and trends. How these phenomena will be evaluated in terms of good or evil, whether by participants in the life of that society or by spectators, does not depend on the exercise of understanding itself. Understanding, for example, will record the tendency of Communist society towards the formation of its own army of workers which society tears away from its natural milieu and obliges to work in conditions which are close to slavery. Understanding shows that this tendency is normal and not the result of the evil intentions of a number of wicked people. Is this a good phenomenon or not? For some people it's good, for others evil. But in itself it is just an objective fact.

TERMINOLOGY

More than once I have heard it said that the term 'Communism' is ambiguous; that Soviet and Western people understand it differently: that it is better to talk about a society of the Eastern or Western type. This is partly true. But advice of this kind hides a fear of calling things by their names, more than it reveals a wish to avoid confusion. Besides, this advice expresses a wish to present the ulcers of Communism as something specifically 'Eastern' or Soviet and not as something intrinsic.

It isn't a matter of words. In the last analysis it is pretty clear to everyone what we are talking about. There is no need for hypocrisy. We are talking about a society which was, and still is, the dream of downtrodden classes, all manner of starry-eyed Utopians, including the classical thinkers of Marxism, Western Communists and the 'progressive forces' of humanity. We are talking about real-life Communist society which is the actual embodiment of Marxist ideals. Demagogy and doctrines can take different forms, but the laws of things in general, and social laws in particular, do not change with regard to place or time. The laws of the Communist type of life are the same for all times and all peoples. And what is called the Eastern or Soviet type of society in fact presents to the world an example of a universal type of society and not something unusual or exceptional. To reject the term 'Communism' is to pretend that the discussion is about something which has no connection with Marxist plans for the reconstruction of society; or with what Communists and their sympathizers fought and fight for, or with the objectives of many 'progressively' disposed people in the West. On the contrary the word 'Communism' here is exactly appropriate. In this book (as in my other books) I give a description of that reality which inevitably results from the embodiment in real life of humanity's most 'progressive' ideals. No other reality has resulted from these ideals; and no other reality will.

The power of words over people is indeed staggering. Instead of using words to record the results of their observations of reality people see reality only in so far as the words themselves induce them to see it. And often they turn to reality only as a secondary source in the course of their main business, which is to manipulate words. Thus people see the very object they are thinking and talking about only via the heaps of the words, sentences, texts and books produced by other people, who are mostly the same slaves of words as they are themselves. Here I prefer to take another path; to speak about that Communism which I personally discovered in the course of a long life without the help of other people, especially of those who discoursed about it long before it appeared in history or obtained knowledge of it at second- or third-hand, or based their opinions on brief and fleeting impressions.

'SCIENTIFIC COMMUNISM' AND A SCIENCE OF COMMUNISM

Marxism makes a distinction between the lowest stage of Communism which is Socialism and the highest which is full Communism. At the lowest stage the governing principle is: 'from each according to his ability, to each according to his needs'. The term Communism is normally used in relation to the highest stage. It is reckoned that society has not yet achieved this highest stage. Even in the Soviet Union the situation is still only one of developed Socialism; very close to full Communism, but all the same not quite the real thing. Khrushchev in his day promised full Communism 'in the lifetime of the present generation'. But the Soviet authorities soon suppressed this particular piece of Khrushcheviana, because it was actually the forerunner of a period of deterioration in the country.

For Communist ideology this distinction between the lowest and highest stages of Communism is very useful. By means of it Communism at the same time sort of exists and sort of doesn't exist. One has a bit of it but the rest is due to come sometime later. All the actual drawbacks of life in Communist countries can be ascribed to the fact that full Communism has not yet been attained. Just wait, as it were, till we build the whole thing and then these drawbacks won't exist! But for the time being just be patient!

But in fact such a distinction between the stages of Communism has a purely speculative character. In actuality the principle of full Communism is capable of being realized even more easily than the principle of Socialism. True, these principles are not realized literally in such an idyllic form as in the dreams of classical Marxists and the exploited classes. Their realization is fully compatible with a low standard of living for the basic mass of the people compared to Western countries, and with huge differences in the standard of living of the different social classes in the Soviet Union. So I shall ignore the Marxist distinction between Socialism and Communism as a purely ideological phenomenon. I shall examine the type of society that is dominant in the USSR and a number of other countries as the actual embodiment of the aspirations of the classical Marxists and of all the, in the Marxist sense, progressive thinkers of the past. And if, in real history, it turns out that the embodiment of high ideals inevitably entails dismal consequences, then it can't be helped.

The positive pole of a magnet, as Marxist philosophers are fond of saying, cannot exist without the negative pole. The Marxist classics and other good-hearted thinkers of the past could not have foreseen that the road to heaven would lead to hell. Or was it that they did not want to foresee that? Could they really not know of the many cases in history when the 'rule of the people' manifested itself in bloody terror and the most frightful inequality? Besides, the wishes of the masses are reasonable. The experience of Communist countries has been revealed to contemporary mankind in all its nakedness, yet this in no way moderates the intensity of

Communist aspirations. Today's heirs to the classics of Marxism certainly know the real value of the Communist order. But their aspirations are purely mundane: to conquer the world for themselves and for their accomplices and to enjoy its blessings, whatever the cost to the rest of humanity.

According to Marxist dogma full Communism does not yet exist in reality, yet a science of it – 'Scientific Communism'– does. But in reality the situation is exactly the opposite: real-life Communism already exists in the form of numerous societies of a particular type, whereas a science of it does not. Communism is to be conceived of as a definite type of real society and taken as an empirical datum. And any science of Communism can only be empirical too, that is, derived from the observation of facts. If there is no object to be observed, there cannot be an empirical science of it. And so the 'Scientific Communism' of the Marxists, which prefers old texts to new reality, condemns itself at the outset to remain a purely ideological phenomenon.

One can regard Marxist 'Scientific Communism' as a design for a future society, though all the same a design is not an empirical science even if it is drawn with the help of the results of genuine science and has a scientific foundation. But can one at least regard the Marxist design for a future society as scientifically founded? A positive answer would seem here to be appropriate in so far as many prophecies by the architects of this design have come true and continue to come true. After all, even I talk about the embodiment in real life of Marxist ideals!

And that's exactly the point: ideals! But that isn't a scientific foundation for a social design. In the history of mankind a phenomenon such as the embodiment of ideals in life is a commonplace. But nobody except the Marxists has claimed *scientific* status for his ideals. No one would dream of maintaining, for example, that the philosophers of the French Enlightenment provided a scientific foundation for bourgeois society, or that nineteenth-century Russian thinkers provided a scientific foundation for the reval of serfdom, or that Hitler's theorists provided a scientific foundation for the social order of Nazi Germany.

Marxist 'Scientific Communism' is no different in this respect and does not constitute a scientifically based design for a new society. Marxism does not observe even the most elementary rules of scientific groundwork. What kind of science can one call it when even in the Soviet Union problems of 'Scientific Communism' are in the hands of the most ignorant and unscrupulous 'philosophers', when only the most ignorant strata of the population rise to this bait; and not even always then? The broad masses of the population in fact do not accept Marxism as a science or as anything scientifically founded at all, but as an ideology. And they use it for their own personal ends which have absolutely nothing to do with thoughts of the world's future social order.

The Marxist design for a Communist society pays no attention to two factors without which a scientific approach is unthinkable: 1) the inherent qualities of the very substance of society, the human being; 2) the principles according to which large numbers of people organize themselves into a single whole. For Marxism man is an 'aggregate of social relations', and one has only to create the requisite conditions of life and people will then become the embodiment of virtues. But in fact people are themselves the product of history; and as such possess characteristics which do not depend on such social transformations. On the contrary, these characteristics determine social transformations. As regards the second factor, in any large agglomeration of people that forms a whole there inevitably emerges a hierarchy of groups and functionaries which means that hopes of social equality are *doomed* to be transformed into the fictions of ideology.

SOCIAL MODELS

The ideas and concepts themselves which are embodied in a blueprint enter into the mainstream of the social process via the activity of people, activity which is rigorously circumscribed by the constraints within which it is actually possible to plan something in advance, and actually to create what was planned – for example, a house. But building a society is not like building a house. A house is built, for example, by putting bricks in particular configurations, and each brick remains in its allotted position for a considerable period of time. But imagine bricks which had consciousness and will-power and the capability of moving around, changing their shape and dimensions, destroying themselves and producing new bricks; and with the ambition to fight their way to the top of the house and force out other bricks . . . What would such a house look like in reality? But the Marxist design for a new society is like a design for a house with immovable bricks, the equivalent of which in real society, however, are seen not as real people but individuals conceptualized *in abstracto*. This is nothing but an *ideological* design.

In saying this I do not want at all to diminish the Marxist social model. To be unscientific is not necessarily to be bad. To be scientific is not necessarily to be good. If the public were presented with a beautifully made scientific theory of Communist society or a genuinely scientific design for one, it wouldn't meet with any success. How, indeed, could a design for a new society have any success which says that, alas, social differences and inequality are here to stay, that people will be tied to their place of work and residence (not to speak of repression)?! But one mustn't regard an ideological model simply as a deception or delusion. The point is simply that the correlation between the model and its realization is something quite other than that between scientific predication and the realization of the predicted events; or between a projected building and its actual construction.

The Marxist social model is formulated in such a way that it allows different interpretations of its propositions: one interpretation suggesting that they are being realized in real life and another suggesting that they are not. If the interpretation is defending Marxism then the ideological model is treated as scientific, and supposedly confirmed by the building of Communism as it is carried out in actual practice. If the interpretation is a critical one, then the model is treated as unscientific gibberish, supposedly refuted by the evidence of that same practice. And both interpretations are equally justified because an ideological blueprint is sufficiently wordy and ambiguous. For example, under Communism the state will *wither away*; so promised the Marxist classics. But one can understand this 'withering' in two ways. First, it could mean that prisons will disappear along with the police, the civil service, the army and other attributes of the 'state'. Practice has shown that these things don't disappear. On the contrary they grow in number and strength. A second meaning could be that the status of these phenomena in society changes so that they can be interpreted not as the apparatus of the 'exploiting classes' (i.e., landowners and capitalists) but as organs of self-government by the people. And then a prison is no longer a prison, but a means of educating the workers. And the innumerable ministers, generals and party officials are no longer the lackeys of the bourgeoisie but servants of the people.

In the case of the ideological model there is a mutual accommodation between it and the activity which is supposed to lead to its realization in practice. There is always some part of such model which actually corresponds to the activity of people. And people behave as if they are acting in accordance with that part, although in fact any correlation is either coincidental or merely apparent.

As for the rest of the model, people either pay no attention to it or else interpret it in a way which makes it appear that they are being guided by it, while at the same time they attempt to present their own activities in a way which suggests that they are faithfully executing its instructions.

The fact is that social models are subject to laws of one particular kind and people's actions to another. And there can in principle be no compatibility between these two kinds of laws because they belong to different spheres of phenomena. A social model is, in fact, only a symbol, consecrating activity. In this context relationships of truth and untruth do not operate but are replaced by reciprocal relationships of a different kind, and thus there is nothing surprising in the fact that the more vile an activity is the more noble appears the social design that sanctions it. Actions which are obviously good don't need any designs. A social design organizes the form of people's activity. Its worth is defined not by its degree of truth or its descriptive adequacy in regard to the present and the future, but in terms of social success. From this viewpoint the Marxist plan for a new society is a grandiose phenomenon and comparable with the social impact of Christianity. If it were scientifically based, I repeat, it would be unable to contain the features which have contributed to its success.

An ideological social model has as its main content a specific aim. A serious plan for this kind includes objectives for which at least a part can be realized: for example, the nationalization of land, the factories, the banks, transport and the postal system. All this is possible. But an ideological plan does not take into account all the possible consequences of the realization of these goals, especially the negative consequences; for instance the proliferation of the bureaucracy, the fall in the quality of production, bad management and the lowering of incentive to work well.

An ideological plan cannot in principle measure the negative consequences of the realization of its own ideals, because its task is to mobilize the masses to achieve those ideals; and therefore it must promise them El Dorado. An ideological plan, I must emphasize, is preponderantly a teleological phenomenon. But the achievement of goals is something different in principle from the realization of a prediction. Communists and their sympathizers seek to liquidate the private ownership of the means of production, to destroy the class of proprietors and to realize other points of their programme, not because this is some objective material law, but because they want to do it in the hope of getting out of it certain specific advantages for themselves and to win an advantageous position in the arena of history. These wishes they dress up in the noble form 'scientific prediction'.

Once they have seized power in a country and translated

16

their programme (their objectives) into real life, Communists turn out to be in the power of real (not imagined) social laws, which inevitably commit them to a far from noble role; and which brings about unplanned and undesired consequences. In their time Communists have, for example, promised to build a society in which civil servants would receive a remuneration not more than the average working man's wage. Yet from the earliest days of the new society this promise was forgotten. In its place, and with frightening urgency, principles of differentiation began to work which inexorably created such differentials in the actual remuneration of workers and of officials of high standing as would never have been possible even in the capitalist countries of the West.

COMMUNISM AS A UNIVERSAL PHENOMENON

Another Marxist dogma says that Communist social ('productive') relations do not develop in the depths of the old society, but are conceived after the socialist revolution; for their formation the prolonged existence of a society at the lowest stage of Communism is required, i.e. in conditions of Socialism. But the experienced researcher who observes life in the Communist countries and compares it with non-Communist countries and past societies soon discovers the mistakenness of this dogma. Communist social relations in one form or another and to some or other extent existed and still exist in the most different societies wherever a large enough number of people are compelled to live together and where there is a complicated economic and governmental system. They exist in the West. They existed in pre-revolutionary Russia. But only in certain conditions can they become dominant and rule the whole of society. It is then that there arises a specifically Communist type of society. The most important of these conditions is the socialization of the means of production throughout the whole country, the liquidation of classes of private owners and entrepreneurs and the centralized direction of all aspects of the country's life, together with the preservation of a complex economic and cultural system.

Of course, the elements of Communism in a Communist country are not the same thing as those in a non-Communist country. Changes do occur; moreover, changes of such magnitude that at times it is difficult to see what these elements have in common. In particular, Communist parties in non-Communist countries who are seeking power and Communist parties in Communist countries who already have power differ in many respects although both types of party are elements of Communism. Communist parties seeking power, for instance, promise to safeguard civil rights and democratic freedoms if they come to power. But having come to power they are compelled by the very conditions of Communist society to do everything to destroy these phenomena of Western civilization at the first opportunity.

Although we can find elements of future Communism in non-Communist societies (what I have in mind are such phenomena as the relationships of power and subordination, systemic subordination, a hierarchy of social strata and administrative positions, the power of the collective over the individual, and so on), we can only understand their authentic social nature when we consider them as elements of a society of the Communist type. To be able to evaluate such phenomena in non-Communist countries one must observe their place and role in Communist countries. Thus one must judge the Communist parties of the West not by their slogans and promises but by what Communist parties in Communist countries are really like.

And so, in contrast to Marxist dogma, I proceed from the actual existence of societies of the Communist type which have been fully established and regard them as the product of the transformation of the Communist relations common to all humanity to the point where they become dominant and all-embracing. This transformation takes place in certain conditions. Some of them have a purely historical significance. Such for example are the defeat of a country in war, the collapse of the economy, occupation by the army of a Communist country. These circumstances do not interest me. Another set of conditions, on the contrary, lies at the very heart of society and these conditions continually regenerate themselves, by the very fact that society exists. They are the conditions of a given type of society which are built into it. For instance the unification of the structure of business organizations, growth of state power, the commanding role of the Party. To describe these conditions is to describe the essential features of the society which developed as a result of them. Such features are those which characterize the society as it is now and, if seen as themselves developing over a period of time, conditioned its development. The concrete historical conditions of Communism for various countries may differ in that some or others may be absent, but the inbuilt conditions are inevitable. They can vary only in form and not in essence.

So the problem is not how to work out in one's mind an idealized optimum standard of living as the goal for the future but how to observe the empirical data of life in Communist countries and then explain which general social phenomena found favourable ground there and engendered that type of society. I have come to the following conclusion about this: the universal phenomena I mentioned above are connected with one and the same fact: that in Communist societies the majority of people are obliged to live and work together as a single whole, to form standard units (communes) of individuals and units composed of these units (supercommunes). That is why the term 'Communism' is more suitable than any other.

COMMUNISM AND CAPITALISM

I do not intend here to examine the interrelationships between Communism and Capitalism. I will only make a brief observation in connection with the idea which I formulated at the end of the foregoing section.

There are a number of opinions which are fairly widespread: Capitalism engenders Communism; Communism is the successor to Capitalism; Communism is a higher stage of social development than Capitalism; Communism is state Capitalism; and so on.

The Marxist version of these assertions is well known: Capitalism socializes production, which leads to conflict with the conditions of private ownership, and this conflict is resolved by the transition to Communism, i.e. by the realignment of forms of ownership with the mode of production. This is merely a bit of verbal tight-rope walking. Capitalism may be one of the historical conditions for the appearance of Communist society, but the latter has its own roots and origins, its own historical lineage which itself is not at all continuation of the one which produced Capitalism. Capitalism grew out of economic relations. Communism arises from relations of quite another order: from relations which I shall designate as *communal*. The lines along which Capitalism and Communism developed historically came into contact and intersected each other but they do not form separate sections of an identical line of development. And Marx's historical materialism which is appropriate in connection with Capitalism (albeit on condition that we accept numerous abstractions and then only as a starting point for analysis) becomes meaningless when applied to Communism. It is not that it is wrong. It is simply that it is irrelevant. Other instruments of cognition are required. Appraisals of Communism as forms of state, collective or even Party Capitalism can only be adequately described in terms appropriate to a discussion of mental deficiency.

There is one circumstance which makes it utterly senseless to regard Communism and Capitalism as equal-ranking forms of society. Capitalist economic relations are merely the preponderant ones in so-called Capitalist countries. They in no way alter other aspects of human relations, communal ones included. Communal relations, once they have become dominant in Communist society, give Capitalist relations no chance whatsoever. Communism is a much deeper phenomenon than Capitalism.

DREAMS AND REALITY

According to Marxist dogma, a Communist society is built to the blueprint of 'scientific Communism' and embodies the centuries-old dream of humanity of an ideal social order, in which there will be an abundance of commodities and of the means of consumption (spiritual as well as material), the most favourable conditions for the development of the personality of the citizen and the very best human relationships. In a word, everything that the philistine consciousness can imagine in the form of human bliss is ascribed to Communism. How in fact things turn out can now be taken to be a matter of public knowledge.

Critics of Communism usually affirm that the Marxists deceived the people; that when it came to it, after seizing power, they refused to fulfil their aspirations. What these critics overlook is that the majority of those who seized power in the new society had nothing whatever to do with Marxism and bear no responsibility for the incautious promises of the progenitors of the ideology which they espoused.

But that is by the by. I part company with these critics of Communism and assert that Communist societies are indeed constructed to the plan of 'scientific Communism', although this plan has nothing in common with science, and although the creators of the new society know nothing at all about the plan or know it only by hearsay. I assert further that in the Communist countries that have been created there *is* an embodiment of the dream of millions of what is best for them in life (for them, be it noted, not for everyone). But I enter one qualification: having been given real form these dreams bring with them, in addition to what was desired and planned, something which the dreamers and planners do not suspect, from which they strive to escape, which they do not even allow themselves to think about.

Psychologically this is understandable; it simply cannot be possible that the noblest intentions have in reality produced the vilest results! True, at first glance the illusion does seem a strange one, because down the centuries people have known that the road to hell is paved with good intentions. But mass psychology behaves according to laws which differ from those which apply to the psychology of the individual.

Here I will make a brief digression. In the example before us two such principles of mass psychology are at work (among others). The first principle is this: good causes produce good effects, bad causes bad effects; good effects are produced by good causes and bad effects by bad causes. For example, if a Socialist revolution is a good thing, then its effects must be good. Mass repressions are evil, therefore they are a deviation from the essence of the revolution. If mass repressions are an effect of the revolution then that means that the revolution was an evil. If power belongs to the people (which is very good) then the life of the people must also be good (full and free). Here we have a confusion of value-relations and causal relations which are in fact quite independent of each other.

The second principle of mass psychology is the following: the social goals and perspectives are so beautiful and important that any sacrifices on their account are justifiable. As a consequence of these (and other) principles it seems that the broad masses of the people never listen to the voice of reason and never draw any lessons from their own or anyone else's experience. And so they make easy sacrifices for demagogues and make others into sacrifices too. Further, they are unable to understand the root causes of their miseries.

The most stable and self-perpetuating basis of the negative phenomena of Communist life is contained in the most positive ideal of Communism and in its most positive qualities as an actual type of society. This is the heart of the matter. The ideals of Communism have been fully realized in the Soviet Union and in a number of other countries. But reality seems less beautiful than was originally envisaged. The reality of Communism has created problems, contrasts and ulcers no less painful than those which earlier engendered those very Communist ideals and which Communism should have, in theory, overcome. The reality of Communism has shown that the exploitation of some by others and the various forms of social and economic inequality are not eliminated under Communism but only change their forms; and in some instances become worse.

The tragedy of our epoch lies in the fact that within the rational measures to overcome social evils there are elements which during implementation create new evils and strengthen some of the old evils merely by giving them other forms. People do not have the power to change the general direction of social evolution. All they succeed in doing is speed up the movement in the same direction. They lack a mooring strong enough to allow them to anchor and think about changing course. But consideration of this problem goes beyond the purpose of this book and so I will say no more.

For a considerable part of the population on earth the standard of living which obtains in the Soviet Union and the Eastern European countries may seem something beyond their wildest dreams. But Communism has greater pretensions than merely to raise the standard of living of the poorest part of the planet. It intends to surpass the standard of living of the richest countries in the world, to solve all painful problems and to create on earth a just and secure paradise. And the fact that living standards in the USSR are higher than those in eternally famine-stricken India does not itself demonstrate that these intentions of Communism are in any way realistic. But let us return to our basic theme.

In human history it is not at all the case that people can establish the social order that their leaders and themselves want, and predict. In reality people try to bring about changes in their own living conditions. But what happens in these new conditions and what type of society will be forthcoming does not depend on their dreams and plans. One cannot predict it with full scientific confidence. Here all predictions have a prophetic or ideological character. Predictions can be made about some banal phenomena to do with human activities, or else phenomena can be predicted in language which allows of differing interpretations. At a later stage the most suitable interpretation is supplied *post factum*. Besides, human consciousness records only that which is more or less coming true and ignores that which isn't coming true.

People do not have the power to choose the type of society which is formed in the new conditions resulting from their combined activities. Moreover, the more grandiose the changes in society, the less obedient to people's will are the social processes whereby the new society is formed. The more deeply these changes affect the foundations of social life, the more closely the processes of social formation seem to approximate to the processes of inanimate nature. The illusion that the society that is being created anew is built according to the will and the wishes of certain people arises from the fact that the new society *suits* some people, the people who settle happily in it and who have the power to foist *their* interpretation of what has happened on other people.

What would be wrong, one might ask, if some people in the West decided to destroy Capitalism, while safe-guarding the values of Western civilization and in its place build a Communism that avoided the shortcomings that have appeared in the USSR? An excellent intention: but one, alas, that in principle simply cannot be implemented. There are certain indissoluble links between social phenomena which nobody has the power to break. The removal of the shortcomings of Western civilization cannot happen without the loss of the values linked to them. One cannot obtain the values of Communism without obtaining the shortcomings linked to them.

For example, many people want to abolish private property, considering it to be the source of all evils. But even if

24

we suppose this wish is fulfilled, by itself it does not produce a social order. The measure is a purely negative one from the viewpoint of social construction. Either it doesn't figure as an element in the new social order or it figures in a way that had not been planned. Abolition is only a condition for the emergence of the new social order. The latter takes shape thanks to the activities of people and according to the laws of organization of the broad mass of the people in certain given conditions (in particular the nationalization of factories, banks, land, transport and communications). When the goal has been reached, a complete reorientation of the historical process takes place on the new base. Unexpected actors appear in the historical arena. Things which no one thought about before become more important. Matters of originally great theoretical importance become secondary or disappear altogether. An example in the case under discussion would be the fact that the whole subject of property-relations becomes, so to speak, a blank space in the new society.

As in nature, so in society there are phenomena that are indissolubly linked. And it would be useful to know just a few of them so as to be able to decide for oneself: is the game worth the candle? I appreciate that the posing of such problems and even their most reasonable solution makes little difference to events. People are obliged to decide their daily problems in a particular way that depends hardly at all on their knowledge of the consequences of their actions. People try either not to think about the future or to think about it in a deceitful and reassuringly cosy way. The behaviour of the West towards the USSR in recent decades provides striking instances of this. The West has spared no effort to help the Soviet Union to strengthen its army and to avoid economic catastrophe. What has been the result? It would be a big mistake to think that this result was not known in advance. To predict it was an absolutely trivial matter. Many did predict it, moreover with convincing arguments. And all in vain.

COMMUNISM AND CIVILIZATION

Communism is not something invented by evil-thinking men contrary to all common sense and alleged human nature, as some opponents of Communism assert. It is exactly the opposite: it is a natural phenomenon of human history which fully corresponds to human nature and derives from it. It grows from the aspiration of the two-legged creature called man to survive in a habitat with a large number of similar creatures, to make better arrangements for himself in it, to defend himself and so on. It springs from what I call *human communality*. The things which are contrived and invented are precisely the defence mechanisms against communality which have given rise to civilization: namely law, morality, publicity, religion, humanism and other means which offer the individual a measure of protection from other people and from the consequences of their numerical strength. Man as we know him – and we pronounce his name rather grandiloquently with a capital M – is a being who has been artificially bred within the framework of civilization from the two-legged communal creature which we mentioned above. In general, civilization springs from the resistance to communality and from the effort to limit its (communal) unruliness and to confine it within certain boundaries. Fundamentally, civilization is above all man's self-defence against himself. And only afterwards is it to do with comfort, which has other foundations. If communality can be understood as a movement with the current of history, then civilization can be regarded as a movement against the current. More vividly still, if we imagine communality as a process of falling into the potholes of history and sliding downwards, then civilization can be seen as a clambering up.

Civilization is effort; communality is taking the line of least resistance. Communism is the unruly conduct of nature's elemental forces; civilization sets them rational bounds. Communism springs from communality, uses it, unleashes it, creates favourable conditions for it, organizes and enforces it as a specal type of society, as a special form of life for the many millions of the popular masses.

It is for this reason that it is the greatest mistake to think that Communism deceives the masses or uses force on them. As the flower and crowning glory of communality Communism represents a type of society which is nearest and dearest to the masses no matter how dreadful the potential consequences for them might be. At the same time in order to defend itself against these self-same masses, Communism invents its own particular means of curbing communality. But these are secondary and are used only in so far as they preserve intact the crystallization of a society that has sprung from communality and give it support. And initially that crystallization is a manifestation and organization of communality for the purposes of taking over society and fighting its constant enemy – civilization.

People have several different potential and actual means of self-defence against their own communality. Not all of them derive from civilization. Among the weapons of civilization, as I have already said, are religion, the legal rights of the individual, morality, publicity, civil rights, humanism, great art and so on. But mass killings of people and their enslavement also sometimes played a role as a means of defence against communality, to the degree to which they either destroyed communality or prevented its appearance.

Communism borrows certain aids from civilization for the control of communality, but only to a certain extent. And when they are combined with the other measures of Communism these measures begin to play quite a different role. For instance, certain moral and legal ideas, humanism and items of sacred art, here assume the function of fooling people and of ruling them ideologically. In other words they have a role opposite to the one they have in the framework of civilization. But more usually, Communism elaborates its own means of defence against communality (or its restraint) which however are destined simultaneously to encourage it and become transformed themselves into elements of com-

27

munality for they are phenomena of the same order. And from this viewpoint Communism appears in history as the opposite pole to civilization, as the negation of the very foundations of the latter, and as its regeneration.

Communism, as an aspect of life and as a tendency, is a natural phenomenon in every society with a sufficiently large number of people formed into a single whole. But the civilization in which we live constitutes in fact a resistance to that tendency. It also became just such a natural phenomenon once it had risen and revealed its values, and it has become a ceaselessly active factor of human life. The struggle between the two tendencies goes on always and everywhere. It goes on in the Communist countries, in the West, in the Communist parties and in the parties hostile to Communism, in government and in the popular masses, in the privileged and in the exploited classes.

Here one can compare the situation with that of an aeroplane in flight. If the engine is running the plane gains height and moves rapidly. If the engine stops running the plane falls to the ground. Communism operates in accordance with the laws of gravity; civilization on the other hand is a flight which makes use of the laws of gravity but resists them. It stands out against the laws of gravity while observing the laws of gravity and is in constant interaction with them.

The struggle against Communism is in the interest of everyone. But because historical circumstances affect people's lives and force various aspects of their life into relatively autonomous compartments, the forces of Communism and the forces of civilization in the end are in fact actual people and groups of people, different countries and groups of countries. It is only as a result of uninterrupted resistance to Communist pressures (and not thanks to their elimination which is not possible in a living society) that civilization can be preserved and can continue.

I have dwelt on this theme to such an extent because I wished to stress the following thoughts: there is a widely-held view in the world that Communism is something new, invented by a group of criminals (or geniuses); something introduced from without, and imposed by fraud and force. In fact, Communism is something well known and familiar to everyone. What is new is merely the transformation of an old acquaintance into a new master. Only on this basis does that great, historic, creative process begin whereby people give to their lives a whole new range of aspects, among which the defects of the new society, which have become well known to everyone, must be given a place of honour.

So the problem becomes not one of choosing between two things, Communism or civilization, for there is no choice; but one of finding the effective means of resisting the first and defending the second. Not stability, but struggle between these two forces is the unavoidable fate of humanity, no matter which countries come out on top in the world, which survive, and which perish. There can be no rest from it. It will cease only when the two forces have been destroyed. Only this destruction will provide the final solution to all problems. But while humanity is alive it is doomed to be beset by problems. A society which exhaustively solves all problems and satisfies everybody is a practical impossibility. And theoretically it is nonsense. There will never be a situation in which people say to themselves: 'Now we've got what we need; no more rushing about, now it's bliss for all time.' And Communism is no exception. Even if it conquers the whole world, a struggle for everything that forms a part of human civilization will start up once more. If that struggle isn't renewed and doesn't consolidate itself in the form of various outcomes and traditions, then humanity will simply degenerate. For the moment predictions of this kind have no sense. But even an outcome like the one just mentioned is not the end of the world. Even if Communism is victorious in this or that part of the world, with the passage of time it is compelled to develop anti-Communist forces within itself in the interests of self-preservation and as a result of popular resistance. The dissident movement in the Soviet Union, for instance, is just as much an organic phenomenon as the repressive activities of the authorities against it. And the present Soviet government itself appears as more of an opponent of Communism than does the Soviet people. It is obliged to limit the operation of the laws of communality, as it struggles to raise production, tighten industrial discipline, improve the economy, stop bribery, shoddy work and all kinds of general eye-wash. Although it is the logical product of the forces of communality, Communism is compelled to confine and moderate them ostensibly in order to preserve them. This is an example of the same dialectic the application of which Marxists authorize in relation to past societies but do not allow in relation to their own offspring whose 'dialecticality' is quintessential. The above-mentioned contradiction appears with the passage of time to be one of those internal reasons which will lead even Communism to its grave; the same Communism which was intended by its prophets to last for ever.

The history of humanity cannot be reduced to the two tendencies discussed above. If we isolate them in this way we are only using an abstraction to help us understand the phenomenon that interests us, namely Communism. One cannot understand the matter unless one has separated it conceptually from its permanently antagonistic companion, anti-communality, which is the source of civilization. As we examine the two types of society we must be able to distinguish the antagonistic tendencies which belong to each of them, but which are different from them, or can be examined from some other point of view.

THE PHILISTINE AND THE SCIENTIST

When I say that Communism is a normal and natural phenomenon my statement is sometimes interpreted as a defence of Communism. This sort of thing enables one to distinguish two types of thought: the philistine and the scientific. For the philistine, if something is normal and natural it means that it is something good. He does not distinguish between the subjective evaluation of a phenomenon and its objective properties. For the scientist even death is a normal and natural phenomenon although there is little about it that people find pleasant.

Here I cannot give a detailed description of these two modes of thought. I shall simply name a few of their characteristics and illustrate them with examples. The philistine takes note of directly observable facts and makes hasty generalizations without any analysis. His judgements are subjective, i.e., they bear the imprint of personal predilections. The scientist tries not only to establish the individual facts and to analyse them from the viewpoint of their random or non-random character, he tries to understand the laws which govern them, laws which cannot be identified by immediate observation. He tries to prevent his predilections from affecting his judgements. The philistine claims that his ratiocinations are directly supported by observable facts. The results of scientific thinking, however, do not coincide directly with observable facts. They merely give the means whereby concrete facts can be explained and predicted.

From the scientific viewpoint, for example, it is possible for people to be discontented with the Communist way of life and at the same time to accept it, prefer it to other ways of life and be ready to defend it, as in the Soviet Union. For the philistine critic of Communism this is unthinkable. He assumes that once people are discontented with the Communist way of life, it means they reject it and are ready to get rid of it at the appropriate time. For the philistine supporter of Communism this is equally unthinkable; he assumes that once people accept the Communist way of life it means they are content with it.

Or again, it is well known that Soviet people officially condemn dissidents. The philistine apologists of Soviet society explain that fact in terms of the trust felt by the Soviet people towards their government, of their love of their type of society and their dislike of dissidents who, for them, are parasites, slanderers and spies. For philistine critics of Soviet society this behaviour is allegedly motivated by the fear of repressions.

But for the scientist both views are devoid of sense. The majority of Soviet people condemn dissidents sincerely, but for reasons which are social in origin and which are independent of their emotions and of their trust, or lack of it, in the regime. The philistine thinker is inclined to confuse his personal feelings with the truth. For instance, he notices that a number of Soviet physicists, biologists, and mathematicians are involved in the dissident movement, while many others privately express their sympathy with dissidents. From that he reaches the conclusion he seeks, namely that Soviet scientists are against the existing Soviet regime.

One doesn't have to be a scientist to show the absurdity of such a conclusion. The same scientists who sympathize with dissidents in private conversation condemn the same dissidents at meetings in their own institutions. But the very concept of scientist is in any case devoid of substance when used of the mass of bureaucrats who are employed in Soviet science.

I have come across more than one instance of inferences that are quite monstrous in their absurdity, although they have been made by educated people. For example, on learning of cases of young men refusing to bear arms for religious reasons, or to serve in the army (for which they were ready to suffer severe punishment, refusal being a crime under Soviet law) someone with whom I happened to be conversing developed from that a whole theory of the weakness of the Soviet army. When I adduced in argument against him the fact that many millions of young people did bear arms and were willing to obey any orders whatever from the authorities, including the suppression of their own countrymen, let alone foreigners, my interlocutor merely waved his hand dismissively. The fact that a few people deviated from the norm seemed to him more convincing, although that kind of refusal exists in all armies and is predictable purely statistically.

The identification of subjective evaluations with the objective state of affairs has now gone so far among philistines that most concepts used in discussions on sociological questions have lost all their scientific character and become value-judgements. Such, for instance, are expressions like 'tyranny', 'dictatorship', 'power of the people', 'democracy', 'bureaucracy', and so on. If the power of the people exists then for the philistine this is jolly good; and he cannot even admit the thought into his head that massive repressions in the Soviet Union were themselves a manifestation of the power of the people, taken to the absolute extreme. He is incapable of understanding that the power of the people also has a social structure and that the latter includes modes of hierarchy, and the means of coercion.

The philistine looks at the life of other people as if he were himself in their position and extends to them his own attitude to life, his own scale of values, his own feelings and experiences. He cannot understand how these people perceive and judge their own position. This type of identification is as characteristic of people in the West *vis-à-vis* Soviet people as it is of Soviet people in relation to the West. It applies not only to the present, but also to the past and future. When a Soviet person is told, for instance, that the standard of living in the West is three, or even five, times higher than in the Soviet Union, he understands this quite simply: he multiplies his own salary by three or five, leaving all other aspects of living conditions unchanged. The Westerner correspondingly divides *his* earnings by three or five, and usually both parties begin to doubt the truth of statements about the standards of living in the West and in the Soviet Union. The scientific mind, however, knows that the standard of living of people is inextricably bound up with the general conditions of life: i.e. with the price which people have to pay for the standard which they have. Consequently only a comparison of the *aggregate* of conditions in which people live makes any sense.

The following conception of the social structure of Communist countries is fairly prevalent: 1) the people are sacrificed to the regime: 2) the authorities are the persecutors of the people: 3) the dissidents are the defenders of the persecuted people.

Whatever ideas people are guided by and whatever their personal circumstances, when they make pronouncements like these they reveal themselves as typical exponents of the philistine method of thinking. The population in a real Communist country has in fact a quite different structure, although it also includes victims, authorities and dissidents. And the structure is not only infinitely more complex than the primitive scheme instanced above, it can only be described in terms of a quite different conceptual system.

The expression 'the people' in this context is totally meaningless; it is impossible even theoretically to separate the people from the authorities inasmuch as power is enmeshed in the whole of society on every level; and, as for dissidents, the same social conditions condemn them to be the defenders only of themselves; and, moreover, not just against the authorities but also against 'the people', on whose support the authorities can rely.

THE HISTORICAL AND SOCIOLOGICAL APPROACHES

Historicist ideas have now become so natural to the understanding of the phenomena of human life that even the suggestion that any other ideas could contend with them seems blasphemous. It is often thought, for instance, that the essence of Communist society can only be grasped from a historical viewpoint; i.e. via an examination of the history of its formation. (The authentic history, of course, and not the one falsified by pro-Communist historians and philosophers.) If, it is said, it can be shown what actually happened, and how this society was actually formed, then it will be clear what sort of society it is.

But, we shall ask, what is the authentic history? If we discover that Stalin really was an agent of the Tsarist secret police, that Lenin really did receive money from the German government, that the exact number of victims of repression was such and such, will this knowledge be the authentic story? Will it do much to clarify our understanding of real-life Communist society? There have been more than enough discoveries of the 'authentic' history of Soviet society. But has a scientific understanding of it been thereby much advanced? And indeed, one might point out *en passant*, that apologists of Communism also rely on the historical approach and they are not at all interested in revealing the defects of that society. Is this just an accident?

I do not deny the usefulness of the historical method in investigating phenomena such as the social order of a given country. But I consider that the leading role in this task should belong to the sociologist. Certainly we need to know what in fact happened as the result of the historical process in order to satisfy ourselves as to the nature of that process. We also need to consider the society which has come into being as a given, on the basis of which we can grasp the sense of certain historical events which preceded and, apparently, produced the society. But the task of actually investigating the society is one for the sociologist.

Sociology also examines the life of society as it flows in time. But there is an essential difference between the role of time in the sociological approach and its corresponding role in the historical approach. Sociology attempts to apprehend forms of social life, as they reproduce themselves in time in a regular and constant manner. It tries to grasp their universal rules and tendencies. For the historian, on the other hand, the important thing is to know by what road these forms of life once arose in time. If, however, we put the question this way: how in general do such forms of life arise? – that is, pose a general question, then only the judgements of sociologists as to how in fact these forms of life in a given society reproduce themselves can provide a scientific answer.

The historian cannot in pure logic provide any scientific explanation of this or that type of society. Historical explanations are illusory. It is no accident that up to now a whole army of learned men has been unable to explain the emergence of language, of the human being himself, of Christianity and of other complicated phenomena of social life. Not because there are not enough facts – often there are all too many of them; but because the explanation is impossible in principle. In the case of the emergence of Communist society, we know too many historical details. But we still have no scientific theory of that society and until we do all we have is a story of a given bit of the world at a given time. And such a theory can only be created in abstraction from history, by treating a given society as an empirical fact.

Illusions about the ability of history to explain social phenomena arise because the image of society that has been formed in one way or another hovers in the consciousness of historically-minded people and influences their awareness. But suppose for a moment that there is no image, only an accumulation of evidence about the existence of a huge number of diachronic and synchronic events. What can one get out of that? When critics of the regime set out to unearth the 'genuine' history, they already have fixed in their minds the figures and the events of the society that has emerged. Why is their attention drawn to the fate of an agent of the *Okhrana* called Djugashvilli? Why does an insignificant Russian émigré called Ulyanov interest them?

Moreover, a historical orientation in this case actually prevents a scientific understanding of the society that interests us because here history has been given functions that are alien to it. Historical science establishes which events took place in a given context of space and time and in what sequence, and it also establishes obvious causal connections between events. For instance, it is quite evident that Lenin and his companions made the journey to Russia because a revolution had occurred there. It also has its own criteria for the selection and the evaluation of events. For instance, it turns its attention to events which achieved a certain prominence when they occurred, and which made a deep impression on people at the time, but which have absolutely no significance from a sociological point of view. How many words and chapters have been written about the activities of Rasputin, about the fate of Samsonov's army, about the personality of Kerensky, although these events and people offer precisely nothing to help us understand the essence of the new society in the Soviet Union and the Russian revolution! A historical orientation deflects the attention towards events from which in the first instance it should be *with-*

drawn if we wish to understand a new society that has grown up and developed in a manner dictated by its history.

The historical process is, of course, also reality which disappears into the past. The society which has matured through that process (a new society), seeks to cast off its historical garb which has become stifling and alien to it. It will then don another, but one which corresponds to its essence and does not reveal its origins. Sociological reality is orientated towards what has come to stay. It looks towards the future.

Millions of people took part in the historical process which led to the birth of Communist society in the Soviet Union. They did billions of different things. They did these things in their own personal interests. They acted according to the laws of communal behaviour, according to the laws of history – in human behaviour there are no such things. Some of these actions worked in favour of the new society, some against it. Some of them worked both for and against it, depending on the circumstances. The people who were in favour of the new society did not always act in its favour. Nor did those who were against it always act against it. Some revolutionaries unwittingly did much to harm the revolution and some counter-revolutionaries did much to help it.

It is practically and logically impossible to distinguish between what worked 'for' and what worked 'against'. Only after the process was complete was it possible to make a judgement about the actual result and its past with more or less plausibility.

A historical orientation leads inevitably to the acceptance of everything at face value. In particular, only those who accept Communist doctrine and act accordingly are deemed to be the sources of Communist society, whereas those who do not accept that doctrine are seen as the source of opposition. The historical mind is, for instance, incapable of understanding that without the help of the privileged classes of the old Russian society the new society could not have survived for more than a year. Try to convince the citizens of the Western European countries that many anti-Communists in the West in effect do more to help Communism than convinced Communists, and see how many of them are able to understand you. In this particular context the historian is only a variant of the philistine.

Even in those cases where the historical process itself becomes the object of attention, sometimes only a sociological approach can provide the necessary guidance in the murky flow of history. This is so in our case. There are several general methodological principles for understanding the processes leading to the emergence of complex systems of phenomena such as a whole organic society. In the case of the Soviet Union, and in a very simplified form, the situation is something like this (from the point of view of the extent to which there is any correlation between Marxism and reality). Communism emerged in the Soviet Union as the result of a specific combination of circumstances and as a part of the natural process of the country's survival in the terrible conditions of the collapse of the Russian Empire. It was the road which it was forced to take by circumstances and not at all something which developed according to a previously elaborated Marxist plan. The Communists only used the circumstances in order to play their desired, or inevitable role in history (psychologically the one easily merges into the other). The destruction of a social order, consequent upon the destruction of the way of life of a population of a given country, depends on people. But what is built in place of the society which has been destroyed depends on general social laws governing the organization of people into large collectives and on the concrete conditions in which this happens.

What happened in Russia coincides in many ways with what the Marxists were talking about. But what *didn't* they talk about? A lot happened which in no way coincides with the substance of these Marxist conversations. Nowadays, of course, Marxists only pay attention to what does coincide, and what does not coincide they ignore. It is senseless to deny the influence of Marxism on the process. But it is absurd to imagine that Communism as it actually developed in Russia was the realization of the projects of individual people and political parties. What happened were some favourable historical coincidences plus a muddy river of words which allowed any kind of *post factum* interpretation.

Actual Communism could have developed without Marxist ideology. The only thing which is sociologically indisputable is that a mass process of that magnitude needed *some* ideological formulation and would, in one way or another, have worked out a suitable one. Marxism was on hand as suitable material (I repeat, only material) but it was by no means the prerequisite or source of the new society in the way that it seems to those who are historically minded.

The grandiose process of the conquest of the world by Communism is taking place before our eyes, and no amount of revelation of the horrors of the Communist way of life in the Soviet Union and other countries will stop this process. Why? The Soviet Union has seized vast territories in the world and is striving to penetrate all the corners of the planet, while it has at home immense untamed land. Why does it do this? What has the historical thinker got to say about it? Something, perhaps, about the continuation of the old Russian imperialist tradition and other platitudes, but nothing more. The spread of Soviet Communism throughout the world entails enormous sacrifices for the Soviet people and the risk of the collapse and rout of the Soviet Empire. Why can't it stop the process of expansion? Because of the idea of world revolution? What rubbish! The fact is that it is impossible to explain the behaviour of this frightful beast (the Soviet Union) without a detailed sociological analysis of the mechanics of its Communist society. It is only possible to guess at and record its separate actions. Even the behaviour of the shark is still a riddle for science; but the Soviet Union is somewhat more complicated than a shark.

When it comes to examining what has not yet happened but might, i.e. the future, the historical approach is, of course, utterly powerless. Take the problem of a new world war. Can one convincingly prophesy its beginning and its character by analysing wars which happened in the past? And what about the general prospects in the struggle between Communism and Western civilization? After all, it is precisely the prospects for Communism as a type of society and its struggle with the West, and not past history, that constitute the main problem of our time. For the sociologist, on the other hand, this is precisely his concern: to explain the laws and tendencies which are operating now and will do so also in the future by virtue of their universality. Even when they look at the past, people are interested not so much by what happened as by whether what happened might happen again, and to what extent. But for this we must know what was inevitable in the events of the past and which social mechanisms mattered.

A SOCIOLOGICAL LOOK AT HISTORY

In the kind of cases we are considering here historical science provides factual material for investigation but only sociology has the means of understanding it. So-called 'conceptual history' is only a sociological analysis of the historical process itself. I shall now set out some principles for such an analysis.

The historian and the sociologist do not simply look at the same thing in different ways. They distinguish separate processes within a single more complex process and offer different interpretations of their interrelationship. The point is this: not everything which happens in the spatio-temporal setting in which a new society is formed furthers the appearance of that new society. Not everything may be included among the causes and conditions that engendered it, or indeed be connected with the new society at all. The new society in its turn has origins and sources which are not specific elements of events occurring in a given spatio-temporal context. It has its own life-line (in the palmist's sense) which extends beyond the framework of this context, both into the past and into the future. Different evolutionary lines are interwoven in the world as a whole, and sometimes they coincide so that it seems that they form one single line. On the other hand, the cut-off point of one line is not necessarily the starting point of another.

Thus the end of the Russian monarchy was not the beginning of the Communist order. The evolution of the latter has its origins deep within the complex mechanisms of social life and in the past, where for a long time its line of development and that of the monarchy coexisted. When a new society evolves, the form it takes and the conditions under which it develops are historically determined. What we have in fact is a social process taking place within the framework of historical process, albeit covertly. At any rate, when the process is finished its participants and activists usually discover to their bewilderment that what they thought they were building has vanished somewhere and has been rudely replaced by something they had never remotely dreamed of. When a new society is sufficiently established there occurs a fundamental change in its relationship to its historical form. As before, it exists in some kind of historically individual form, but now the social process becomes predominant and thereby determines the nature of the historical process for the future.

What is historical in a given instance is not purely accidental and transient. Historical consequences can last for centuries. For example, one can ignore national frontiers *in abstracto*, but this is not so easy to accomplish in reality. One can dream of moving Moscow to some more advantageous position, but in reality this cannot be done. Communist society, like everything else in the world, takes shape in history and exists as an individual and unique phenomenon. But it does so in certain standard and persistent forms (again, like everything else in the world).

The Marxist scheme of evolution was created in the following way. Different bits of human history were taken from different parts of the planet and from different epochs, selected according to particular criteria and arranged into a speculative ordered sequence which was regarded as the natural stages of the development of society. But fragments of history scattered in space and time are not the history of any one thing, however much they are put into order by theorists. An ordered sequence of the possible conditions of different societies is not a sequence of the successive stages of evolution of one and the same society.

We must distinguish two senses of the expression 'human society'. It can mean the aggregate of the earth's inhabitants; and it can mean separate human collectives. In the first instance I will simply use the expression 'mankind', and for the second I will reserve the expression 'human society' (which can be shortened simply to 'society'). Thus I shall understand society as being a larger or smaller collection of people united into a relatively self-contained system. It is preserved in this form for a long time and its essential features are continually visible in the activity of its members. The history of mankind is the history of the rise, the existence, the change, the collapse, the collision, the inter-penetration and so on of societies. The history of a specific society does not coincide with the history of mankind, although it introduces into the latter its own particular element. Mankind is not something as uniform as a specific society.

If a given society exists for long enough that means that some stable system for the maintenance of that form of life has evolved within it. In this sense one can differentiate between different types of society. In itself, the idea of introducing comparative criteria in regard to types of society and of using them to place the societies in an orderly sequence from lower to higher is not wrong, provided that the abstract order that results is not viewed as an objective law of social development. For science only the following is permissible: we can describe a given society's type, we can elucidate the laws whereby this society functions and we can discover the general laws of every type of society. We can elucidate the laws of evolution within a given type and of general laws within any type. But there are no laws which govern the conversion of one type of society into another. They do not exist, not because of any empirical reasons but because of the particularity of the modes of cognition without which there can be no science. There is no law for the conversion of societies, just as there is no law for the conversion of flies into elephants, elephants into cows, or rabbits into lions or boa-constrictors. In the course of history some forms of human social units collapse and others arise and indeed perhaps create another type of society. For instance, when the Russian Empire crashed, a new form of society took its place. But it took shape not because of some mystic law of transition from one social form to another of a higher degree but in accordance with laws regarding the shaping of large human formations in certain historical conditions.

If we compare different types of society with regard to certain characteristics, we can observe the superiority of some over others and talk about progress in this sense. We can even clarify why such progress takes place. But in the nature of things in general and of society in particular, progress is by no means inherently inevitable. It is not inherent by virtue of the principle which governs all comparative concepts; namely the rules of logical comparison and of definition. Progress is possible if facts of a certain kind are known (everything which exists is possible). But it is not inevitable, because not everything that exists is inevitable. If there are occasions when progress does not happen, then it is logically irrefutable that progress is not inevitable. If progress does happen, then that means that specific historical circumstances were such that changes came about in a given sector of nature. Only by comparing the result attained with the previous situation according to definite criteria can we speak about progress or its absence (or about stagnation or degradation). The word 'progress' is a value-concept which presupposes a subjective operation: comparison between different phenomena in time.

I shall now introduce some general principles relating to every type of society. The time during which a particular type of society evolves out of a conglomeration of human individuals and takes its shape is so short in relation to historical time that we can understand it as a historical 'moment'. If a given type of society evolves then it happens 'at once', otherwise the attempt will not succeed. People do not manage to grasp intelligently what type of society has been formed before that formation has been completed. It then begins its life, perhaps with a few finishing touches and alterations which do not change its essence. And it is naïve to count on the ability of reformers or oppositionists to change the type of society. They can affect the lives of people in a given society for better or for worse, and they can help to strengthen it or ruin it. But the type is unshakeable. It is formed 'once and for all'.

When people offer examples of types of society which allegedly change, they are not in fact offering examples of normal societies, but abnormal abortions, deformed by circumstances. They may offer examples of changes in society as a whole, but not in types of society. A particular type of society is an abstraction from observed, variegated material. Therefore to speak of the possibility of change with respect to something which is *in abstracto* immutable is to destroy that initial abstraction.

The longer that a society of a given type exists, the harder it becomes to change its type granted the given human material and the conditions of its existence. Attempts to change the type usually end in the collapse of the community itself or a return to an earlier regime with certain changes that take account of altered circumstances. When the normal form of social life is infringed a society tries to restore its type, its 'traditional social order'. When a social community collapses and the type of society that it created is destroyed, and when a new society is created on its ruins with the same human material, then the latter turns out to be a restoration of the earlier society, or a society close to the earlier type. The social order that was established in Russia after the revolution took shape is in many ways a reconstruction of the Russian serfdom which had existed for centuries.

Every type of society has specific parameters (coefficients, constants, degrees) that characterize all facets of its social life: the productivity of labour, the degree of freedom, the level of remuneration, the extent of parasitism, the coefficients of systemization, the coefficients which measure the extent of hierarchical relationships, and so on. There are definite bounds within which the associated magnitudes fluctuate, so that a particular type of society contains in itself internal restrictions on that society's potential. And talk about the limitless development and perfectibility of society on the basis of Communism is just typical ideological rubbish. For example, from the purely technical viewpoint, there is no limit to the growth of productivity. But the technical aspect is always submerged in the systemic organization of the life of the given society, in which each step is increasingly costly and at one point or another begins to be counter-productive. Technical achievements are cancelled out with a vengeance by the losses made by the bureaucratic *apparat*, by bad management, by red-tape, eye-wash, parasitism, managerial play-acting and so on. The establishment of a given type of society is at the same time the establishment of internal limitations on all the vitally important indicators of that society. The Communist type of society is wholly and fully subjected to these principles and can be described by means of a corresponding system of concepts and magnitudes.

THE PROBLEMS OF METHOD

The object of our reflections (a multi-million-strong society of rational beings of a particular type in particular conditions) is an actual Communist country. Such a society is a particular instance not only of a society of the Communist type, but of society in general, of a large social system, and, finally, of a large empirical system. Within it there coexist and intertwine simultaneously the properties of all empirical systems, the properties of social systems, the properties of every large community, the properties of the Communist system and the individual peculiarities of a particular country, its history and its peoples. There is no such thing as a 'pure' Communist society. Real countries do exist with a Communist order, but they have their own individual history. Further, we must be able to distinguish in a particular country that which derives from Communism as such and that which arises from other sources. Sometimes this distinction is obvious: (for instance Communism is not guilty of causing earthquakes); and sometimes not (for example shortages of foodstuffs may be caused either by bad weather conditions or by the system of agriculture).

The Soviet Union, as I have already said, gives us a classically clear model of the Communist order. But here too that order is submerged in a mass of relationships of another kind as well as in the general history of the country. Here too, this problem of distinguishing specifically Communist phenomena from phenomena of another sort remains, and it is naïve to think that the specific features and laws of the Communist order can be observed constantly in the streets and in the villages, in the corridors of institutions and the shop-floors of factories. One can observe directly only millions of people, billions of actions and some buildings and events. Considerable intellectual effort is needed to distinguish in the flux and jumble of passing events those phenomena which specifically exemplify the Communist system, to recognize their regularity, to divine their mechanisms, to trace their importance in the life of the people and to ascertain their decisive role in society. Add to this the consequences of the fact that any given country is itself an element in a system of other countries. Add to that the coexistence and intertwining of different social systems in the real life of peoples and countries. Unless we distinguish all of this and take account of all the perplexities of social processes, we cannot make very much sense of even the simplest phenomena.

Our object of consideration has already been delineated. Assuming that we can study the subject freely and that we have access to any facts we want, what can we do with them? Where do we begin? What particular sequence should we follow? What can we jettison altogether? What can we postpone for the time being and then return to later? How does one split up the whole study into parts?

I could formulate scores of purely technical, methodological problems to which the representatives of dialectical materialism can give no answer any more than can those who regard dialectical materialism with disdain. You won't find them in Western scientific methodology or in Western sociology either: from the point of view of the problems which interest us they provide as dismal a spectacle as Marxism itself.

But the conditions in which we are to make our enquiry are in reality not as ideal as I have assumed above. The concrete data are either secret or falsified, whether unconsciously or deliberately; or they are generally inaccessible for practical reasons. Moreover, even the subject itself is unfavourable for our purposes. It is unusually complex, cumbersome and muddled. Its components are protean, inconstant and interactive. The very same phenomena engender contradictory effects and can themselves be the effects of contradictory causes. Precise measurements are too cumbersome, impossible in practice, expensive, and meaningless because of the inconstancy of what is being measured. It is impossible to establish exactly the actual distribution of the different elements of the whole at any given time or place. Also our means of receiving and processing information are limited. And, in addition to all the rest, we have problems which in principle are insoluble. An instance of this would be a situation in which obtaining evidence about some phenomena excludes the possibility of obtaining evidence about other problems. In short, the very subject itself and the possibilities for tackling it are such that we are going to meet thousands of different kinds of 'not'; 'no', 'not known', 'cannot be established', 'has no sense' and 'without meaning'.

In such conditions we shall be compelled to work with judgements which cannot be verified empirically and which we cannot reach by the general rules of deduction. So we must somehow compensate for our lack of information and our impotence. We must invent a special method of investigation for such a situation. One won't discover the method in the situation itself because it simply doesn't exist in it. It doesn't exist at all; and so we've got to invent it. So what remains to us? Should we abandon attempts at scientific understanding and rely on prophetic intuition, on the amateurish guesses of reformers and the emotions of dissidents? No, there is a way out of this situation. There *is* a way of studying society which coincides with a scientific approach in its purposes and methods but differs from science in its aims and results: one must develop in oneself a scientific mode of thought and learn to interpret the facts of life we observe *as if they were* objects of scientific examination. The results of this approach will not be precise magnitudes and formulae but approximate valuations and guidelines for our understanding of life around us. The approach will be free from illusions and free too from the influence of propaganda, demagogy, deceit and self-deception. Later on I want to expound certain elements of such a mode of thought when I come to apply it to Communist society.

COMMUNISM AS SUCH

When one begins to think about Communist society one naturally does so within a particular linguistic system. The latter contains a system of concepts, and so in one way or another orientates the critical faculties and predetermines the instruments and possible modes of cognition. The first requirement of the mode of thought I am talking about is this: one must examine the object of study (in our case Communist society) as such or in itself, from the point of view of its own intrinsic values, and not from the point of view of possible comparisons with other objects (with other societies and countries). Our method must avoid received opinions that are foisted upon us via our own familiar linguistic system (conceptual system) and via mental associations with other objects.

Often when talking about the Communist way of life I would find myself in the following position. I would be talking, for example, about social contrasts under Communism. What of it, my opponents would object, there are also rich and poor in the West, exploiters and exploited, the privileged and the underprivileged. When they said this my opponents were completely forgetting that whereas social contrasts in the West had long been a *banal* object of criticism, Communism was conceived of as a society without exploiters and exploited and as the kingdom of universal justice. But the important point here is not so much that as the following: If Communist society has some particular positive or negative features, and if societies of a different type have analogous features, it by no means follows that Communist society suddenly no longer has these features, or that their role becomes different. We must observe the properties of Communist society independently of the question as to whether or not they exist in societies of another type. I do not deny the usefulness of comparisons in general. But in this case comparisons should not play a decisive role. They acquire sense only after we have gained an understanding of a particular society in its own terms and without reference to societies of another type. The fact that in other societies there is a repression, exploitation, a low standard of living and other unpleasant features does not at all mean that these don't exist in Communist society. They do, and that is an empirical fact. We must examine them as objective properties of the society in question, we must explain why they arise, and this without reference to their fate in other countries. Our task is not to decide which society is better but to draw an objective picture of a particular society without comparative and subjective value-judgements.

Amid a host of factors that prevent such an approach to Communist society I want especially to draw attention to the following two. The first is Marxist phraseology. Although Marxism was born historically with pretensions to being regarded as scientific, and still claims to be a science (moreover, the most advanced of its kind and unique), it has in fact been converted into a classical form of ideology and its terms and expressions have become purely ideological phenomena which have been deprived of any scientific sense, and which are designed to disorientate thoroughly those who seek to understand real-life Communism. Marxist expressions and terms were conceived in the context of bourgeois society of the last century and were inspired by the specific desires of members of that society. But now they are applied to Communist society as it actually exists. Here they fulfil the ideological role of diverting attention from life as it really is and are a means of concealing the reality of the social order. For example, Marxist teaching about social classes concentrates on social distinctions which are not important for Communism (workers, peasants and intelligentsia) and their relations, thereby diverting attention from the characteristic division of the population in Communist countries into the privileged and underprivileged, the rich and the poor, the exploiters and exploited. The real social structure of the population is simply never taken into consideration. Moreover, the critics of Communism fall into the Marxist phraseological trap themselves by indulging in a completely hopeless polemic with Marxists, having had foisted on them Marxist linguistic terms. Or, let us take the example of poverty. Under Communism there is indeed no private ownership of the means of production. But to say this is to say absolutely nothing about how things in Communist society really are.

The second factor is the habit of examining the phenomena of Communist society using the same system of concepts as one uses to examine similar phenomena in other countries. For instance, concepts such as 'party', 'trade-union', 'elections', 'law' and so forth are used in the examination of Communist society in the same sense in which they are used in respect of societies of the Western type. And suitable phenomena exist in Communist society to fit these expressions, but people fail to see that these things in that context have a qualitatively different nature. If we compare Communist society with other societies (for example with Western states) it is not hard to notice many similarities between them. One can see under Communism many things that exist in the West. But the significance of these phenomena is often utterly different in principle from their counterparts in non-Communist countries. And these phenomena must, I repeat, be understood as above all belonging to Communist society independently of their similarity with certain phenomena elsewhere. It is only on this basis that a meaningful comparison is possible, and not conversely.

For example, in pre-revolutionary Russia there was never a serious trade-union movement analogous to the Western one. Now there are trade-union organizations in all the institutions of the USSR. But these are the Communist system's own product and not the continuation of a past tradition. And their social role has very little in common with the role of the trade-unions in the West. Yet Soviet trade-unions (*profsoyuzy*) are seen as being analogous to those in the West; and the managers of Soviet and Western trade-unions conduct relations as if they belonged to the same category of phenomenon. If Soviet trade-unions are viewed in the same way as Western ones then it is absolutely impossible to understand their role in Soviet society. They can only be properly understood as part of the structure of Communist society quite independently of whether or not they have any antecedents in the past or in the West. The word 'trade-union' could well be exchanged for another in the interests of greater clarity.

The requirement that an object be examined 'in itself', 'for itself', 'as itself', i.e., leaving out of account for the time being its comparative characteristics, was well known in the philosophy of the past and in particular in German classical philosophy (the philosophy which served as one of the sources of Marxism). But this methodological requirement, like many others, is habitually ignored even by specialists when judgements are made about Communist themes, not to mention ordinary mortals who have no idea whatever of past philosophical achievements.

To understand Communism in itself means to elucidate that particular social animal from the point of view of its inner processes and outward behaviour; to be clear about what one should expect of it and what one should not expect of it in any circumstances. One can, for instance, adduce as many external analogies as one likes in order to reinforce a thesis about the possibility of there being Communism with civil rights in certain countries. But from the point of view of an internal analysis (i.e. one without recourse to analogies), that thesis is just as nonsensical as one which postulates a Capitalism without money, capital and profit. One can propose analogies on which to base hopes that the Soviet Union will curtail its penetration of all corners of the planet and give up its claims to world hegemony. But an analysis which eschews analogies makes it quite evident that the USSR *cannot* exist without expansion, without the penetration of other countries, and without the quest for world hegemony.

COMMUNISM AND TOTALITARIANISM

The social order in the USSR and the social order in Hitler's Germany are sometimes regarded as being phenomena of the same species, as particular cases of totalitarianism. This is an example of the non-observance of the methodological principle which we noted above. Of course, there is a similarity there which it would be senseless to deny, but from the sociological point of view these are phenomena which are in principle qualitatively different. German totalitarianism occurred within the context of Western civilization. It was a political regime which in itself did not destroy the social basis of the state. Of course, Hitlerism had as one of its sources the same elements of communalism from which Communism grew. And to a certain degree it was a training for future Communism. But all the same it wasn't Communism. Stalin's totalitarianism was a social rather than a political phenomenon. Stalinism was born of a revolution already accomplished, and it was a manifestation of a maturing Communist society. Hitlerite totalitarianism was born of fear of the Communist revolution and of the possibility of the rise of a Communist society.

The system of each leader's personal power, the phenomenon of mass repression and much else were similar in both countries. But the conditions of life of the mass of the people remained different in principle. One could cast aside totalitarianism of the German type and preserve the social order of the country. One could not cast aside totalitarianism of the Soviet type without destroying the whole social order of the country down to its very foundations. German and Soviet totalitarianism came to resemble each other in many ways because of the law that social systems which are in contact with one another tend to become alike; that is, through the effect of certain general laws of large empirical systems; and not because of any inevitable development from the inner laws of each individual system.

The use of the term 'totalitarianism' in connection with Communist society hinders an understanding of that society. Totalitarianism is a system of coercion foisted upon a people 'from above' *independently of the social structure of the population*. The Communist system of coercion arose from the social structure itself, i.e. 'from below'. It marries well with the social order of the country. It only occasionally looks like totalitarianism (especially during the maturation period of a social structure of the Communist type), and mainly as such to outside observers with a penchant for deeply intellectual comparisons.

FROM THE ABSTRACT TO THE CONCRETE

During the last century an appropriate method was discovered for the investigation and understanding of such complex and changing phenomena as human societies and described in general outline. It was a method for moving from the abstract to the concrete and was described by Hegel and Marx. Marx made considerable use of it in writing *Capital*. In 1954 I myself finished a philosophical dissertation on this theme (*Method of ascent from the abstract to the concrete*). The dissertation had some success among young philosophers (we were then approaching the liberal period) and it was distributed in manuscript copies. But it had a hostile reception from the luminaries of Soviet philosophy, and this was not at all surprising. The conversion of Marxism into a ruling state-ideology was accompanied by the conversion of the dialectic from an instrument for understanding the complex phenomena of reality into a weapon of ideological dishonesty, and for the deception of the population. Any attempt to describe the dialectical method of thought as an aggregate of logical methods of a special kind (and such indeed was the orientation of my work) was doomed to failure because of the conception of the dialectic, by then prevalent in Soviet philosophy, as a doctrine of the general laws of existence. When the dialectic became the kernel of Marxist ideology, it compromised itself in the eyes of scholars and philosophers in the West. Thus these otherwise unimpeachable methods, which in one way or another lay at the root of the dialectic method of thought, were consigned to oblivion, including the method of transition from the abstract to the concrete. To know what real Communism is without using this method is quite impossible. Below I shall describe it very briefly, sticking to the essentials.

When one has to study and describe a complex, many-sided, differentiated, changeable subject, one cannot at once take account of all its properties and manifestations. Something or other has to be left out. Nor is it the case that everything is equally important for our understanding of the subject in question. Much is of no relevance while much prevents our understanding of it. But suppose that we have managed to isolate everything that we must include in the subject in order to understand it properly. Even in this abstract form it will still remain complex and many-sided enough. We still have to grapple with the inconsistency of its manifestations and the continually changing consequences of their interaction. In these conditions we must isolate different aspects of our subject from their general context and while we are studying them we must desist from a consideration of other phenomena, establish some kind of sequence and then somehow or other take account of the phenomena whose consideration we postponed.

The judgements arrived at in this way are more or less abstract; that is to say that they have sense, meaning and truth *by virtue of their abstraction from circumstances*. As we continue to take account of different facets of the subject under study we gradually arrive at more or less concrete judgements, i.e. judgements which have sense, meaning and truth in the context of actual circumstances.

Here I am examining abstract or 'pure' Communism, which means this. I accept as a fact that this or that Communist country has definite dimensions, geographic conditions, a population of certain numerical order, a national structure, a historical past and traditions. But I am abstracting from all that: I am examining any Communist country in isolation from its dimensions, the size of its population, its history and a whole series of other characteristics.

Of course one may examine some of these with the purpose of making certain assertions concrete. For example, the very low living and cultural standard of the population of Russia made it suitable for Communist experiments. The natural conditions and dimensions of that country were convenient if one wished to execute mass repressions. The dimensions were a help in the war with Germany. Furthermore, I am examining any Communist country in abstraction from its non-Communist neighbours and from its relations with other Communist countries. Again, these problems of mutual relations between Communist and non-Communist countries and between Communist countries, can be examined later; they will give a more concrete picture of the society compared with the one to be had from an examination of individual Communist countries. What I am doing ultimately is viewing a Communist country in its *ideal aspect*, as if all the norms of the Communist form of life were strictly observed. For instance, according to the rules of Communism, every citizen fit to work is obliged to offer his labour to the state in some institution or other and receives a livelihood only in respect of that work. In practice this rule is constantly broken. Thus a man may receive an inheritance, he may win money in a lottery, he make take a bribe, he may moonlight. But these phenomena do not derive from the essence of Communism itself. They are not accidental, but they must be understood only on the basis of those results which are obtained from the study of ideal, abstract, 'pure' Communism.

The method of approach or 'ascent' from the abstract to the concrete is an indispensable technical element for scientific study in conditions in which one cannot make use of laboratory experiments; when one cannot in fact isolate the object under study from others, separate the components and study them in isolation from one another and in differing combinations; when, in short, all this must be replaced in Marx's words by the power of abstract thinking, the ability to manipulate the object under study, as if all our imaginary experiments were really taking place but at the same time preserving the integrity of the object. Nowadays in the context of a general passion for mathematizing everything, for cybernetics, modelling, deductive system, empirical measurement, it is not at all *à la mode* to work out a method of 'ascent' from the abstract to the concrete or even to remember that it exists. This is a pity. Contempt for this method is suitably rewarded by the fact that the efforts of many thousands of well-qualified specialists produce in real life either quite derisory results or else errors.

A REMARK ABOUT THE DIALECTIC

The method of moving from the abstract to the concrete can be itemized as a set of cognitive steps in the understanding of the subject under study. In particular there is the device of moving from an examination of a phenomenon taken individually (i.e. in isolation from the coexistence of the interaction between many phenomena of the same sort) to the examination of aggregates of many phenomena of the same sort (i.e. taking into account the fact that there will be interrelationships between these phenomena such as will affect their properties).

Many people know, for instance, from personal experience that Soviet man, viewed in isolation from his position in the collective, differs from Soviet man seen in terms of his behaviour within the collective. In the first case he is quite capable of cursing the Central Committee or the speech of the Party's General Secretary upside down; in the second, in the collective, he will exalt them to the skies. From the point of view of the method we are considering this is a trivial example: in the one case our judgement of the man will be abstract; in the other concrete (compared with the first case). Moreover the concrete judgement may appear to contradict the abstract, but no logical contradiction is present, because in fact we have the following pair of judgements: 1) if we make an abstraction from certain factors (exclude their influence, suppose that they do not exist), then our subject will have Property X; 2) if we include these factors (admit their influence), then our subject will have Property Y. Here X may contradict Y but judgement 2) as a whole does not contradict judgement 1) as a whole. In its time the dialectical method of thought was first and foremost an aggregate of logical steps of that type, and not a doctrine about the general laws of existence which, one may add, do not exist in reality.

Not only the apologists of Communism and Marxism but their critics as well equally reject the dialectic as a set of logical methods for comprehending a phenomenon as complex as human society. Although Marx did not invent dialectic in this sense, he consciously applied certain of its logical methods in his analysis of bourgeois society. He was, incidentally, the only thinker who understood and consciously used the methods of transition from the abstract to the concrete. Engels regarded this as a flirtation with Hegel. And Lenin stated that, fifty years after the publication of *Capital*, only a few understood it, and those imperfectly. Marxists who live in the society of triumphant Communism, where Marxism is the state ideology, are hostile to the dialectic as understood in our sense, because when it is applied to Communist society itself it inevitably gives a result that contradicts the depiction of the Communist paradise offered by that same Marxism.

I attempted to describe the dialectic as a set of logical devices at the beginning of the 1950s. The reception given to this attempt by Soviet philosophical officialdom was deeply hostile. The critics of Communism and Marxism tie the dialectic firmly to Marxism, interpreting it in the same way as Marxist apologists. That is why, when they reject Marxist ideology, they also reject a scientific method of arriving at an understanding of Communist society, moreover the only method which provides a theoretical weapon against that ideology and one which has no necessary connection with Marxism at all.

LAWS AND EMPIRICAL FACTS

The method of abstraction of which we spoke above does not exhaust the methodology of scientific reasoning. Here I shall offer a few more remarks on this subject.

In many cases when social themes are discussed confusion and misunderstandings arise because different categories of logical assertion are not differentiated; assertions about facts, about scientific laws, assertions about the laws of the subject under discussion itself and other types of assertion. For example, in a certain country facts can be observed to justify the statement: 'In X country the forces of repression *vis-à-vis* dissidents are growing stronger.' At the same time the statement may also be true, when arrived at by means of scientific analysis, that 'In country X the authorities are trying to avoid intensifying their repression'. At first glance there is a contradiction between the two statements, and moreover the second seems to be false, since the first is true. But there is in reality no logical contradiction at all between the two statements. They have such different logical pedigrees that they simply cannot be used to form a contradiction. A contradiction of the first statement could for instance be the statement: 'In the country the repression of dissidents is not being intensified,' and of the second: 'The authorities are trying to intensify repression.'

It is very important to distinguish between statements with the logical status of scientific laws and statements with the logical status of a statement of facts. A classical example of statement of the first type is the well-known law of mechanics: 'A body remains at rest or moves at the same speed in a straight line until external forces remove it from this state.' An example of the second type is the statement about the displacement or point of rest of observed physical bodies. Statements of these two types differ in many respects, but particularly in the following one: scientific laws have validity only in strictly identified conditions. Thus the same law of mechanics when formulated more clearly runs like this: 'If no external forces act on a body, it will maintain its position of rest or movement in a direct line at the same speed.' Under those conditions scientific laws are universal, i.e. true always and everywhere without exception. And the statement in its entirety (both that which identifies the condition and that which takes place under it) is also universal.

Statements of facts, on the other hand, can be true in some conditions and false in others. Statements of facts in the case of mechanics identify the positions of concrete objects in space and their displacement. People observe the facts regarding the stopping of moving bodies, their acceleration, changes in their trajectory; but nobody will ever *observe* what it is that the laws of mechanics under consideration expresses. For it was invented according to strictly logical rules which are distinct from the rules governing the observation of facts. And despite their apparent non-correspondence with facts, it is precisely scientific laws of this type that enable us to describe factual displacement of bodies and to predict their position in the future. Scientific laws do not require explanation or substantiation because *they themselves* are the ultimate grounds for the explanation of phenomena of a specific kind and their ultimate mechanism. What we sometimes think is a substantiation or an explanation of scientific laws turns out to be either an interpretation for students or a popularization, or the invention of new laws from which the first are deduced as consequences.

The theoretical part of a new scientific law is not always clearly expressed. Often people make guesses about it out of context. Often it is left out altogether and special expressions such as 'tendency', 'purpose', 'preference', are used instead of it. In our example from mechanics sometimes the statement is made in this form: 'A body tends to remain . . .' At times this leads to muddled and senseless discussions, especially in unenlightened circles and among people who are self-assertive at the cost of verbal clarity. This is the usual situation in the field of social analysis.

In the field of statements about social phenomena there is the same distinction between statements based on scientific laws and opinions that state facts and immediately generalize from them. Here cases continually occur in which the observed facts apparently contradict statements generally taken as scientific laws. For example, in a certain type of society there may be laws in operation by which the authorities try to destroy the opposition and to lower the remuneration of work. But observation may show that in fact members of the opposition are not being severely persecuted and that the forces of persecution are weakening, while real earnings are increasing. In society the law of the periodicity of economic crisis may operate; but there may not be any economic crises. Well, what does all this mean? The point is that we must not confront scientific laws with facts directly. They are only the means to help us to obtain explanations of facts. If we use scientific laws together with factual evidence about a concrete situation then we can explain why the situation exists and what its perspectives are in the future.

NORMS AND DEVIATIONS

We shall now examine the concept of the norm or normal

phenomenon. I have more than once encountered the following situation. I would say that the social order in the USSR was a normal phenomenon and not some kind of deviation from the norm. This statement of mine would be interpreted as meaning that I thought that the Soviet social order was something good: an example of the philistine mode of thinking. But the concept of the norm (or normality) is not a value-concept.

A poisonous snake complete with teeth in the desert is a normal phenomenon within a particular natural zone. A snake with broken teeth or a healthy snake on the streets of Moscow is a deviation from the norm. In social life a certain model is taken as the norm in respect of phenomena of a certain variety with which examples of such phenomena in one way or another are compared. When people use the concept of a norm in relation to a certain set of phenomena they abstract from concrete instances and make certain assumptions. Some properties of the individual examples of events of a given type are left out while other properties are attributed to the norm which individual examples of the type may not possess. For example, when we talk about a normal human being, we abstract from him his height, sex, hair colour and so on. But we don't consider a person to be normal if he or she has no legs or eyes. This is a trivial point. Only, for some reason or other, such trivially simple points are immediately forgotten when important social problems are discussed.

A Communist country in which dissidents are persecuted, people are tied to their dwelling-places and to their work and in which there are no civil freedoms, is a normal Communist society, i.e. it is the norm for this kind of phenomenon, even if, in practice, facts may be observed which contradict the ones mentioned. A Communist country in which dissidents were not persecuted and people could move freely about the world, on the other hand, would be a deviation from the norm. I have adduced this example in order to draw attention to the following point with respect to the concept of the 'norm'.

There are various ways of establishing an abstract model of a particular type of phenomenon, in comparison with which empirically given examples are evaluated as conforming or not conforming with the norm. In our case we regard as the norm that which conforms with the social laws of the society in question, derives from these laws and appears as their consequence. What the norm is, however, is not always clear, even after prolonged study. But there are many fundamental cases when the concept of the norm *is* simple and clear. For example, one can describe a normal Soviet institution – I shall do this later – in terms of a certain abstract model. Proceeding from these assumptions, one can test the normality of phenomena of social life whose correspondence with the norm of the society in question may not be so evident. Furthermore, having examined examples of a phenomenon which we deem to be 'normal' we can then examine deviations from the norm, some of which may themselves be the regular outcome of the operation of other laws of that particular society. And they can be understood as such only by reference to some other norm set up earlier. For example, instances of connivance at the activities of dissidents in the Soviet Union constitute a deviation from the norm; but a deviation which is itself a normal manifestation of the life of that society in one of its other facets. Because of the complexity of social phenomena and the intermediacy of their connections there can be cases where both the norm and its infringement can be the effects of the same causes. For instance, the abstract law of equivalent exchange between man and society operates in the concrete conditions of society as the law of remuneration according to social position; a law which itself engenders the infringement of the principle of equivalence. And that is exactly the way it is with all the laws of the social organism. For people who are mostly accustomed to look upon their comparatively primitive life and psychology as the model and measure for all other people it is psychologically very difficult to recognize the 'dialecticality' of complex social phenomena. Here nature plays a dialectical joke at their expense: it convinces people of their cosmic importance, while condemning them to play the role of unstructured grains of sand.

DIRECTING THE ATTENTION . . .

How important a particular logical method is for under-standing the complex and shifting phenomena of social life is shown by the fact that, without it, neither the professional investigator nor the man in general who wants to make some sort of analysis of social themes can even direct his attention properly. It is widely known that human society acquires the means of its subsistence from surrounding nature. The production of the means of subsistence, which is called 'work', forms the basis of the existence of society. But this is not to say that by stating that fact and examining it we thereby arrive at a basis for understanding any parti-cular type of society. At any rate, such an orientation will be of no use for the understanding of every type of society. It is adequate for some social phenomena and possibly for some types of social organization. It seemed to provide a suitable starting point for the understanding of Communist society: the latter was considered to be heaven on earth, in which all problems of human relations would be solved in the best possible way and it would only remain for people to pro-duce in abundance the means of subsistence and supply all members of society according to their needs. It is, therefore, no accident that this orientation has occupied such a large place in Marx's historical materialism. The orientation is only apparently scientific. It is in fact purely ideological.

To understand real Communist society one must act in precisely the opposite way. If we take the relationship be-tween human society and nature in which the production of the means of subsistence takes place as a given and as a condition of human social existence, it is precisely that relationship which we must ignore in order to define the real source of Communist social relations. They do not spring from the fact that human beings interact with nature in order to work and thereby produce the means of subsist-ence, but from the fact that large numbers of people gather in collectives for the purpose of common life and action. What we must isolate as the object of our attention are the relations between people in collectives which occur independently of the activity undertaken in these collectives. Currently this orientation of attention is strengthened by the fact that everyone is capable of noticing general features of the relations between people in Communist countries in the most varied types of human collective: in factories, in institutes, in towns, in villages, in the organs of power and in the public services.

Communist relations between people operate, of course, in the life and activity of human collectives. But neither the type of activity in the collective nor the activity as such forms the basis of these relations or determines them; on the contrary these relations themselves form the basis of all other social phenomena, *including the character of people's productive activity*. Only on this basis can one grasp the character of the people's attitude to work in this society and the forms of productive organization which the society is forced to adopt because of these relations. In particular, it is only in this way that we can explain to what extent the hopes of the apologists of Communist society are realistic when they speak of increasing productivity or of transforming labour into something as vital to the human organism as food and water or into something which will bring about the happiness and contentment of the workers. At any rate, you will in no way be able to explain the actual tendency of Communism towards compulsory forms of work and enslavement if you proceed from the Marxist orientation of social science and 'scientific Communism', whereas that task is trivially simple if you adopt the approach described here.

If we take as the object of our attention the properties of individuals and the rules underlying their behaviour to each other (i.e. their relationships), behaviour which is conditioned by the fact that people are gathered in collectives for the purposes of communal activity, we should not take account of data which are either exceptional or of short duration, but other normal, everyday data which are widely prevalent and which become evident only with the passage of a considerable period of time. For this to happen a Communist society must exist for a sufficiently long period for the social relations under examination to emerge as factors determining the life of that society. It is no accident, therefore, that a scientific understanding of Communism is becoming possible only now; i.e. when the Communist countries (and in the first place the Soviet Union) have had a sufficiently long period of peace to enable the actual mechanisms of Communism to start working and to reveal themselves to those who seek to understand them.

. . . TO COMMUNALITY

Historically, Communist society is formed along numerous different lines. It is a mistake to regard it as arising from one single source. If we take it as given, i.e. as it exists, and if we isolate the phenomena which are of vital importance, we can then trace via these phenomena the sources of Communism retrospectively. Not for the purposes of carrying out some kind of historical investigation but in order to analyse the society in question and study these phenomena from the point of view of their universality. A case in point is the phenomenon to which I give the term 'communality', which finds in Communism a favourable environment and in which it blossoms forth luxuriantly. I shall explain this important point in greater detail.

Let us take any sufficiently large number of people who relate to their surroundings as a unit, occupy territory, defend themselves against their enemies and secure the means of existence. In this respect people enter into certain relations with each other; moreover these relations materialize in the interests of the relationship of the society as a whole to its environment. But there are other relations between people which derive simply from the fact that there are many people and that they are forced to come into contact with each other in one way or another, to associate, to split up into groups, in some cases to subordinate and in others to be subordinated. In this respect people are obliged to regard each other as their own external environment. In this context, people also perform actions, but now they do so in the interests of their own position within the whole.

There are connections of different kinds between these aspects of the life of the collective. It happens sometimes that the first aspect is the dominant one, subordinates the second to itself and suppresses it. But the converse also happens: the second aspect becomes the dominant one in people's lives. Moreover, either aspect can concern individual people, groups of people, the minority or the majority of the collective, or everyone. In large human organizations like contemporary societies, the second aspect is predominant, at least for the majority of the members of the society. They are not even aware of their participation in the first aspect which is always at one remove and remote. They know of its existence but it has no real meaning for them and it does not influence their behaviour. Even those members of society who have a professional duty to implement the first aspect of collective life do so as a means of attaining their own aims in the second aspect. There is no need to adduce examples to make this clear. Look at your own position in society and try to decide to what degree you feel yourself to be a small part of the whole of society in its relations with nature and other countries and to what degree you perceive your environment to consist of other members of society. What part of your activity relates to the first aspect of the collective and what to the second? An individual's place and behaviour in the internal life of the collective is determined by definite rules or laws. If that individual doesn't observe them, he or she cannot have a normal existence in his or her social milieu nor attain success. Communality as such consists of these rules and the behaviour they enforce taken together.

The essence of communality was already known to thinkers of the past many centuries ago. It is fairly well expressed in the formula: 'Dog eat dog', which subsequently has been attibuted to bourgeois society only. The essence of communality lies in people's struggle for existence and for the betterment of their position in the social environment. The latter is apprehended by them as something given by nature, often as something largely alien and hostile, always as something which does not yield its blessings without effort and struggle. From this historical perspective the struggle of all against all forms the basis of human life.

The essence of communality as we have described it is not an absolute evil any more than it is an absolute good. It is an objective fact, in the same sense that the negative pole of an electron is not evil any more than the positive pole of a proton is good. Everything which we regard as good or evil springs from the essence of communality in equal measure. Within communality, moreover, evil forms the basis for good and good inevitably begets evil. In the nature of human society there is no inherent embryonic morality or criteria for the evaluation of what goes on. These are the artificial inventions of civilization.

THE BASIC IDEA

One cannot say that Communism as a type of society derives directly from communality any more than it would be true to say that Capitalism derives directly from economics or from commodity-money relations. The rise of Capitalism required the appearance on the market of the commodity known as free labour and a series of other conditions. The rise of Communism is similarly conditioned. It was only because these conditions were present that communal relations between people have proliferated through all the spheres of social life and become dominant. Communism derives from communality in these conditions.

The conditions we are speaking of are not the actual historical circumstances in which the Communist order arose in this country or that. You will remember that we have agreed to abstract from these circumstances. These conditions are something that always exists in the life of any society: they are constantly regenerated and serve as the basis for the very continuation of that society's life. These conditions should be looked for not in the pre-history or the history of a society but in its present-day life. Moreover, they should appear as something evident, generally known, usual, mundane. Here the intellect is required not for the purpose of discovering something hidden in the crannies and depths of the system, but for the identification of what is determinant for the formation of a certain type of society in what is obvious and well known.

If we look at such a classical model of Communist society as the Soviet Union, it is easy to see that it has a very complex structure; a variegated industry and agriculture, a system of administration and culture of immense ramifications and a particular territorial composition. We shall notice, moreover, that some elements of the structure protect and preserve its integrity, while others in a sense form autonomous parts of it which themselves are also integral, albeit on a smaller scale. And these parts have an interesting quality: in some respects they are a microcosm of society as a whole. This is evident not only in the case of such large territorial units as whole republics, but also in the case of smaller, but still quite large entities like the district (*krai*), the province (*oblast'*), and the region (*raion*). But this resemblance can go still further and embrace individual institutions (plants, factories, institutes, collective farms). We find the limits of its extent in the smallest components of the society which themselves possess some of the essential features of the larger components and of the society as a whole. They are what we may call the elementary cells or nuclei. Indeed it is in these cells which are common to all parts of the social structure from the smallest nuclei up to and including the whole, that one must look for the most unshakeable foundations of that society.

Historically, Communist society, as seen in its classical model offering almost laboratory conditions of study, took shape along many lines at once. It was formed in a way which united the country. Its various components were differentiated and combined in various ways. Life was standardized in all regions, in all spheres, at all levels. It was this standardization of life in all its aspects right down to the level of elementary cell and the formation of a standardized cell structure for all areas and organs of the society as a whole which form the essence of the historical process whereby contemporary Communist society came into being. In many other countries history seems to have taken a different course from the one it took in the case of the Soviet Union, yet essentially the result has been the same: the formation of a standard structure and the standardization of life in all the cells of the whole.

Of course the process of standardization was two-way, involving the influence of the whole on the part and the part on the whole. There was a process of mutual adaptation and 'levelling out'. But once that had happened this reflection of the parts in the whole and of the whole in the parts became the norm for that society.

George Orwell, in his remarkable book *1984*, did observe some features of Communist society. But despite my admiration for this author, I should say that he understood little about its essence. In particular, he did not know what is most important – the way in which the life of society is enacted at its fundamental level, at the level of the cell. It is a mistake to regard Communism as something foisted on people by force and fraud from above. It constantly wells up from below, from the cells. And it is here that the system obtains its constant support. It is only on this foundation that it grows and is supported from above. Here 'above' is a relative concept: 'above' also has a cell structure, but occupies a special position in the cell hierarchy.

Of course, the isolation of the cell as the starting point for the analysis of the whole entails a whole series of abstractions. For example, not all citizens enter society directly via its cells. Children and old men, pensioners and invalids, people in the 'liberal' professions live outside them. They are not tied to institutions nor do they figure at a definite place of work. Or if they are connected with the cells it is only via people who *are* tied to them. The majority of the population, however, are members of society because they are members of its cells. All the rest of society is in one way

69

or another subordinate to this base and is dependent on it, or at any rate has no real influence on the standard style of social life. Any exceptions to the rule can be considered at a later stage.

COMMUNALITY

I have described in some detail what communality is in the books to which I have already referred. Many people took that description to be some kind of literary device or at best considered it as a description of a Soviet society in which the people had been corrupted by the conditions obtaining within it. But in fact it was a fully scientific description of the phenomenon of communality, which has a universal human character. I emphasize the word 'scientific', because the description is valid by virtue of a whole series of abstractions about which I spoke earlier. Here I shall only present a part of that description together with some additions and explanations that are appropriate to the context of this book.

The laws of communality are the same always and everywhere where there are numbers of people large enough to allow one to speak of society. These laws are simple and in a sense generally known, or at least known to a significant number of people. If this were not so then social life in general would be impossible. People in practice live in society according to communal rules and are aware of them out of necessity. For the laws of communality it is a matter of indifference what unites people in society. They operate in one way or another once people have come together for a long enough period in large enough collectives.

The laws of communality are the rules which determine people's actions and conduct in relation to one another. These rules stem from the struggle of people and groups of people in society to defend themselves and better their lot, as they have done throughout history and always will do. Examples of such rules include the following: give less and take more; risk the minimum to gain the maximum; minimize personal responsibility and maximize the possibilities for distinction and social standing; minimize dependence on others while maximizing the dependence of others on oneself. The ease with which people discover these rules for themselves and acquire them is striking. This is explained by the fact that these rules are natural and correspond to the socio-biological nature of human individuals and groups as it has evolved historically.

People learn to behave according to the laws of communality. They learn by experience, by watching others, or via their upbringing by others, or their education or by experiment. The rules insinuate themselves of their own accord. People have the nous to discover the rules for themselves, and indeed society offers people immense possibilities for practice. In most cases people do not even take account of the fact that they are undergoing a systematic apprenticeship for the role of communal individuals as they act out what seems to them their normal daily lives. Nor can they avoid this apprenticeship, because unless they have mastered the rules of communality they will be unable to cope with life. Although communal laws are natural, people prefer to keep silent about them and even conceal them.

The progress of humanity has been to a considerable degree a process of inventing means of limiting and regulating the operation of communal laws. These means include morality, truth, religion, freedom of the press and of opinion, public opinion itself, ideas of humanism, and so on. For centuries people have been taught to adapt their behaviour to forms which are acceptable from the viewpoint of these limiting factors and to hide whatever is reprehensible. It is not surprising that communal forms of behaviour seem to them something disreputable and sometimes even criminal. Individually people are so formed that the communal rules appear to them only as possibilities which need not exist, or as specially cunning inventions of their own. When they do talk of this or that law of communality, however, they deprive it of actual human status and ascribe it to some rotten form of society. (The Marxist ascribes it to Capitalism, naturally.) They suppose that in a different, noble type of society (Communism, of course) there will be no place for communal behaviour. But this is a great mistake. There is nothing inhuman about the laws of communality, which are no more inhuman than the laws of friendship, mutual help or respect. The latter are fully compatible with the former and fully explicable as having derived from them. But whether a human or inhuman type of society takes root in this or that country does not depend on the communal laws themselves, but on whether the population has been able to develop institutions which counteract and limit the force of these communal laws. Only where such institutions do not exist in a society or where they are weakly developed, will the forces of communality gain great strength and determine the physiognomy of the country, and indeed the character of the institutions notionally designed to protect people from their effects. What will then develop is a type of society in which there will flourish hypocrisy, together with violence, corruption, bad management, irresponsibility, poor workmanship, cheating, boorishness, idleness, disinformation, deceit, drabness and a system of perks for the *privilegentsia*. In this respect a perverted valuation of the worth of the individual asserts itself; nonentities are exalted, significant personalities are debased. Morally superior citizens are subjected to persecution, the more talented and active are brought down to the level of the mediocre and incompetent.

Moreover, it is not necessarily the authorities who do this. Colleagues, friends, neighbours, co-workers do everything they can to prevent a talented man from revealing his individuality or the active man from rising in the world. This tendency takes on a mass-character and pervades all aspects of life, and nowhere more so than in the creative and administrative spheres. The threat of the society's being turned into a barracks begins to prevail and affects the psychological state of the citizens. Boredom and depression reign and people constantly expect the worst. A society of this type is doomed to stagnation and chronic decay if it cannot find in itself forces that will oppose this tendency. Moreover, this situation can last for centuries.

COMMUNAL INDIVIDUALS: THE BASIC UNIT

The simplest communal (or social) unit is the individual. He possesses a body and an organ for controlling his body which allows him to foresee the most immediate and vitally important consequences of the majority of his own actions and of the actions of other people affecting him. His basic principle here is this: do not act in a way that harms yourself, prevent other individuals from acting to harm you, see that your living conditions don't get worse, do all you can to make them better. This principle derives from man's biological evolution. But it is precisely as the product of that past evolution that man enters communal life and operates according to that fundamental principle. He is incapable of changing it. He can overcome it only by subjecting himself to it.

Applied to the communal environment the principle works like this: the individual tries to preserve, consolidate and improve his social position, or at any rate to prevent its getting worse. But how is he to achieve this? The most typical and basic position in which the individual finds himself in society is that all the most tempting places have already been allotted, that either there are no free places left, or only the worst ones and that there are other people wanting the better ones. It is quite obvious that in this state of affairs the principle can only be realized for the individual at the expense of other individuals: he is forced to prevent others strengthening their social position and seeks to weaken their position. In the conditions of the communal environment, when an individual is sufficiently and securely protected from the collective, another individual becomes the enemy; one on whom the realization of the fundamental principle for each of them depends. Moreover, social life not only does not weaken the principle, it strengthens it many times over by creating countless temptations and seductions for people.

Are there any possible deviations from this principle? Yes, of course. Here are the main ones. The first is opting out of the communal environment itself; for example, an individual can isolate himself and be content with the most miserable scrapings. The situation is like the one which obtains in respect of the laws of gravity: one can avoid falling by not going anywhere high. The second possibility lies through the expansion of the sphere of social activity: for instance, one can seize new territory, or create new institutions. The third entails the coming into play of other human relations which paralyse or obscure the operation of the forces of communality. (There would be, for instance, family relationships, or relationships with friends, intimate or otherwise.) A fourth possibility involves a degree of intermediacy, whereby an individual seeks to help others consolidate their position as a means (so he calculates) of consolidating his own. Fifthly, people can join forces for the joint strengthening of their positions.

Furthermore, not everything that a man does on his own account is necessarily to the disadvantage of his neighbours. And, even if it is, it isn't for all of them. It will in fact suit many. One might also mention the mistakes people make in their calculations and the unforeseen consequences of their actions. Finally, there are people in society who make the happiness of others their own egotistical goal: this is how they assert themselves. There are other sources of deviation, including certain typical psychic illnesses.

These deviations in no way change the operation of the fundamental principle that governs the behaviour of communal individuals. First, the number of instances of behaviour that conform to it far exceeds the number of instances that do not. Second, deviations from it are in most cases caused by the fact that, in one way or another, it still lies at the heart of human behaviour: as, for instance, when one individual does another individual a good turn in order to improve his own position or to damage someone else's.

It does not follow from what has been said that man is a born evil-doer. By nature he is neither good nor bad. But if he is obliged to do something because of the fundamental principle of his communal existence, and he can do it with impunity, then he does it. Nothing in him prevents him or inhibits him from acting in this way. From this point of view man is a creature capable of anything. It is society which develops the limiting factors which constrain this creature's behaviour, and it is only in the framework of such factors (whether prohibitions or encouragements) that man acquires virtues. What is perceived as deriving from man himself is in reality only the reflection of social inhibitions in the consciousness and behaviour of individuals. Self-control is only external control at one remove. The only inhibitors of man's behaviour are other individuals; but he experiences them as something within himself.

COMMUNAL INDIVIDUALS: COMPLEX UNITS

Two or more people form an integral *communal individual* if, and only if, the following conditions are fulfilled: 1) this group of people relates to the environment as a unit; 2) there takes place within it the same distribution of 'body' and 'brain' functions as was observed in the case of the individual person, the former being governed by the latter; 3) there is a division of functions among the individuals who are governed.

This formulation is not a generalization from empirical facts, nor is it something discovered in the observable world. It is a definition of the term 'communal individual' applied to groups of two or more persons. More exactly, it could be formulated like this: in respect of groups of two or more people, we will term 'communal individual' that group of people for whom such and such conditions are fulfilled.

The relationship of such expressions to reality is not

characterized according to concepts of truth or falsity, but quite otherwise; namely, are there in reality groups conforming with the definition 'communal individual' or not? If we define a rhombus as a quadrangle with equal sides, then the statement 'the rhombus is a quadrangle with equal sides' is neither true nor false. It merely introduces the word 'rhombus' into circulation. So it is in our case. Communal individuals of still greater complexity are formed, not out of separate people but from groups of people who are themselves individuals. Here the division of 'body' and 'brain' functions is replicated and their functions are distributed among different people, or indeed among the different individuals which make up the unit. In complex individuals the functions of the governing organ can be carried out by individuals which in their turn are also complex and by combinations of such individuals. What is significant here is that people do not thereby lose their 'body' or their 'governing organ'. The division and distribution of functions concerns combinations of people: in a complex individual its functions as a new whole with respect to its parts are carried out by different people and groups of people who retain all their own functions as whole entities at a lower level. On this basis there develops what we might call the 'alienation of functions'. Just as in the case of the human body a certain percentage of the cells is singled out for the role of member cells of the governing organ, in complex individuals a certain percentage of the people present themselves as suitable for membership of governing organs on the new, more complex whole.

Although this is a trivial and generally known phenomenon, for some reason all the critics of 'totalitarian' and 'bureaucratic' regimes obstinately ignore it. They dream of a society which lacks these defects, i.e., a society which in effect would be without government or organization. Of course, such an ideal society is possible, but only in the short term, as an anomaly in some larger and more normal whole or at the most primitive organization level.

If an entity which can be considered as a communal individual is sufficiently complex then there will be a division and distribution of other essential functions of the individual such as an information function enabling the governing organ to monitor the state of what it is governing, the functions of disseminating truth or falsehood, threats and encouragement, and others. In my books I have given a description of this phenomenon which is valid for a wide range of such functions. Here I want to make the point that in a sufficiently large human collective all virtues and defects which are theoretically inherent in man are *personified* as functions of separate people and groups of people who fulfil these very functions as the functions of some huge social individual.

In a division of functions at that level their distribution between different people and groups of people becomes a matter of chance. Thus virtuous functions can fall to the scoundrels, and the scoundrel's role to people who are decent. Very often, at any rate, these functions do not coincide with people's personal characteristics. In differing situations one and the same individual may fulfil different functions, and one and the same function may be fulfilled by people of different character. The apparent instability of people's character and role can be explained by the simplicity of these roles and their accessibility to everyone, but also in terms of the impressive adaptability of people which allows them to play different roles. In actual fact this engenders a high degree of stability in social groups and enables the mass to organize itself speedily in standard forms.

COMMUNAL BEHAVIOUR

The basic principle of the communal individual is realized in a whole system of people's behaviour. To describe it would need a whole science, and people spend many years of their lives mastering it. In my books I have given many examples of the operation of these rules of behaviour in very different social spheres. Here I shall offer a few important general remarks on the subject.

Any conscious act performed by a person (including voluntary acts) which influences his social position or that of other people I designate an instance of communal behaviour or communal act. A person is aware of the communal significance of such behaviour. In time much of it becomes automatic but that does not alter the fact that it is fundamentally or potentially conscious. Such behaviour is learned consciously as a set of skills and if necessary the conscious nature of such activity can be re-established. A person may deceive himself and others about the nature of his behaviour, but objectively it remains the same. For instance, he may imagine to himself and indicate to others that he is concerned with the good of the state when he rejects the candidature of another man for the Party bureau on the grounds that he is unreliable in his living habits (he drinks a lot or is unfaithful to his wife), but in reality this behaviour is dictated by the basic principle of behaviour of the communal individual: it weakens the position of that candidate as regards membership of the Party bureau, an aim which the man rejecting the candidature achieves by denouncing the other man publicly. Toadying to authority quickly becomes a habit. But even when he has toadied a thousand times, the toady will be perfectly aware of the reality of his toadying. One of the most dreadful forms of masking the disgusting character of a whole series of communal actions is 'sincerity'. But do not believe that this sincerity is natural, because there is no such thing in nature. The most extreme fanatics will act, and indeed do act, according to the rules of communal expediency.

Not all instances of communal behaviour are equivalent. Many have trivial consequences, many have none. But there are instances of communal behaviour which determine the physiognomy of society, its soul and its nature. They also provoke other instances of communal behaviour and influence people's behaviour in every aspect of their lives. The percentage of such communal acts in the general mass of human actions is insignificantly small. Usually they are performed in such a way that they cannot be distinguished from other actions, or are simply not noticed at all.

They go unpunished and are even encouraged. Once again I refer the reader to my other books where I give a more detailed description of communal behaviour.

If people commit communal acts in certain situations in a more or less stereotyped way, one can speak of the stereotype of communal behaviour for the society in question, or about the persistent communal atmosphere of a society. People live their lives in that atmosphere as if it were something natural and habitual. They usually do not even notice that it is oppressive and that it forces them to behave according to the generally accepted stereotype much more effectively than the fear of punishment by special organs of suppression such as the KGB. Since people in the West are only dimly aware of the communal atmosphere in which Soviet people live, they are always inclined to regard their behaviour as something unnatural and performed out of fear of the organs of state security. In fact, the latter intrude in people's lives only exceptionally, when individual members of society escape from the influence of the usual communal atmosphere. In the overwhelming majority of cases there is no need for the incursion of these organs. Soviet people already reproduce the behavioural stereotype that is appropriate to their form of society from generation to generation and preserve their own communal atmosphere in a stable condition. But this would not have been possible without the development in society of more or less standardized living conditions in which this behavioural stereotype, the product of communal rules, could become natural.

There is a whole unwritten (or not yet written) science of communal behaviour. Many citizens master it in its entirety. Here is what was said on the subject in *Notes of a Nightwatchman*.

Every individual who wishes to get a tastier or more generous helping at life's banquet must convince those surrounding him that, as bastards go, he is average, run-of-the-mill and of only moderate talent. This law is inevitable. But there are other laws which mask it and modify its outward appearance. Imagine someone coming forward in a circle of Soviet writers, artists or academics and saying this: 'I am a real shit. Just ask me and I will write a denunciation. I will sign any letter smearing dissidents. I will write an arse-licking portrait of Brezhnev.' Would such a person meet with success? No. Yet this is the sort of thing that everyone does, and that is precisely why they are successful. So what is the point? The point is that there is another law of behaviour which is this: in this society mediocrity must take the form of talent, vice must take the form of virtue, denunciations must become a matter of courage and honesty, and slander sacred truth. It is for that reason that the individual must operate the first law for the achievement of success in a form that satisfies the second law. The fact that everyone knows that he is a bastard doesn't matter. What is important is that he is a bastard who conforms to the rules of communality and accordingly makes an impression of decency. He has to behave correctly (according to the rules!) so that, formally, there is no way of revealing him for what he is.

Further, every individual begins to fight for his share of the cake when all the roles have already been distributed, all the good places taken and when those in possession won't give them up without a fight. Can the individual afford to wait until somebody notices him and recognizes his true worth? Society tries to encourage people to moderate their career expectations, that is to persuade them to wait until others recognize that worth. It happens of course that people *are* noticed and given their due. But rarely. And in unimportant positions. In the most important posts the principle operates which exposes the total vacuity of the proverbial 'everything comes to him who waits'. The individual usually knows that people around him are capable of noticing and evaluating his worth, but that they will do what suits *them*.

And what if there isn't any worth? An individual has to display a certain minimum of activity in order to be noticed and evaluated formally. But how? Will he succeed if he sets his sights very high and, for instance, begins to denounce the high-ups in his sphere? No, of course not. There is another law of communal life, the law of proportionality. According to this law a person must convince those who surround him (or at least the most influential number of them) that his own claims do not threaten their position. If the individual is to risk breaking this law, he must make use of another law from the same category which is this: put the powerful and influential into a position in which they will be compelled to satisfy the inordinate claims of the individual.

But this doesn't often happen. Usually the law of proportionality operates in conjunction with the law of gradualness. The individual should claim a big piece of the cake only after he has received a smaller piece, got used to it and accustomed those around him to regard it as well-deserved. In this way his growing claims look like the natural reward for his services. Besides, for every bastard who is beginning his career there is another bastard who has the reputation of being an even bigger one. This is also a law: communal individuals throw champion bastards out of their environment in order that their own behaviour should not be noticed and should seem to be the norm. And the path the bastard takes when starting out on his career should look like the path of the development of Communist society from greater to less skulduggery – i.e. like progress. To be a participant in progress, to be in the forefront and to be progressive: that is also demanded of individuals in Communist society.

In my books I have presented numerous rules of communal behaviour illustrated by examples taken from my experience of Soviet life. I shall give two more hypothetical examples in order to illustrate some general propositions. Here is the first example. Imagine some sphere of activity where the participants are more or less the same, or at any rate comparable. It has its prominent figures and its below-average individuals, but, as they all know, there is not a great difference between them. But then they notice that someone has joined them who quite possibly will quickly and decisively surpass them all. Will they welcome this event which promises to do considerable damage to their own prestige? Of course not. They will be embittered and will want to get rid of him. That their attitude is thoroughly natural is precisely the point. The rules of communal behaviour are generally natural. If these people have the chance, without damage to themselves, of preventing the appearance of an individual who threatens, they will do it. But can the individual nevertheless make it in the end? He can if there are other people who are interested in his success for their own private purposes and who can preserve him from his colleagues who are trying to get rid of him. Such cases constantly occur in sport, in science, in art and in other spheres.

These other people who help the individual to fight his way through are also acting according to communal rules. They have their own concerns. In real life people's actions and interests are intertwined in such a complex way that the detection of communal rules in this jungle is only rarely possible. Over everything there reigns a hypocritical atmosphere of friendship, mutual assistance, and willingness to cover up for each other. Consequently, the real mechanisms of human behaviour remain deeply hidden in the confusion of actions and words.

The second example is this. Suppose that author A has written a good book. Suppose author B is an enemy of A and wants to cause him harm. To the casual observer he appears to defend A's book. But there are several ways of defending a book, and so B, in his defence of A, reduces the status of the book to some mediocre level. He can't severely criticize A because that would discredit B and draw attention to A. So B praises A, and thereby preserves his own reputation as a decent fellow, while at the same time he reduces A to the level of mediocrity. In these conditions B causes damage to A in a way which suits his own interests. This example is hypothetical in terms of its exposition, but it is not contrived and is wholly characteristic. In our comparatively highly educated age people develop surprisingly refined and effective skills in the matter of harming their neighbour without harming themselves. Occasionally this behaviour can even enhance their own reputation. The rules of communal behaviour retain their full force in the deep workings of our lives, however decorous society may appear on the surface.

The communal behaviour of complex individuals (that is groups of people and groups of these groups) is replicated in the behaviour of their governing organs and the behaviour of the latter in that of the most basic individual units. Of course the complexity of large populations comprising single individuals can give rise to new rules which govern the behaviour of the latter, but in general the behaviour of complex individuals and single individuals is analogous. From this point of view, for example, the Soviet Union as a whole behaves like the average Soviet citizen: it is unreliable, mendacious, hypocritical, it is boorish from a position of strength, cringes in the face of superior strength, and in addition is absolutely sincere.

In the West people are surprised at the behaviour of the Soviet Union in the person of its government. Yet, its behaviour is perfectly natural. The country is the classic example of the communal individual. Within it the coincidence of the types of behaviour of individual people, individual communes and of the country as a whole is very striking indeed.

COMMUNAL RELATIONS

The basic communal relations of individuals are those they have with the group to which they belong, the relations of the group to individuals, and the relations between individuals within the group. Derivative communal relationships are, for example, those of the individual to other individuals outside the group, or of the individual to society as a whole and of society to him.

The overwhelming majority of individuals do not enter society directly, but via a group or hierarchy of groups. The relationship between the individual and his immediate group is determined by the degree of dependence of the individual on the group, and vice versa. The individual's dependence tends towards the maximal and the group's towards the minimal. The group tries to put the individual in a position in which he is dependent on it for everything he receives from society, and for everything which he contributes to society. The group tries to control the individual's rewards and punishments, his productive activity and his personal life. And the group has the basis and the obvious means of so doing, because it is the group which pays the individual for his participation in social life. I emphasize again that he participates in society as a member of the group and not as an individual person.

There are, of course, people who enjoy a large degree of independence from their immediate group, but these are exceptions. Besides in such circumstances there is another imprecisely defined group to which these people belong in practice. The dependence of the individual on the group is in reality his dependence on those members of the group who fulfil the functions of watching over him on behalf of the group. These individuals who exercise this monitoring function can change depending on the situation, but the tendency is against change. Usually the head man, boss or leader of the group fulfils this function together with his official or voluntary helpers. Other members of the group, especially those who are hostile to the individual, help them. This kind of supervision is a perfectly natural and healthy phenomenon, without which the integrity of the group as a communal individual is impossible. The individual tries to weaken his dependence on the group, to which the group reacts in conformity with the principle: 'nobody is irreplaceable'. The individual knows this and usually restrains himself within reasonable bounds. The bounds are exceeded when the individual deserts the group or regards himself as only nominally a member of it. If the individual cannot rely on strong protection when he has deserted the group, then it will punish him in one way or another. Conflicts between the individual and the group normally end with victory for the group, unless the individual is protected from without. The relations between the individual and the group are very well known from the evidence about certain types of groups, especially gangster bands. Here I am only establishing their general rules. Gangster groups can be regarded as laboratory examples in which scientific abstractions are strikingly embodied.

Communal relations within the group are divided into relations of subordination and co-ordination. Subordinate relations are those which exist between those who manage and those who are managed. They reflect the division of functions between the governing organ and the governed body. Of course in these relations there is an element of compulsion, and sometimes they are established as a result of force exercised by some people over others. However, this compulsion has a voluntary basis. The rank and file recognize the bosses as such and carry out their wishes, which gives them the means of existence. The bosses for their part depend on the rank and file in the sense that their position and prospects depend on the latter's behaviour. This relationship is one of mutual advantage, and helps to ensure a stable society. Instances of conflict between the bosses and their underlings, and attempts to destroy this form of dependence, should be understood as deriving from the positive aspect of the relationship.

The relations between boss and underling are a particular instance of domination and submission. Its special character derives from the fact that the people on top are chosen or designated by law or custom. They are not in office because of privilege of birth, economic advantage, physical force or any other non-communal circumstances. Of course these circumstances play their role too, but one must exclude them at the outset because they are not of the essence of the matter. The children of the ruling élite, for example, have more chance of attaining important posts, but nevertheless they become bosses according to the rules of selection or designation which are recognized by the members of society as rules which are just.

The relationship between those who govern and those who are governed is obviously one of inequality from the very beginning. In principle it is ineradicable once society exists. Inequality is intensified by virtue of the hierarchical ordering of the groups, for the rank of the social position of the boss increases with the rank within the hierarchy of the group under his charge. The relationship between the bosses and the bossed is one of the bases of the different forms of coercion in a society where communal relations are generalized and encouraged. The general principle of the relationship is this: the social position of the boss is higher than his subordinates; he is seen as being of more value to the group than his subordinates; his remuneration is higher than his subordinates'. This principle is recognized by everyone, since otherwise there would not be any unity within the group. The boss seeks to maximize his subordinates' dependence on him, and to minimize his dependence on them. The rank and file naturally try to minimize their dependence on the boss and maximize his dependence on them. It is only through this struggle between the two tendencies that some kind of balance emerges. It is constantly being upset because social life is an organic process which is constantly in flux. But means exist for re-establishing the balance one way or another or for re-ordering the individual composition of groups.

Co-ordinate relations (of co-operation, collaboration) are regulated like this. For the individual the greatest danger is another individual who has greater possibilities than he has in terms which are important from the social point of view: e.g. intellect, artistic talent, eloquence, versatility, self-interest. This provides the motive for attempting to weaken the social position of the superior individual; or where it is impossible to weaken him, at least to prevent him strengthening his position; and if that can't be done, at least to prevent his getting it all his way.

Thus the two-facedness, denunciations, slander, intrigue, double-crossing which we normally encounter are not deviations from the norm but the norm itself. Indeed, it is the opposite qualities that are the exceptions. Individuals protest particularly vigorously when people in a similar social position (actual colleagues or otherwise) achieve success in some endeavour which rises noticeably above the average level (this happens especially in scientific work, in art and in sport). Then unbelievable efforts are made to prevent or reduce a colleague's success to the very minimum. On the other hand, it is not desirable to weaken the positions of other individuals too much because that threatens to create problems and stir up trouble.

The inescapable result of the principles of 'co-operation' that we are examining is a tendency to make everyone mediocre. Be like everyone else: that principle is the very cornerstone of a society in which communal laws are paramount. The individual aims at maximum independence from all other individuals and to maximize the dependence on him of at least one or two of them. The individual tries to shift unpleasant tasks which are his responsibility on to the shoulders of somebody else. If an individual can get away with breaching the moral code in his relationship with other individuals and needs to, then he will breach it. If the individual can get away with doing somebody a bad turn and needs to, he will do it. If an individual can get away with stealing the product of somebody else's labour and needs to, then he will. Examples of this are numerous: one can instance the practice of adjudication for prizes, the issue of patents, journeys to congresses, and plagiarism. The individual tries to duck responsibility and to transfer it to somebody else. The list of such principles of behaviour is endless, and everyone knows them from his own experience – merely, of course, in the guise of other people's shortcomings.

Communal relations outside the group between individuals are formed on the basis of principles transferred from the rules governing relationships within the group. There is a reason for this. Firstly, people acquire particular behavioural habits. Secondly, every individual from outside the group with whom a given individual has to do business is perceived by the latter as a potential colleague, boss, or subordinate. Besides, there are numerous occasions when the individual in the course of his work has regular business with other individuals (shop assistants, militia-men, government servants, university lecturers) and stands in relation to these individuals in exactly the same position as he does in his own group. In this way unofficial quasi-communal groups are formed which act like communal ones. Moreover, in such cases communal laws work more openly because of the circumstances that here there are fewer inhibiting factors. The boorishness and capricious behaviour of functionaries, important or otherwise, the coarseness of shop assistants, the arbitrariness of the militia, the open corruption in the public services and in teaching institutions, the endless red-tape: all these are not minor defects, but the essence of the whole matter.

The position of the individual in the quasi-communal groups does not necessarily coincide with his position in the communal groups. In the case of the former, the boss of a normal group may be in the position of a subordinate and conversely (although that more rarely happens). The sociopsychological law of attention-switching and compensation is more often realized in relations outside the group. The law in essence can be reduced to the following: if an individual needs to do a bad turn to another individual but is unable to achieve this, then, as compensation, he chooses someone else as a sacrifice, that is to say a more or less suitable candidate to whom he can do a bad turn with the least risk to himself.

What is typical in communal relations is not the competition between independent individuals but their mutual involvement and their attempts somehow to weaken that involvement and to overcome it.

MANAGEMENT

The question of the ruling élite (the bosses) and of government generally should receive special examination because that élite embodies the mind* the honour and the conscience of society. I shall begin by formulating the basic abstract truth which underlies the following analysis of leader-

* This is a reference to a familiar CPSU slogan.

88

ship in Communistic society. Leadership posts are filled by suitable people. Naturally bosses fulfil certain functions connected with the particular group enterprise. This requires a minimum of education, intelligence and practical capability, but not more than is possessed by very many people in the general population. These qualities are taken for granted; they do not play a decisive role. When hundreds of thousands and even millions of managers are needed in society, then it is senseless to talk about choosing those with the most managerial flair. This is all the more so in Communist society in which competition in the bourgeois sense is excluded and in which the question of competence practically loses significance. Here the situation is more like the one in which millions of people have a motor car: there have to be special circumstances to prevent someone from becoming a driver.

In my book, *The Yawning Heights*, I gave a brief but fairly adequate description of management in a society in which communality is the rule. I shall reproduce it here, with some slight abbreviations, because I feel it to be sufficiently exact from a scientific point of view.

The leadership/management question is one of the central questions of sociology since it is a question about the nature of the social groups which make up a particular society. From this point of view the manager is in principle adequate for the groups. The social type of the society is largely characterized by its managerial type.

The position of the boss is socially better than that of the underling. That is obvious to all normal people. Therefore management is not a function that is fulfilled for the good of the people by high-minded martyrs. It is a position for which people struggle bitterly, and the higher the rank, with its concomitants of greater security and greater benefits, the more intense the struggle.

The most important principle for the manager is the one which allows him to present his own interests as those of the group, and to use the group in a way which serves his own personal ends. If the boss does undertake certain activities in the interests of the group, this is only because it is one of the means of achieving his personal goals; and, above all, one of his means of making a career. A man who has organized things well can sometimes, but by no means always, improve his career prospects. But more often a career is more successful on account of its apparent (but illusory) accomplishments and improvements, which is one of the causes of eye-wash, disinformation and deliberate deceit.

Any hopes that the management will 'take steps', 'look into it' or 'sort things out' are childishly naïve. The management prefers demagogy about improvement to real improvement; and if it does go after improvement it will do so from fear of weakening its own position because of the lack of improvement, or from the wish to strengthen its own position, or because of its own internal intrigues. As regards the operation of communal laws, management not only does not try to limit it but tries to encourage it, for the reason that management itself is quintessentially a product of these laws.

The position is analogous with respect to the relationship between what is in the interests of the enterprise and the manager's interests. Only as a result of external, non-communal reasons can it occur that the manager of the group fulfils personal goals by way of securing the interests of the enterprise itself. As a social norm the tendency is for the affairs of the group to move independently of the manager, not only from the point of view of his social position but from the organizational angle as well. The social position of the manager tends towards independence, and is a particular instance of the general law which applies to all members of the group. The business of the manager is not the same as the business of the group but has to do rather with moving up the managerial ladder, or consolidating his current position and exploiting it for his own purposes, including that of making a career.

The rules by which people are promoted and make a career develop historically and become traditional. According to these rules managers at the lowest level are appointed from the ranks of the averagely incompetent (or competent, which is the same thing) and the averagely dim (bright) who are suitable from many points of view. This principle of selection applies also to higher levels of management insofar as these posts are filled by incumbents from the lower levels, and so as the managerial level increases there is a deterioration in the individual manager's real worth, including his intellectual potential, cultural level and professional competence.

There are, however, circumstances which compensate for this tendency. Firstly, there are the huge staffs of assistants, assessors and deputies as well as the possibility of calling on the assistance of different types of institutions. Moreover, the higher the manager's rank, the larger is the group of people who carry out his management for him. For instance, the speeches which are read out by the top leaders (party bosses) are put together by hundreds of qualified people. The leaders themselves who read out these speeches not only are incapable of writing them, they usually scarcely understand them. However, all the aforementioned people are themselves communal individuals, and they become members of the leader's entourage in accordance with the laws of career-making, so that the compensation we are talking about is largely fictitious. Secondly, there is the systemic effect whereby a sufficiently large group of specialists, if they adhere to the operational rules of that system, achieves in one way or another the desired result.

Thirdly, there is the circumstance whereby the functions of management become more primitive as the rank of the manager increases. The point is that the individual, whatever position he holds, can only, because of his physical limitations, make contact with a limited number of people and express a limited number of judgements, none of which is even minimally well-formed. Any ordinary individual of average competence or education can master with average speed the functions of management on any level so long as he has negotiated the associated steps on the career-ladder. The difficulty here has nothing to do with management as an intellectual activity but has to do with making a career, as such, which of course in itself constitutes a special kind of professional activity. The profession of manager consists mainly of being able to hold one's job, to fight one's way up the ladder and to manoeuvre. Only to an insignificant degree is it connected with its supposedly real function of managing people. For that reason the people who seek managerial positions are those who are least concerned with moral considerations and most incompetent from the professional point of view.

The individual who sets out on the path of a managerial career is soon convinced that it is an extremely easy one as regards the demands made upon his intellect and capability, and a very advantageous one as regards remuneration. The number of people who give up this profession later is so small as to be practically non-existent. So there is nothing abnormal in the fact that old men who have lost their faculties should occupy the top posts and be unwilling to give them up. Besides, the manager in such cases, once a certain stage is reached, is only the symbol of a large group of persons who have positions of power.

Finally, we should notice that management (or government) in conditions where there is no higher authority or more powerful body to whom it is essentially responsible engenders a system where there are masters, but no one with a proprietorial sense of responsibility for the welfare of the enterprise who invests in it something of himself, in other words, a system epitomized by poor stewardship, irresponsibility and endless buck-passing. The masters are only intent upon grabbing a more advantageous position for themselves and holding on to it, without regard for future consequences. For reasons we have already stated, the system of management (leadership) acquires a gangster mentality which informs its behaviour and engenders an attitude of disregard for moral laws and an awareness of the precariousness of one's position, which in turn induces the need for everything to be constantly justified, corroborated, confirmed, or eradicated.

It is characteristic of the individual to try to make the positive results of the work of others his own, and to shift responsibility for the negative results of his own actions on to others. In the case of individual managers (leaders) it takes the following form. All successes that are somehow or other achieved by a given society or social group are counted as successes achieved thanks to the wisdom of the management. Moreover, the nature and extent of the participation of the management in the achievement of the results is immaterial. Even if they have been achieved in the teeth of the manager's opposition they are, nevertheless, in terms of the law that we are examining, regarded as successes of management. Successes achieved under a given management are, of course, the successes of that management. This law operates with such force that even all the cultural phenomena that once were persecuted and then rehabilitated are depicted as the product of the highest governmental wisdom. Even phenomena which have nothing to do with government at all (for instance good weather, the monuments of ancient culture and natural resources) tend to be regarded by the ruling élite as something they have personally given to the people.

Furthermore, responsibility for all the negative consequences of the government's throwing its weight about do not belong to the government, but to those people, classes and organizations to which the government considers it suitable to have the blame attributed. The government is able to do this and does it. The government as such makes no mistakes. Usually suitable guilty people are easily found, but if it is hard to find suitable culprits, then they are invented. Insofar as it is difficult or practically impossible to distinguish phenomena that are really the results of bad management from phenomena that would have happened under any management just the same, culprits are sought for any and all phenomena in life that might be *thought* of as being the result of bad management.

In such cases the management acts with blind formality. The well-known cases in which political leaders tried to present their own criminal activities as an expression of the popular will, or as having been approved by the people, are a particular case of the working of the laws that we are examining. Hence the efforts of the leadership to present its own activity as being for the good of the people, or as willed by the people, and indeed as activity of the people itself. This is convenient. Successes of the people can always be represented as successes of the government of the people, while negative phenomena, *in extremis*, can be represented as the result of the action of the people or as actions expressing its will and interests. The efforts of criminal or amoral political leaders to make as many people as possible co-participants of their crimes or immoral actions is not the evil design of individual persons, but a product of the operation of the laws of communality which people follow – often with a great deal of personal pleasure.

CAREERISM

When people speak about careerism they normally do not distinguish between two phenomena: 1) careerism as a human characteristic which is open to condemnation on moral grounds; 2) careerism as a natural desire to move up the career ladder, such as exists in every complex, hierarchical society. Careerism in the first sense is to be found in all societies, and is also condemned in Communist societies. In Communist societies, however, careerism in the second sense is developed to the highest degree, because only a very few people can reach a high standard of living exclusively on the basis of their own effort and talent. They include, for instance, writers and painters, but even then by no means all of them. In this area, too, there are ranks, titles, posts and privileged positions. In the academic sphere the number of steps in the hierarchy is close to that of the army. Even people who are born into the highest strata of society use their advantage to further their career. In itself social advantage is not yet a career. The number of posts in Communist countries is enormous. The number of degrees in the hierarchy is also enormous. Movement up the career ladder, therefore, is a normal affair for many millions of people, and is the chief (and for the majority the only) way of raising one's standard of living and of satisfying practical needs, as well as the requirements of personal vanity and other elements of social life.

There is a detailed and elaborate system of unwritten rules for the making of a career which forms part of the system of the rules of communal behaviour. I have written about it in detail in my books. I shall reproduce a few excerpts from them here so that the reader may get at least an initial impression. In *The Yawning Heights* I formulated the following three principles for making a career: one does not make a career; a career makes itself; if it is making itself there is no need to interfere. Every help given to a career that is making itself leads to obstacles. If a career is not in the making one has to wait until it begins to take off. If this doesn't happen the idea of a career is nonsensical. The only thing that is demanded of an individual who is desperate to make a career is to reveal himself to society as a potential careerist and wait for results. As a rule the desired results happen. All one need do is be able to wait for them and to recognize them in time. The careerist who has skipped over even one step of a normal career must convince everyone that he is content with what he has got and does not intend to skip further. No matter what 'advanced' or 'progressive' ideas might be in the air, the careerist must convince all those that matter that he is less 'advanced' and 'progressive' than these ideas are.

And here is what is said in *In the Ante-Chamber of Paradise*. There are several career channels. Each of them has a particular ceiling, offers particular chances of reaching that ceiling, promises particular advantages and exacts a particular price. Between the channels there are different types of interrelationship. Here is one of the laws governing them. Let us say that there are three channels, A, B and C. B and C are such that A takes precedence over B, while B takes precedence over C as regards their relative ceiling. Suppose you were making a career in channel B and decided for some reason, or were forced, to change channel. If you transfer to channel A, regardless of the position you occupy, in the eyes of the people on whom your further promotion depends, you revert to a career level one step lower than you were in channel B; i.e. your promotion will be relatively retarded. But, conversely, if you switch to channel C your promotion is relatively accelerated. Thus a kind of career constant is preserved: in the first case you pay for the improvement in your prospects, in the second you are paid for their deterioration.

Just as in the army there are general staff officers and separate army commanders, there are generalist careerists and those who are more specialized. Generalists take the road of general Party work or of Party-representational work: they become secretaries of Party organizations in institutions, district committees, town committees, regional committees. Many people would like to take this road but few succeed. The total figure of those who succeed is colossal in the country, but is small compared with the number who fail. Selection for a general Party career is done most carefully and along many parameters. The system is the holy of holies within the system which perpetuates the Party's power, and because the selection is done by many people, by many ranks of the hierarchy and along parameters, it is the most ordinary and mediocre person with an irreproachable curriculum vitae who is chosen. It is similar to the situation which would obtain if there were a sports competition that included a hundred compulsory events; the champion would be pretty mediocre in any one event.

The Party apparatus channel differs from the general Party channel, in the same way as the career routes of staff officers and commanders differ. Party careerists taking the generalist route are elected to Party office, to regional, municipal and Party conferences and congresses, and become district and municipal Party secretaries, or members of the Central Committee and the Politburo. Although these elections are a sham from the Western point of view, officially they are elections. Members of the Party *apparat*, however, are selected in the usual fashion: strictly, by special criteria, but they are not formally chosen in open assembly. People enter the *apparat* quietly and inconspicuously. No publicity is given to their selection. Here people are chosen who are neither particularly competent nor particularly mediocre, but who can fulfil official bureaucratic functions, and who are reliable by other criteria, because the *apparat* has to deal with real power and affairs which really *matter*.

The career-problem is problem number one for the overwhelming majority of the most active part of society. To describe the system of rules for career-making in Communist society is in large measure to describe that society itself, and the type of person which dominates it. To occupy a definite place on the hierarchical official ladder, to keep it for oneself, to behave in such a way as to have a prospect of taking the next step constitute the basis and mainspring in the life of the most active and creative section of the community. Incidentally, the need to take the next step in one's career is from the beginning a means of holding and strengthening one's previous position before attempting to move a little bit further up. This compulsion to observe the rules whereby a position is acquired and retained turns the best part of the citizenry into creatures who evoke the horror and anger of every kind of moralist. But the creatures themselves and those surrounding them do not regard this as anything frightful. They perceive the rules of career-oriented behaviour in the same way as high society regards the rules of *bon ton*. Rules are rules, and as a matter of fact there is a certain justice which arises out of these rules by which careerists are guided: on average, in the main, people tend to be adequate for their positions. Of course, other people could also be adequate and even a tiny bit better: but what can you do? You can't make everyone ministers, generals, academics, or directors.

To this can be added the following. After a certain level in the hierarchy the way things go does not depend on the person nominally in charge. It depends on the general context in relation to the matter in hand and on the general rules of the system. The manager operates within that framework. He may have taken part in the elaboration of the system, but this doesn't change his own position very much. If a man wants to get the job of managing some enterprise or other he must recommend himself in some way to those who have the power of appointment. Moreover, usually those who are desperate for a managerial post are not counting on a particular post in question. They are counting on *a* post *somewhere*. But the people who decide their destiny and the offices which select the candidate do so from a given number of careerists who are after a given vacancy. In this situation the personal interests and calculations of the majority of the people who take part in the selection and in the nomination of the manager play the decisive role. Among the parameters which influence the selection the intellectual level of the candidates is of decidedly secondary importance. This gives an advantage to people of mediocre ability. In any particular case this does not matter all that much: as a rule the mediocre people fulfil their functions well enough. But taken as a whole this contributes to the tendency towards a decrease in the intellectual level of management and of society as a whole.

The case of careerism is characteristic from the methodological point of view. Many of the negative qualities in people and in the society as a whole can also be seen in other societies. But this fact in no way vindicates Communist society. It is important to state that these negative qualities exist in Communist society as well, and that as such they flourish. Furthermore, it is important to me to show why they continually appear and by what mechanism they do so. In the given case of careerism we see the following: Communist society, because of its irreversible laws of organization and government, has an enormous quantity of managerial posts integrated in a complex hierarchy. People's promotion up the career ladder is a natural and inevitable phenomenon deriving from the very existence of this society. Outstanding talent and industriousness play a comparatively small role in the efforts of people to better their own position. They are of use only to the few. And even for most of those who do possess these qualities they are only of indirect use in their career. Average, even minimal, ability and training is enough for the fulfilment of all (or nearly all) managerial functions. For these and other reasons (which I have already touched on and shall speak about later) there is a ceaseless embittered struggle in society for managerial positions, which naturally engenders the morally reprehensible phenomenon of careerism. Moreover, within this general maelstrom of careerism a brand of individual is beginning to appear whom even the officially recognized careerists find disagreeable.

ASSUMPTIONS AND REALITY

I want to remind the reader that although I have been talking until now about communality as a general human phenomenon, I have been examining it in terms of the way in which it becomes a dominant factor in people's lives. This is clearly what happens in a developed Communist society. In addition I made a number of assumptions, some of them obvious, others perhaps not. The most typical of them are these: 1) individuals perform all communal actions of their own free will: they are free actions: 2) every communal individual holds a position in society which corresponds to his personal worth: 3) everybody receives from society according to his contribution: 4) the needs of an individual are suited to his social position.

From these assumptions other statements follow logically, for instance: 5) the individual's remuneration fits his social position: 6) the individual's needs are always satisfied. These assumptions with their consequences are not arbitrary: they reflect the norms and the tendencies of society. I arrived at them from the observation of facts. But to make such assumptions I had to perform a complex operation and abstract from the circumstances which were concealing and modifying the manifestations of these principles or laws of social life in a Communist regime. That was, however, a purely intellectual operation, a research method which reflects nothing in itself, but acts as a kind of mirror for the attainment of understanding.

By themselves these assumptions do not mean anything

unless we show how such principles are realized in real life. I will try to make clear the principle of *equivalence* as regards the exchange between the individual and society (principle 3). In all probability the principle of equivalence of exchange is a general natural principle. Only the mechanisms of its realization differ.

Let us take the relationship: individual–society. The individual gives something to society: his work and services. But what he gives is one thing and what he receives is another. What he gives and what he receives are not in themselves comparable. How can we judge whether the exchange is equivalent? For this purpose society has a very effective mechanism which in its simplest terms I describe as follows. Let us take the relation to society not of one individual but of at least two of the same social level, and let us call these individuals A and B. The principles run like this: 1) if individual A gives to society more than individual B (and here a comparison *can* be made!), then he cannot receive less than B: 2) if individual A gives less to society than B, he cannot receive more than B. From these principles it follows that if A and B give identical labour or services, then they should receive an identical remuneration. The collective through which A and B give their services to society will see to it that these principles are realized. And they usually *are* realized, more or less accurately, with deviations and after a struggle. But the source of the struggle lies in other principles which derive from the individuals themselves: 1) an individual tries to ensure that another individual does not receive more than he does for the same services: 2) but at the same time that same individual tries to receive *more* than the other for the same services.

That type of comparison of which I was speaking is appropriate only if the individuals occupy the same social position. But what happens if they occupy different social positions? How, for instance can you compare the input into society of the director of an institute and that of one of his subordinates? Here it would be senseless to be guided by the 'cost-of-training' principle. Training a good interpreter, for example, is more laborious than training a director. Only a few can do the work done by the director's most junior colleagues, whereas at least a third of his colleagues are capable of being the director. A cost-benefit analysis in this context is senseless.

There are no means of comparison other than the positions which people actually occupy. This is all the more reason why, in accordance with my basic assumption, the individual's position is commensurate with his value to society.

Here the following principles operate. Let us assume that position A is higher than position B. The principle of rank from A's point of view looks like this: A gives society more than B. Consequence: A receives more from society than B. The same principle from B's point of view: A gives society no less than B. Consequence: A should not receive from society less than B. Thus B recognizes the possibility of a certain inequality as just, while A insists on the necessity for inequality. The degree of inequality is established empirically and depends on tradition. But the principle of perceived inequality of remuneration is a general one, without which the structuring of society into groups would be meaningless and society itself would be condemned to disintegration or ferment, at best to a system encouraging misuse of official positions and illegal revenue. Inequality in distribution, if it is not recognized officially, will be introduced unofficially in one way or another. It flows from the most basic principles of the organization of society. Inequality in no way contradicts the principles of Marxist socialism and Communism. On the contrary, it is only through inequality that these principles can actually be embodied.

In addition to the difficulties that are encountered in the realization of communal principles in life, principles which force people into a cruel struggle, whether they want to observe them or transgress them, there is also the effect of people's actions in the mass which constantly muddies the hypothetical clarity of our basic assumptions. Take for example, assumption 1, according to which individuals execute communal acts of their own free will. These actions are free. This doesn't exclude actions due to *force majeure*, but basically they are voluntary. Only here we must clarify what we take the concepts of free will and compulsion to mean.

Let us take a simple hypothetical instance. In time of war the enemy has surrounded you with superior forces. You are asked to surrender and if you refuse you are threatened with destruction. You agree to surrender. Is this an act of free will or not? If we leave aside unnecessary casuistry then we must regard your act as one of free will. You had the freedom of choice: to surrender or to fight. You were not compelled to make this choice; you chose to. But you made a social calculation; that is to say you considered the consequences of one choice or the other and preferred capitulation. In an analogous sense communal acts taken separately are also free and voluntary.

But when we begin to consider a large number of communal actions by a large number of individuals, i.e. regard them as mass phenomena, then because of the very definitions of the concepts a quite different correlation between free will and compulsion comes into being. Under Communism a standard mass reaction develops in regard to particular types of social action; and individuals pay attention to this possible reaction before they decide whether or not to perform these actions. This does not mean that in the mass people rack their brains to calculate the consequences. The latter are more or less obvious and people follow communal rules semi-automatically. And from this point of view free will or freedom of choice are reduced in practice to a very small magnitude; and the rules of communality acquire the force of compulsion.

This is an example of how we can make contradictory judgements on one and the same theme. But there is no logical contradiction here. One judgement is true if we abstract from the individual act of the individual person; while the other is true if a large mass of people is performing standard acts in standard conditions. When they are applied to concrete reality both judgements are valid simultaneously. But there they simply lose their meaning and give place to other judgements and concepts, or a different focus of attention.

Real Communism provides enough evidence for us to be able to make the following statement which is of the very highest importance: the people who come out with slogans and all sorts of programmes for the transformation of society have to think about how they will be realized in the practical life of the mass of the population. Moreover, for many of them at least one can predict at the outset certain inevitable results when the measures are implemented, inasmuch as large social systems have general regular properties which no reformer or participant in the social process can escape. Our example above of the mechanics of equivalent exchange is a fairly obvious example of this. But something of this kind operates for any social principles and their realization.

In my investigations of Soviet society I have always been guided by this principle: make the best possible assumptions about this society such as only its most inveterate apologists are capable of and then show how, when these assumptions are accomplished in reality, they produce the worst possible results, and provide ammunition for its most inveterate denouncers. This is neither a literary device nor a personal inclination towards paradox, but a completely dispassionate method of scientific investigation. It is a method that enables us to clarify complex and shifting reality, and indeed to surmount the paradoxical nature of our first impressions.

THE CELL IN COMMUNIST SOCIETY

In order to understand why communality is of such fateful significance in Communist society we need to turn to its smallest structural nuclei or cells, which make up not only the larger elements of society but the fabric and structure of the society as a whole. These cells are the *primary collectives*. Then we shall see that there is the greatest possible coincidence between the laws governing the life of the primary collectives and the laws of human communality itself. Such a complete coincidence of communality with the way in which the cells function is not to be found in any other type of society known to history. Here the coincidence is so strong that it seems as if communality were the direct product of Communism and not its historical source. Moreover, there is an element of truth in this: on the basis of Communism communality blossoms forth luxuriantly and reveals all its potentiality. The cell is formed by the smallest part of the society which can be said to incorporate the basic properties of the whole. It should have a certain integrity and independence. It is the society in miniature. At the same time the whole of society must be built from these little parts. But it would be wrong to suppose that one can deduce the properties of the whole system from an analysis of the cell. Communist society is the product of a long history. It presupposes a large number of people comprising a whole country with a long history. The society is formed along several different lines at once, including the creation of those social formations which, now that the society has been established, we can regard as its cells. It is also formed via the creation of a hierarchy of personalities and institutions, of power-systems, transport, education, armies. Simultaneously, the formation of a particular way of life for a large population takes place in such a way that some of the formations included within the total fabric become cells of the whole and combine groups of people in this population according to a few, unified principles. Thus the cell can only be discovered in an empirically given society which has achieved an integral form. This also is an experiential fact. The very idea of cell-separation and the realization of this operation have their origin in scientific technique. Moreover, the type of society and the observation of it as a whole define in advance what will be taken into account when it comes to the examination of the cell. When we examine the cell we shall be examining the whole society, but in its simplest form. Or, to put it another way, we shall be examining society by means of its simplest model.

What concrete form does the Communist cell have? Communist society is contained within territorial frontiers, divided into regions, provinces and other parts. However, its social foundation is organized not territorially but in terms of activity. The expression 'productive principle' is no use here, inasmuch as it is associated with the production of material or spiritual goods which is an individual form of activity, and not a basic one either. Activity to do with the destruction of dissidents, or the stifling of genuine creative literature, or government, is not the production of goods; but it plays here a very important role.

The functional cell of Communist society is an organization created to execute certain practical functions and has in relation to its own business a relative degree of autonomy. It is the primary socio-economic organization. It has its own direction and management, its own accountancy section, its own division of cadres, its Party organization. These cells are the very familiar factories, institutes, shops, offices, collective farms and schools and so on. For every adult member of society who is fit for work the cell is where he obtains a job, gets paid, achieves success, makes his career and receives rewards and decorations. It is through the cell that the socially active member of society (the employee) engages with society, gives it his own efforts and receives his remuneration.

Primary functional cells are established and exist according to particular rules, irrespective of the purposes for which these cells were formed. The nature of the business is not important, as long as influential forces in society consider the business necessary and allocate to a particular cell the necessary means. The functional cell is merely the means whereby one or other group of people acquire their livelihood and realize their plans and interests.

Communist society can be differentiated in many different respects, but in each one of them the cell (cellular structure) forms the basis. Moreover, the functional cell is, I repeat, society in miniature whereas society as a whole is a multiply partitioned, functional super-cell. People's behaviour and their mutual relations within the cells themselves determine the whole remaining system of behaviour and the mutual relationships in society as a whole. It is in the cell that the citizens' standardized form of behaviour is established, and from then on this human material is reproduced as a product of normal social activity. The product then produces in its turn the social order that produced it. All the rest is only the struggle of the social order for its existence, consolidation and extension.

Of course, the social structure of society cannot be reduced to the cellular structure. We must also take into account other aspects of the composition of society: elements of co-ordination and subordination, hierarchies in the fabric of society; classes, organs, and organizations. But to understand all this systematically one must begin with the understanding of the social cell. I repeat, the average and typical institution of the country, the cell, reproduces all the essential features of the life of the country as a whole: relations between the governors and the governed, relations between colleagues, the hierarchy of posts and privileges, the distribution of goods, the surveillance of the individual. If you want to comprehend society, start by studying its individual cell. It is well known, for example, that it was only possible to understand feudal society by taking as one's starting point its basic unit: the individual seigneurial household.

Communist cells differ in many ways: in terms of the number of their workers, their task, their place in the social hierarchy, their prestige and their internal structure. For example, the most menial worker in any division of the Central Committee or the Council of Ministers has greater emoluments than the highest ranks in an ordinary scientific research institute. On the other hand, even the youngest workers in the institute don't wear out the seat of their pants in their institute in the way that the senior people in the great organs do. In Moscow the car factory has 50,000 workers on its strength, while an average humanities institute of the Academy of Sciences has only 500. However, all institutions have some general features in common which allow one to regard them as social cells of the same species. They have in common, for instance, a hierarchy of authority, colleagues appointed from above, a Party organization and the supervision by Party organs of the life and activities of the institution, a *Komsomol* organization, similar relations between people, similar avenues of promotion, similar rewards and punishments and a similar relationship between the individual and the collective.

In any institution the management has officially more of this world's goods and privileges than its subordinates. But the main thing is that the rules of people's behaviour are everywhere identical. If you have thoroughly studied the life of one establishment, it is naïve to reckon that things will be different in others. Everywhere you will find yourself under the vigilant surveillance of your co-workers and colleagues. Everywhere you will find sucking-up, eye-wash, careerism and money-grubbing. There are, of course, deviations from these general norms, some of which are conditioned by the norms of social life itself, and these must be examined at a later stage. Others are linked to the conditions in which social phenomena are enveloped and one must distance oneself from these inessentials and regard the general picture as an abstract model, but as one which gravitates towards reality. Society makes fairly successful efforts to ensure that this average model is adhered to.

Henceforth I shall also be using the term 'commune' to designate the cells of Communist society. The use is justified, because immediately after the revolution experiments began with the formation of communes, and those functional cells which are now standardized did not immediately take shape. The cells have turned out to be the most viable and the most effective units. They differ a good deal from the first communes, but they are their successors. These are communes, and society as a whole is Communism or the grouping together of a multitude of standard communes.

Communes differ in the degree of complexity of their internal structure. One can have primitive communes which do not fall into recognized social groups. Groups, for example, which are created for a short period (scientific expeditions, brigades for the unloading of potatoes), small

107

enterprises consisting of one man who combined in his person the functions of ordinary worker, manager and accountant; for instance, the manager of a beer-counter. But these cases are 'degenerate' ones which play no social role. You can have gigantic communes consisting of tens of thousands of people. Such are the giant aviation and automobile factories and the metallurgical combines. Such huge communes are in fact aggregates of communes. In practice their subdivisions acquire the functions of independent communes that are attached to other communes by business interests somewhat differently from the way in which ordinary communes are attached.

The more important and typical communes have a complex internal structure based on two principles, one which has to do with the interests of the business and one which concerns the management and control of people. In practice the position here is fairly variegated and inconstant, but the two principles tend to coincide. Usually functional groups are formed which are rational from the management point of view. Where the requirements of the enterprise demand the participation of a large number of people and there is officially no subdivision of these groups of people into smaller social groups they will still group themselves according to general communal rules all the same, and one way or another leaders (or managers) will emerge. For example, some scientific research institutes have the hierarchy 'group-sector-department-institute'. In some industrial enterprises the hierarchy is 'brigade-section-factory-combine'. It sometimes happens that parts of the commune are dispersed and the members of these groups associate with each other less than they do with members of other communes. The fact remains that an understanding of the life of all kinds of groups of people which appear to be deviations from some ideal commune is only possible if that ideal commune is analysed first. What is found in the ideal commune will still be found in all sorts of departures from this ideal, albeit in a slightly modified form. Moreover, the modifications are easily explained.

A NOTE ON METHODOLOGY

I shall make a brief methodological digression. There exist objective, general, combinational laws for the grouping of any individuals of a particular type. You can only assemble a limited number of human beings in the environment of any one of those human beings, and similarly you need a minimal number of people before it is impossible for another human being to squeeze in between them. Social groupings are determined by analogous *a priori* circumstances. The structure of communes is not a subjective, arbitrary matter. It emerges empirically, but nonetheless in conformity with these laws. For example, if a sector in a research institute mushrooms beyond a certain limit it will split up into several groups, or even sectors. If too many sectors appear departments will inevitably spring up, i.e. the intermediate groups between sectors and a whole institute. All this is rather obvious and yet somehow seems to escape the attention of theorists. Given this situation, the emergence of a huge social stratum of managers (bosses) of all ranks is an irreversible phenomenon of social life; and just as irreversible is the corresponding stratification of levels of consumption.

What is interesting is the manner in which the grouping of individuals and the differentiation of society depend on the level of the elements of the group (primary or complex individuals). The more primitive the elements of the group, the higher is the upper limit of the group (the larger the group can be) and the higher its lower limit. The larger the group, the more primitive its elements. The higher the level of the elements of the group the lower are the upper and lower limits of that group. The smaller the group, the higher should be the level of its elements. The more primitive the elements of the group, the larger is the range of its potential dimensions. And the higher the level of its elements, the lower its range of potential dimensions.

If the elements are of different levels, the group will gravitate towards the more primitive of these. These are all laws of nature just like the laws of physics, biology and chemistry. I try to avoid such general discussions, but the reader should bear in mind that everything I have talked about and shall be talking about reveals the workings of the general organizational principles underlying large empirical systems (including social systems).

PROPERTY AND OWNERSHIP

To carry out its official functions a commune acquires from society indispensable material resources (buildings, machines, instruments, furniture, transport, etc.). The commune possesses these resources and exploits them, but they do not constitute its property. It can transfer some part of these resources to other communes or even individual persons. It can liquidate part of them as defective ('write them off'), but this requires the permission of particular authorized bodies. And these facts in no way have anything to do with property relations.

According to Marxist doctrine in Capitalist, feudal and slave-owning societies there is private ownership of the basic, vital resources: land and the means of production, whereas in a Communist society these resources come under a system of social ownership. But this is a purely ideological contention without any scientific meaning. It exploits a confusion between the concepts of ownership and the right to dispose of property. Ownership entails the right to dispose of property, but not every such right entails ownership. Hegel knew this very well. One can dispose of something without owning it, dispose of it for reasons other than ownership, for instance as a result of physical seizure, custom or tradition. Ownership is a juridical relationship. If a person or group of people dispose of something by virtue of ownership they have the right to transfer it to others of their own free will, to sell it, exchange it or destroy it. A collective of people working in one and the same institution in Communist society disposes of premises, tables, machines, instruments and much else besides, but it does not own them. The state as a whole disposes of its territory and its natural resources but it does not own them. The existence of external trade and the fact that the state sells to other countries some of its natural riches and may even yield a piece of territory creates only an illusion of ownership, but not ownership itself. The fraction of what seems to be property but which cannot function as property is insignificant and can generally be disregarded.

The situation is just the same with regard to what is called private property. A huge part of citizens' 'private property' is in fact not property at all, for instance flats and villas. One can also add here a large proportion of objects of consumption: you can't give the dinner you've just eaten to someone else or sell it to him. Valuable things circulate on the black market, but this fact does not derive from the nature of society. In principle society wages war against the black market. True, valuable things are accumulated in certain families as a result of inheritance, which are disposed of as if they were private property. But all that is a secondary phenomenon and one that does not determine the type of society.

The ideological propaganda of the Communist countries asserts that in these countries, for the first time in history, the workers feel themselves to be the masters of all the wealth which those countries contain. In actual fact their position is exactly the opposite. Of course there are masters, but they are far from being all the citizens of the country. Those of them who *are* masters act as lords not because of anything to do with property, but according to the laws of communality. As regards the workers, they look at their possession of the collective as something given by nature and as a means of livelihood to which they are indifferent. This attitude of indifference extends to everything over which they dispose by virtue of their status as members of the collective and is manifested by an extreme lack of husbandry, damage, theft, carelessness, poor workmanship.

Attitudes to these same assets change abruptly when they become the property of citizens. 'Private' property and 'state' property are looked after and exploited quite differently. The sharply differing length of the working life of the respective assets bears witness to this.

The expression 'social ownership' is a logical nonsense. Even in the cases where a collective appears to be the proprietor, this is simply a special case of private property; and it is best simply to say 'property', because the expression 'private property' is like the expression 'bread and butter with butter'. In the USSR the land was given to the collective farms 'for their eternal use'. But the collective farms did not become collective proprietors as a result of this, for they not only could not sell their land, they could not even manage it at their own discretion.

THE INDIVIDUAL AND THE COMMUNE

The commune receives a certain share of the social means of people's subsistence which it uses according to established norms for the remuneration of the workers in return for their participation in the business of the commune. These include sums of money for wages, prizes and loans, the building-fund, rest homes, sanatoria and means of transport. Communes are thus the channels through which the citizens contribute to society and receive the means of subsistence in return. They are the points at which people as individual elements slot into society as a whole. People do not enter society directly as sovereign individuals but only via these primary collectives, that is to say, the communes. Communist society is not composed directly of people but of communes, and so the basic personality is not the individual person but the whole collective. Here only the commune is a personality while the individual person is only a small part of the personality, or a featureless precondition of a personality. For that reason the slogan: 'the interests of the collective are higher than the interests of the individual' is not simply a demagogic declaration: it is an actual operating principle.

The active citizen who is fit for work in Communist society acquires the indispensable means of subsistence for himself and his family only via the commune. He is obliged to go to work in some commune or other, to fulfil the duties that it stipulates and to occupy a particular position in it. For him this is an economic necessity, juridically enhanced to the status of a sacred duty. The juridical formulation of economic necessity expresses the fact that if the citizen has the means of subsistence and is not a worker in any commune, he is infringing the most deep-rooted norms of the society. For such people there is a special term '*tuneyadyets*', or parasite. The parasite is Public Enemy Number One. Moreover, in most cases the parasite gains the means of subsistence dishonestly and is criminally prosecuted. But that is not really the point. A person who can live in society independently of a primary collective is a threat to the very foundations of society. He is like a soldier who doesn't walk in step with the rest of the platoon but wanders about at random independently of the rest. He annoys the rest.

A person may change his primary collective for another and obtain thereby some advantage, something that happens fairly often. However, it doesn't alter the fact that he must be attached to some primary collective one way or other.

If he has left his collective, a person must look for another place of work, since he won't last long without wages. There are also other reasons which compel him to look for a new collective. There are, for example, the problems of maintaining an unbroken length of service, career considerations and juridical norms. Frequent changes of job are not encouraged. People who work a long time in one institution have an ascendancy over the others (priorities for improvements in living conditions, rewards, free trips to rest homes).

A person can improve his living conditions and make a career, that is, improve his social position, mainly within the framework of a primary collective. Thus his well-being, destiny and prospects do depend on the collective. Everything he has is at the price of subordinating himself to the collective and behaving in such a manner that the collective will not stand in his way and may even help him. Of course he does have some degree of independence from the collective. For instance many people solve their accommodation problems not through the commune but through local organizations in the district where they live. The levels of pay are sanctioned by law not by the communes. A person also accumulates useful connections. However even these phenomena which lessen a person's dependence on the collective operate only as a function of his particular position and of his reputation in some collective or other.

SOCIAL POSITION

The workers in a commune fulfil different functions within it and correspondingly they occupy different social positions. Although these functions vary according to the special nature of the commune's business, there is a fairly stable system for grading them so that it is possible to examine them from one particular angle and to speak of standardized social positions. These positions are officially recognized and buttressed by the law. The acquisition of skills appropriate to each position in different institutions of the same rank requires approximately the same amount of training and effort. And the fulfilment of the duties attached to these positions in institutions of the same rank requires approximately the same expenditure of energy and talent. The remuneration likewise is approximately the same.

These positions together form a hierarchy from lowest to highest. The lowest positions are occupied by the least qualified workers who do the least pleasant jobs. The highest positions are occupied by the managers of the institution. The hierarchy of social positions is officially consolidated in a hierarchy of rates of remuneration. True, the workers often use their position in the hierarchy to obtain supplementary sources of subsistence. But this concerns only a comparatively small fraction of the workers and often leads to prosecutions. To what extent this obscures communal norms and to what extent it strengthens them we will examine later.

Although people differ in their ability to fulfil their functions in a commune, they need no more than average ability and an average training. If people take on these roles and enact them, they usually perform more or less satisfactorily. Of course it sometimes happens that people execute their duties badly and then they are punished, demoted or dismissed. Or, conversely, people do their work very well, and are encouraged, praised, given prizes and holidays. But on the whole there are some average social norms for fulfilling the functions of a given rank; and people one way or other acquire the average necessary skills. In the case of large masses of people who do one and the same thing, differences in ability and skill lose their meaning. What we have, taking the masses as a whole, is the operation of the principle of congruence between the worker and his social position.

Of course, many workers who occupy a given position could fulfil higher functions and hold higher positions and they struggle fiercely to be transferred to them. The best do not always succeed. But then neither do the worst. Here again we have the congruence principle, according to which the people who are chosen to carry out duties at a higher level in the collective will be capable of carrying them out with average efficiency. These people often come from other institutions, i.e. they are nominated from outside the institution in question. But they are nonetheless selected by someone, somewhere, and on the assumption that functions for which they will be responsible will be carried out normally.

Of course, for real people doing a specific job even small differences in ability and training play a role. They are a source of discontent, envy and hatred. Very often good workers receive less than workers whose performance is much inferior. Very often people make the transition to a higher social position who in the opinion of their colleagues do not deserve it. These phenomena play a real part in life and influence the psychological atmosphere of society. But when we talk about social position as a whole and its underlying laws, we must proceed from the fact that there is a kind of abstract justice whereby, all things considered, people in an institution are distributed among the various levels of the social hierarchy. And we must admit that at the level of the primary collectives people recognize this hierarchy as something normal.

The hierarchy of social positions in institutions serves as a natural basis for the material, social and psychological inequality of people. It is accepted by the overwhelming majority of citizens. Naturally some are discontented with this inequality, but their discontent has no socially significant role. Either it is subjective and partly neurotic, or it is transient. As soon as such people begin to improve their own social position they usually forget about their past discontent and indeed become fierce defenders of justifiable social inequality. The attempts made in the first years of the Soviet Union to introduce equal pay, the *uravnilovka*, in the communes met with disaster. Ideas of a Party maximum pay for civil servants never achieved wide popularity; and now only a few dissidents remember them. Such ideas do not meet with sympathy among the population.

FROM EACH ACCORDING TO HIS ABILITY, TO EACH ACCORDING TO HIS WORK

From what has been said it will be clear that the principle 'from each according to his ability' is realized in Communist society, not in the vulgar sense that everyone is at liberty to display all the ability he has, but in a purely social sense: 1) society decides what shall count as the ability of a given individual in a given social position; 2) on average, people appointed by society to fulfil certain functions tend to carry them out adequately. This principle applies not to people's potential ability but to their actual ability as it is realized in practice. Incidentally, if one approaches the ability-problem from a mass point of view, then mass potential ability is realized in the given conditions as actual ability. The latter is an index of the former. In the case of individuals there may be no correspondence between the two. However, even in respect of individuals, assertions about their wasted talents are quite unprovable. There is sense in talking about wasted talent only when a person has revealed his talent in a manner that is noticed by those around him and has then somehow lost the possibility of developing and using it further. One may instance Mussorgsky, Lermontov, Yesenin or Mayakovsky. But these are exceptions from the general rule. As a rule the overwhelming majority of people is averagely able or averagely untalented, which is the same.

Furthermore, from what we have said it should be clear that the principle 'from each according to his ability' is not a specifically Communist phenomenon. It is realized to some degree in any large differentiated human society.

Let us assume that we have decided slavishly to follow the principle 'to each according to his work' as regards the remuneration of the workers for their activity. If people are engaged in identical activity we can compare their work and its results. But what happens if people are engaged in different types of activity and a comparison of their labour based on the results of their activity turns out to be impossible? Try comparing by results the work of a workman who is producing a specific number of industrial components with that of a member of the government *apparat*, a laboratory technician in a scientific research institute, a doctor or a teacher! How do you compare the work of the director with that of his subordinates? There is only one socially significant criterion for comparing work-inputs in such situations and that is the social position which people occupy.

The average, normal performance of his duties by a person in a given social position corresponds to the work which he contributes to society. In real life the principle 'to

117

each according to his work' is realized in the form of 'to each according to his social position'.

This principle operates even in those cases when one *can* compare the work of different people engaged in an identical production process; when many people engage in activity of the same order, this tends to level out the differences between them. In such cases the authorities, in order to preserve 'material incentives' preserve pay by piece-work (related to the quantity of production) and other special forms of incentive. But this does not affect the standard of living of the workers to any great exent.

This principle, 'to each according to his social position', operates first and foremost not as some kind of juridical principle but as an objective tendency in a complex mass process. In real life people learn, they invent dodges, they try to improve their social position. As a result they try to be adequate to that position. A legislative system merely strengthens the tendency by means of formal norms. Gradually a very detailed scale of remuneration is elaborated which acquires the force of law. The scale then begins to work in a purely formal way, and weakens the tendency which gave rise to it. Thus we have here a characteristic example of contradictory consequences of one and the same phenomenon; on the one hand the law fixes remuneration according to the social position of the worker thereby expressing an objective tendency and standardizing it: on the other hand society, having guaranteed the workers a legally determined remuneration, itself creates temptations and possibilities of remuneration and of improving one's social position without the concomitant guarantee of a corresponding work-input.

In relation to the main types of productive activity the principle 'to each according to his social position' is just, in so far as it expresses the just principle of 'to everyone according to his work'. But there are types of activity where these two principles do not coincide and the first is introduced without reference to activity and is not backed up by the second. An example of this would be the activity of people in management. But what is most important is the fact that after a certain level in the hierarchy of functional communes this principle acquires such force that it produces a glaring contradiction to the principle 'according to his work' which engendered it. This is one example of how something which is fundamentally good at the level of the primary collectives can produce the evil of Communist society.

But even on the level of the primary collective the justice of the principle under examination is achieved only as some mean in relation to a mass of examples of relative injustice. And this mean is achieved at the price of an intense struggle which people wage for the consolidation or improvement of their social position in the daily life of the collective. Here the laws of communality are much more reliable.

If we take the statements of Marxism literally and compare them directly with reality, then we can find facts which invalidate them and facts which support them. Besides, they are ideological statements and as such allow different interpretations. In some interpretations the statements appear to be true, in others false. Therefore in order to avoid pointless verbal discussions we must begin by describing the actual state of things in all its complexity, inconsistency and mutability. Afterwards we can see in what sense, to what extent and according to what interpretation ideological Communist principles are realized in real life.

A NOTE ON METHODOLOGY

The contemporary reader is well aware that it is possible to have technical devices with the following properties: you push an object away from you and it moves towards you; it goes in the right direction for a time and then it swerves. Up to a certain moment you can monitor its movements and then you can monitor them no longer. We may imagine society in the same way as a huge aggregate of such structures. Their composition is unknown and the combined results of their actions cannot be measured accurately.

I am ready to concede that Communist society is built with the very best of intentions: to heap blessings on mankind. But its builders pay no attention to the fact that its elements resemble the devices we have just been talking about. They decide, for instance, to introduce an equitable system of remuneration of labour. But where are the criteria of measurement? When the mass of the people is taken into consideration it is not so easy to find criteria for even the simplest cases. In practice the achievement of precise measurement and equitable treatment on the scale of the whole society is impossible. But people do not need that anyway. They find a way of realizing the principle which is significant in real, social terms: it consists of simply attempting to occupy a position in society which corresponds to their abilities and efforts. If we did find a common method for measuring people's work the results would be astonishing: we would be convinced that, on the whole, in the vast majority of cases, the social position which people occupy does, after all, match their abilities and the efforts they expend. And the principle 'according to work' would be identical with the principle 'according to social position'. But at this point it emerges that we are dealing with one of those strange devices which I spoke of at the beginning of this section. The battle for the improvement of one's social position is waged in a context in which the laws of communality are paramount and in which in a large number of cases it is not the best worker who has the advantage but the individual who, in communal terms, is the most flexible and resourceful. As a result the principle 'according to social position', engendered by the principle 'according to work', begins to operate in the opposite direction.

I am not saying that people should calculate the consequences of their actions in advance. That is impossible in practice. When dealing with social problems in real life, people are forced to resolve them according to the circumstances: often there is only one possible solution. People do not make history; history makes itself. If the first post-revolutionary communes had been effective and productive they would have survived and been encouraged by the country's rulers. If the introduction of a Party maximum wage for highly placed officials would have been likely to produce the desired results, the Party would have introduced it long ago. But even if they had imposed a maximum, highly placed officials would still have taken the share that corresponded with their positions, one way or another. Incidentally, these officials do not normally have such a very large salary. But they do not need a large salary. They can have everything they need for little or no money at all. I only wish to draw the reader's attention to the fact that elements of a social organism can play a lot stranger tricks than the technical devices I was speaking about earlier.

Much has been said about how the Stalinists destroyed the real organizers of the revolution and those sincere Communists – Lenin's Old Guard, not to mention Trotskyites and supporters of Bukharin. But this is one of history's paradoxes which has a trivially simple explanation in terms of these same mechanical models. Profound critics of Communism are frightened by the very triviality of the problem and prefer to spout the most unintelligible rubbish on this score rather than to state the much more convincing banalities.

Incidentally, let me remark *en passant* for the edification of every kind of left-wing movement in the Western countries that is attracted by Communist ideas, that they will be the very first people to be destroyed in the event of a Communist society being installed in their countries, for they contradict the very essence of Communism. What they are idealistically struggling for will eliminate them as unwanted enemies.

THE MERITS OF THE COMMUNE

Able-bodied citizens in Communist society not only have the right to work, they are obliged to work: that is, they are obliged to be members of some primary collective and to be attached to it. This has its shortcomings: a person who is fit for work and obliged to be registered in a commune but for a long time has been considered to be without work (i.e. not attached to a commune), is regarded as someone who has infringed the norms of social life, and might even be looked upon as a criminal. There are special laws and organizations that have the right and power to compel those who decline to work (more precisely, who decline to belong to a collective) to be attached to some commune by force, and not in a place of their choice. However, for the overwhelming majority of the population this situation is a boon: they are always guaranteed a place of work that gives them some means of subsistence. Unless a worker in a commune infringes the norms of social life beyond the limits of legality, he cannot be dismissed from his work. In general it is very hard indeed to sack someone if he does not come into serious conflict with society. The collective defends him, as do various social organizations, especially his trade-union. It is for this reason that Communist society may contain numerous unprofitable enterprises which cannot be abolished because they provide work (i.e. attach people to collectives) and provide the means of subsistence for many citizens. Thus open unemployment is impossible. Higher productivity which could lead to unemployment is therefore made difficult; and low productivity has to be paid for by everyone taking what in practice amounts to a decrease in their wages; the burden is thus shared out among all those who work. Here in general variations in people's living standards depend on the situation in the country as a whole (e.g. on whether prices in the country as a whole are raised or lowered, etc. The same applies to wages).

Conditions of work in productive communes are relatively light. Since in order to receive a certain remuneration it is enough to occupy an appropriate social position and then to do one's duty in the generally accepted manner, an attitude to work is established which is accurately expressed in the saying: 'Only fools and horses work'. Only a few enthusiasts try to raise their living standard by heroic feats of labour. The majority is indifferent to its work and obtains what improvements it can by other means, such as bribes, theft, moonlighting and so on. Poor workmanship and eye-wash flourish. This is a society of unconscientious workers and cheats.

I now introduce the concept of a coefficient of remuneration (or exploitation) in order to compare the conditions of work in Communist societies and other societies. If x is the quantity of work in terms of input and y the size of the remuneration, the relation between y and x is the coefficient of remuneration. In Communist society the quantity y is lower than in the West and the quantity x is lower still, so that the coefficient of remuneration, y/x is significantly higher than in the West. This is why the workers in Communist society almost always prefer the conditions of life under Communism to those in the West. Of course, they dream of good food, clothes, flats and cars. But they would scarcely be prepared to pay the price for them that Western workers pay.

Workers in communes are guaranteed a paid holiday. They can obtain trips to rest homes, often at a discount or without payment at all. They are paid while they are ill. Their old-age pension and health insurance are guaranteed. It is still the case that citizens have their place of residence as a result of tradition or local conditions (e.g. houses and flats might have been passed on to them by their parents). It is still the case that a considerable part of living accommodation is distributed by the housing sections of the local authorities. Nevertheless, the productive communes are playing an ever-increasing part in this respect as well. At any rate, citizens' accommodation is cheap. For the majority it is overcrowded. Sometimes the efforts of a lifetime are expended on the acquisition of a small, self-contained flat for one family. But all the same, I repeat, people somehow acquire a minimum of living space, and acquire it cheaply. In Russia, we must remember, even a separate bed with sheets was a great historical achievement. And in general one can say that the living conditions of Soviet citizens have noticeably improved since the War.

Citizens are guaranteed free medical assistance in the

area where they live. Many can arrange for hospital treatment through their place of work. Although the medical service leaves something to be desired, the minimal needs of the citizens are well met. In the areas of education and professional training the situation is similar. In short, certain essential needs are satisfied one way or another. Indeed if the principle 'to everyone according to his needs' is understood sociologically and is not interpreted in vulgar, philistine fashion as meaning 'everyone gets what he wants', then in this society it is actually realized in practice. It does not remove inequality or people's dissatisfaction with their lot. But that is another question.

TO EACH ACCORDING TO HIS NEEDS

I shall dwell on this principle in more detail as it is one of the central points of Marxist doctrine about Communism.

We need to distinguish between the historical conditions in which the idea 'according to need' arose and its original historical meaning; between the philistine interpretation of this idea and its interpretation in the state ideology of the Communist countries (and Soviet ideology above all). Historically Communist society was conceived as a society in which there would be equality in all aspects of people's lives. That this society might breed its own form of social and economic inequality – and to a staggering degree into the bargain – was something that the theorists did not even wish to contemplate. They attributed all evil to private property. And as the latter was due to be destroyed it was supposed that all social evil would disappear with it, economic inequality included. But they conceived of 'need' in the most primitive sense: as need for food, clothing, and shelter. The hope was that these would be satisfied and it was this hope that the principle 'each according to his needs' expressed. The notion of abundance is relative and historically determined. And indeed, if we consider the way it was thought of in past centuries, then it has been achieved in

Soviet society, where no one is destitute or homeless or actually dying from hunger. In this sense the principle of Communism has been realized.

But this satisfaction of basic needs has now given rise to another, contemporary, understanding of the concept of abundance and the principle of 'according to need', which is interpreted as the provision of whatever people nowadays *wish for*. But their wishes have now grown to such an extent that even the official ideology of the Soviet Union has postponed the fulfilment of this principle to the indefinite future. Soviet people already regard abundance under Communism as being at least the equal of the high living standards of some Western countries, which are to be attainable by everyone. The founders of the Marxist doctrine of Communism can hardly have suspected that refrigerators and television sets would be indispensable objects of the first priority, nor that the motor car would be a normal means of transport. But the philistine of today no longer thinks of Communism except in terms of flats with lots of rooms and all modern conveniences, including television and refrigerator, with a private car and a country villa thrown in.

The official ideology of the Soviet Union sensed the danger which lurked in such an interpretation of the very incautious declaration of classical Marxism and gave it its own interpretation. It began to speak of reasonable needs, which could be monitored and regulated by society. This was only an expression in disguised form of the actual state of affairs; namely that a person's needs in Communist society are determined by the feasibility of their satisfaction: i.e., by that person's actual social position. The slogan 'to each according to his needs' is in practice embodied in the principle 'to each according to his social position'. In practice it is precisely people's social position which becomes the guiding principle underlying the distribution of goods and services. Since it is a 'just' principle, both notionally and in terms of its practical and fundamental influence on the structure of society, in the context of a developed social hierarchy of people and collectives it gives rise to socio-economic inequality on a scale which is comparable with that of other societies, and in certain respects even exceeds it.

Official Soviet ideology is not far from the truth in its interpretation of need. The point is that there are two definitions of 'need': one which is subjective or psychological, and the other which is objective or sociological. In the second instance not every human desire is a need, but only what the social milieu recognizes as a need. And that means that there is a generally accepted level at which a person at a particular point in the social hierarchy might expect his needs to be met, i.e. that there is some kind of legitimate norm of consumption. To have 'according to need' means to have within the framework of this norm, and to have 'not according to need' is either to exceed or fall short of that norm. The expression 'he does not have what he needs' refers only to the case in which a person does not receive what is due to him, whereas the expression 'he has what he doesn't need' refers to the case where a person receives more than his due.

In addition, one must distinguish between need as something which society is obliged to fulfil and consequently defines, and need as it is perceived by rational individuals within that society. For instance, in terms of the norms which operate in the Soviet Union in practice, three square metres of living space per person in the lower strata count as sufficient to meet the first definition of need, while in the second sense society has already come to think that each adult member of the family needs a separate room. If we take all aspects of everyday life into consideration then we can pinpoint for every stratum of the population the limits of these 'rational' needs within which the position of any one person fluctuates. And we must recognize that, in one way or another, society tries to keep the living standards of the population within these limits.

THE SIMPLICITY OF LIFE

There is another feature of life in Communist society that we should pay attention to here, and that is the formal simplicity of life itself. After school or some other educational institution a person goes to work. That person is automatically supplied with a work-book. He becomes a member of a trade-union, and all the rest happens by itself. In principle he needs no further documents for the rest of his life. True, from time to time he will need a few certificates from his place of residence and from his place of work. But that is a matter of routine and hardly burdensome. He might have the odd problem when he changes residence or work. But all this amounts to is a waste of time plus a certain strain on the nerves. In principle it does not complicate his life any more than standing in a queue, or being buffeted on public transport complicate it. Under Communism the human being is not ensnared in a formal system of juridical relationships. For example, he is quite unfamiliar with the heavy and cumbersome taxation system which exists in Western countries. In Communist society a small percentage is automatically deducted as tax from all monetary payments made by official institutions. And that is all. For the large number of people who have comparatively large incomes, this situation is immeasurably better than that in Western societies which are governed by the rule of law.

Because of the extreme simplification of the formal-legal aspect of life all people's attention and efforts are transferred to the communal aspect. This aspect is normal, easily accessible and needs no moral or juridical formulation. People in that society are specialists from childhood in living in a turbulent social swim, just as many people in the West are used from childhood to be law-abiding.

DEGREES OF EXPLOITATION AND REMUNERATION

The opinion that the standard of living in the West is higher than in the Soviet Union has more or less become dogma. But what is a living standard? Do its components in the West match those in the Soviet Union, i.e. those in a Communist society? Are the criteria of measurement the same? How, moreover, does one measure a standard of living? Here I want to examine the two most important elements of a living standard and a way of life in general which I call 'the degree of exploitation and the degree of remuneration'. I shall keep my examination as simple as possible.

In one way or another the working man devotes his efforts to society: he expends himself for society. The magnitude of these efforts is a function of the time spent, the intensity of his work, nervous tension, the emotions and risks involved and much else. People differ very much in terms of these indices, so that the production of sufficiently accurate measurements is no easy task. For instance, the scientific worker can idle away his day at his institute, but work at home in the evening and even at night, as often happens. People in important managerial positions often find themselves in a state of great nervous tension. They spend lots of time at meetings, and have no time or energy to read books, or go to the theatre or for culture in general. In brief, it would take a special sociological investigation to measure the magnitude of effort expended in every form of activity, to compare these magnitudes and to produce some kind of statistics for the various sub-sections of society and for the country as a whole.

The working man receives a particular remuneration for his activity, and once again this remuneration is not easy to measure. It comprises much more than just the official wage: e.g. housing, children's institutions, rest homes and sanatoria, the medical service, loans, prizes, privileges, special shops, special bonuses, villas, private cars. One cannot enumerate all the supplementary ways which people find in their sphere of work (including theft, bribes and the use of their official position in general). To this we may add the guarantee of a minimum of this world's goods and the relative security of people's social position.

Let us assume that we have measured the magnitude of remuneration and the magnitude of the efforts expended to receive that remuneration. The quotient from the division of the first magnitude by the second gives the degree of remuneration, while the converse is the degree of exploitation. According to my observations and measurements (greatly simplified and approximate) the degree of remuneration of the most active and productive segment of the population in Communist society has a tendency to grow, while the degree of its exploitation diminishes. Moreover, the degree of remuneration is here higher than for corresponding people in Western countries; and the degree of exploitation is lower. This is the basic advantage that Communism has over Western society and the reason for its attraction for millions of people on this planet.

But do not imagine that the high degree of remuneration means that people live well in the Communist environment. People can have a low standard of living with a high degree of remuneration, and vice versa. In the West the population is much better off materially than in the Soviet Union. The degree of remuneration can grow and at the same time material conditions can deteriorate. These magnitudes are relative, not evaluative. A high degree of remuneration is not necessarily good, nor a low one necessarily bad. From the point of view of the progress of civilization it is just the opposite; an increase in the degree of exploitation and a decrease in the degree of remuneration are the hallmarks of a higher level of civilization. They mean greater productivity. And although there is no direct link between the degrees of remuneration and exploitation and everyday living conditions, large sections of the population feel that the Communist situation is advantageous for them; and having tasted it in practice they can no longer give it up. Of course, there are strata of the population in Communist countries for which the opposite is the case. But they do not play the chief role in society nor do they wield the power.

The tendency towards greater remuneration and less exploitation in Communist society furthers the tendency for the growth of productivity to slow down, at the very least; and it accentuates, too, the tendency towards stagnation and at times even deterioration. Scientific and technical progress balances these tendencies; but there is a limit to its efficiency. It is becoming increasingly expensive. The same tendencies apply to it too, slowing it down and setting it upper limits. There is reason to suppose that in time the tendency to stagnation and deterioration will dominate. At any rate, the fact that the Soviet Union cannot compete economically with the West is clearly not accidental.

Higher remuneration and lower exploitation, however splendid they may appear at first sight, have far less splendid consequences. They lead to a reduction in the metabolic rate of society itself, and of its interaction with its environment. All the vital processes slow down. The tendency of the society to grow purely physically and spatially is accentuated. This is one of the profound reasons for the Soviet Union's attempt to expand at the expense of other places on the planet. The tendency towards the predatory and destructive exploitation of nature is also strengthened, as is the Soviet Union's tendency to parasitism in relation to its immediate environment.

COMPULSORY WORK

In Communist society work is a duty in the sense that every able-bodied person must be attached to a primary work commune. This obligation stems from the objective fact that only by working in such a commune can able-bodied citizens gain the means of subsistence. Here a socio-economic fact takes juridical form and becomes a means of making work compulsory. Inasmuch as the overwhelming majority of citizens need and want to work whether there is legal compulsion or not, the compulsory character of the work hardly registers with them. In this case a situation arises of a type in which Hegel's formula 'freedom is perceived necessity' operates as an element of Soviet state ideology. But with one small correction: compulsory attachment to a work-commune (and the obligation to work in it) is not perceived as a lack of freedom. People perceive this apparent freedom as if it were real. Inasmuch as there is some freedom of choice of profession or of place of work for a significant number of people and these people have some interest in staying in their work-commune, the acceptance of this situation, which is inherited by each generation, taken together with other circumstances so strengthens the illusion of freedom and hides the reality of unfreedom that the distinction between the real and the illusory virtually disappears from the popular ethic. If unfreedom *is* noticed it is seen as natural and inevitable.

The actual position is revealed here (and in many other instances of this kind) only in exceptional cases, only in cases of deviation from the general norm: that is when individual people have sources of subsistence that are independent of work and want to avoid working in a work-commune; when individuals for some reason or other lose their work and cannot find suitable work of their own choice. For such people there is a special term, 'parasites'. And, as we have seen, there are laws which permit the authorities to recruit such people for forced labour, and in places designated by the authorities.

The majority of parasites do not threaten the existence of society. Some of them are criminals and are prosecuted in the usual way. Some live off their relatives or from illegal sources that have not been discovered. Usually they get along with the authorities through bribes, personal connections or forged documents, and society turns a blind eye to their existence. But some parasites attract the special attention of the authorities, and they are severely dealt with. These are people who, in one way or another, come into conflict with society such as dissidents, religious sectarians, individual renegades and rebels. In their case the phenomenon of compulsory work is revealed in all its mercilessness. Moreover, in such cases the authorities will not take into account that someone works at home, for instance composing poetry or scientific treatises or painting pictures or teaching mathematics or languages. In this society only those count as workers who can show documents proving that they are attached to a work-commune. There are those who belong to the so-called liberal professions and work individually and independently of the commune. But they too must in some way or other be attached to some organization, for example by a special contract.

Anyone who is unattached to a work-commune and is obviously able-bodied represents a serious danger to society for many reasons. He infringes the orderliness of the ranks of workers in society, just as a soldier who is out of step with his company prevents it from marching and calls down upon himself the justified wrath of his commanders. He is a bad example to the other soldiers. Some time ago in the Soviet Union there were quite a lot of these parasites. Their behaviour infected literally thousands of young people, and even older people as well. They showed that one could live without being dependent on the commune and earn just as good a living. And be a free man at the same time. They showed that one could get on with people very well with no risk of being an outcast.

The authorities found it hard to deal with this epidemic of parasitism. One of their main difficulties arose from the fact that parasites were very useful in influential circles. They got them books they needed, books that were not to be found in the usual shops, and various articles, bits of jewellery. They coached their children in various subjects, so that they could get a decent pass in their entrance exams into institutes of higher education. In short, they were very useful servants of the middle and upper classes of society. There were even parasites who composed dissertations for learned people and verses for writers. The struggle with the parasite epidemic only became really serious when the ranks of the parasites were infiltrated by a considerable number of dissidents. In a sense the parasites blazed a trail for the dissidents by pioneering and working out a detailed technique of living in Communist society without being attached to a primary work-commune.

The main danger of parasitism for society is not a criminal but a social one. The parasite escapes the control of the primary collective which is in hard fact the highest power society has over the individual.

Compulsory work, which I spoke of earlier, is a normal phenomenon in this society, and even an object of pride as well as of envy on the part of many people in non-Communist countries. There are other forms of compulsion which at the moment appear to be incidental and temporary but which are tending to become the permanent feature of real-life Communism. I will instance two of them: 1) the compulsory despatch of large masses of the population (workers, civil servants, students, school pupils, scientific workers and others) to work in the country, on far-off building sites and in vegetable depots, as well as the use of the army as a labour force; 2) the huge number of prisoners. Although much mention of these forms of organization is made in dissident literature (especially of prisons and labour camps), there has still been no serious sociological analysis of them. Yet this phenomenon deserves the most serious attention because it manifests one frightful tendency of Communism which everyone either tries not to notice or carefully conceals, the tendency towards a special form of slavery: not in a figurative but in a *literal* sense of the word.

The inventors of ideological Communism proceeded from a whole series of more or less obvious assumptions when they described future society as an earthly paradise. And the first thing they disregarded was the fact that in society there are places where people just do not want to live and types of jobs which people do not wish to do. Communism's ideologues excel themselves on this subject, arguing that robots and machines will do the dirty jobs and that far-off places will be linked with other places by modern transport and crammed full of cultural opportunities.

Taken in abstract, everything is possible. But facts, which, as Stalin said, are obstinate things, for the time being tell a different story. Despite technical development, new transport, the proliferation of culture and so on, there are other factors whereby people judge their position, and new problems arise that no one could have foreseen earlier. For instance, who could have foreseen the whole complex of problems connected with the discovery and use of atomic energy? However successful science and technology may be, the vast masses of the population will still require jobs to be done of a kind that has low social prestige and is relatively badly paid. But the main point is that, because of the social hierarchy itself, a significant part of the population must occupy a position in comparison with which all other ranks of the hierarchy must seem to be in clover. In order that the dismal life of Communist society should really seem to be the promised paradise, there must be a hell with which people can compare their lives and thank their stars that they at least are not in that hell.

One must never ignore socio-psychological factors of this kind when one is examining Communist society. At times they play an immeasurably greater role than tangible material factors. So that even if one supposes that there are no unpleasant places in the country and no dirty jobs, they will still be especially invented because of the social laws of that society. One of the reasons for the existence of Stalin's concentration camps was the unconscious execution of an inevitable social wish. That they provided unpaid labour in the form of slaves is of course evident.

Every year in the Soviet Union up to twenty million people are sent for a longer or shorter period to do harvesting work in the country, to join various building sites, or to vegetable depots in the towns. And how much human effort is expended on voluntary work on days off! As for prisoners, the overwhelming majority of them are not criminals but ordinary citizens who have committed crimes because of circumstances, often from sheer necessity. In the Soviet Union it is practically impossible to live without breaking the law. The number of prisoners doesn't depend on the number of crimes but the ability of the militia to detect criminals and of the courts to pass sentence on this or that number of people. These factors in their turn depend on the purposes of the higher authorities and of the demand for labour in those places in which only prisoners, that is to say, slaves, can work.

I want to emphasize that I am speaking here about a rather large and typical Communist country, not about exceptions. It is possible that among the Communist countries a small country will occupy an exceptional position and that such things won't happen in it. In the largest countries there may be regions with exceptional conditions. But in the Communist world as a whole such exceptions do not affect the general trends.

The noble idea about man's obligation to work has, when it comes to be applied to the broad masses, an inevitable consequence, namely, that people are divided into two categories in one of the most fundamental areas of human existence: for some work becomes slavery, for the others it is a source of pleasure. At one end of society there is a concentration of people leading an active social life with all its temptations; at the other there are those condemned to exist like slaves and animals. Communism does not eliminate this polarization. It only changes the forms it takes and intensifies them. I would make the prophecy that in time the army of slaves in Communist countries will exceed the figures of Stalin's time. We have no data about China. What is happening there?

WORK ATTITUDES

The citizen's relationship to his work in Communist countries is determined by the organization of activity in the primary communes and by the principle of remuneration. Here in practice a principle operates which Soviet people express in jocular form: 'it doesn't matter where you work as long as you don't have to work'; 'even horses die of work'; 'work isn't a wolf; it won't run off into the woods'. This doesn't mean that all people work badly or try not to work. First, there are many kinds of work which force people to work and to do their job fairly well. Secondly, for many people the very process of work gives them satisfaction; and they are motivated not by fear but by their conscience. Thirdly, within certain limits good work is better paid than bad. All this of course is true. However, in much of the social activity in which the most active citizens are engaged, the quality of work and the personal capabilities of the citizens play a less important role than do their skills in orientating themselves in the social milieu and in making a career. In this area of society's activities people with mediocre gifts and mediocre training and energy are quite able to carry out their duties effectively and yet are paid as much as, or more than, colleagues who are gifted and who work very hard. Here the most significant kind of behaviour is not work in the accepted sense of the word, but is rather like what used to happen at society balls where the high and mighty would resolve important governmental problems in circumstances which did not resemble work at all. Activities which break up the routine or contain a large fun-element are more prestigious than the activity known as 'work'. Usually even the people who find their real work absorbing end up by being attracted by activity which breaks up the monotony or creates some kind of diversion.

Thus there is a division of activity into work-activity and entertainment-activity. The first consists of the unpleasant and compulsory occupations which are to do with earning one's living. The second, in addition to offering better livelihood, brings to the participants satisfaction by itself. It becomes an end in itself, and is its own reward. But reward for what? Exclusively for the ability to fight one's way into that area of activity and to occupy the necessary social position. The struggle to turn every activity into career activity acts as a disincentive to the mass of the population to show any interest in its work, in better performance, in being conscientious. Poor workmanship, laziness, deception, disinclination to work, infect the whole of society.

Increasing the productivity of labour, on which the ideologues of Communism rely so much in their calculations, has turned out to be one of the most intractable problems of Communist society and to a large extent derives from this particular attitude to work. Communist society, I repeat, is a society of bad workers. This is not a national characteristic of the Russian people. The experience of other Communist countries confirms this statement.

Society tries to surmount this obstacle, which explains the very cumbersome monitoring system, the establishment of model enterprises, the existence of special conditions in some spheres, propaganda, a proliferation of low-quality production sectors of the economy, and the inflation of staff levels. However, all these measures cannot counteract completely the strong tendency of society to slow down the growth of productivity and to further the decline in quality of everything that is produced. Indeed, the measures themselves further this tendency, as is very clear if one examines how the procedures of quality-control actually operate.

The system for ensuring accountability in the Soviet Union is truly grandiose. This monitoring function is carried out by special authorities, social organizations and the whole mass of the active population. Here everyone has to account for the results of his activity, one way or another. And in a huge number of cases the form of accountability acquires much more meaning than the actual state of the business. A special system of procedures is worked out which allows the enterprise to produce an excellent impression on the monitoring personnel when in fact the enterprise's position is very bad. Moreover, the monitors themselves know the real state of affairs and are interested in covering it up while at the same time making it appear that everything is above board. Covering up for each other becomes a form of self-deception which suits everyone. This tendency is greatly strengthened by the fact that individuals and enterprises do not depend on the sale of their products. I will return to this theme later.

SOCIAL WORK

A brief word about one specifically Communist phenomenon: social work. This is a complex phenomenon. In part it has to do with forms of compulsory work; in part with the forms of educational and ideological activity; in part with spending one's time pleasantly and profitably.

I myself have done social work all my life. At school I was the leader of a Youth Pioneer detachment and drew cartoons for the wall-newspapers. Drawing caricatures in wall-newspapers afterwards became my social work all through my life in the Soviet Union, and although it was work, it was also an amusing way of passing the time. Usually when we were discussing the make-up of a wall-newspaper we would get together in a large group, laugh a lot and then celebrate the end of our work with a jolly good booze-up. Often I used to travel about the countryside with the *agitprop* brigade lecturing and giving amateur concerts. And here again I have excellent memories of these journeys. I have drawn on some of them in my books, especially in *In the Ante-Chamber of Paradise*, and in *The Yellow House*. I also read scores of public lectures of every kind within the political education network. And part of these lectures I used in my own books, especially in *The Yawning Heights*.

Although social work is often a disagreeable chore and an empty formality, it would be unjust to regard it as such in general. In my experience, it is a complex phenomenon and one that is very effective in ideological education. Millions of people take part in this work. And how many captive millions does it have as an audience! To dismiss social work in a couple of critical sentences and jokes would be to abandon the principles of scientific investigation. Social work is an important phenomenon.

Social work is done by citizens over and above their professional duties. In theory, this means that it is done outside 'office hours'. In practice it is frequently done *during* working hours, and very often instead of official duties. Many workers who are officially full-time employees are in practice fully occupied with this social work professionally. It is reckoned that this is voluntary, unpaid work for the good of society, and is the offspring of the Communist attitude to work. It is, of course, itself a Communist form of work.

Let us consider the voluntary aspect first. Members of the Party and the *Komsomol* are obliged to do social work, otherwise there are penalties and reprimands. Other people are also obliged, inasmuch as the continuous record of a worker's 'standing' takes account of his participation in social work, not, of course, to the same extent as in the case of members of the Party or of the *Komsomol*, but nevertheless to some degree. If someone avoids social work then that fact is noted and measures are taken. And there are several measures, ranging from pay rises and promotion to the solution of accommodation problems, the possibility of trips abroad or the chance of having one's work published. Only those who have given up all prospects of a career and improvement in their standard of living ignore social work, in addition, perhaps, to celebrities, aristocrats and people with high connections.

Now a word about the unpaid aspect. Most people who take on social work receive remuneration in the form of a good testimonial, official thanks and even prizes. Very often the time spent on this work is made up for in other ways: official holidays and unofficial leave, tickets for places of entertainment, journeys at a discount. Many social workers receive special pay, for example lecturers at the Evening University of Marxism-Leninism; and honoraria, for instance lecturers from various kinds of Party organs and societies such as the society *Znanie* (Knowledge). In many cases social work is very profitable.

The basic form of social work is linked to membership of the elective organs: the Party bureau, the trade-union bureau, the local Party committee, the *Komsomol* bureau. Usually there is a struggle over this. Sometimes a very keen one, because it is a struggle about power and privilege. The secretary of the Party bureau of an institution and the Chairman of the local Party committee, for example, are very influential personages in an institution. People who get on to housing committees and deal with the allocation of trips to rest homes and sanatoria play a very notable role in the life of the collective.

The highest Party and administrative organs judge the activity of an institution by the state of its social work and its record in work of this kind. And this affects the reputation of its management. Social work can lead to prizes and decorations. It is social work which binds the individual and the collective as a whole to the specifically Communist form of social life. Social work does not squeeze out or replace productive work. It is simply another cross-section of life in our society, and is just as indispensable as production.

PRIVATE ENTERPRISE

In theory there should be no private enterprise in Communist society. This means that everyone should work in an official institution, do everything within the framework of the law and be satisfied with only those means of subsistence which are appropriate to their place of work in the primary collectives. But in fact people are not satisfied with this. Most of all they use their official position to improve their conditions. But beyond this phenomenon which the authorities find practically impossible to control (not least because they do it themselves) there exists a very significant sphere of private enterprise. The authorities struggle against it and try to contain it within tolerable bounds or destroy it altogether, but in one way or another it breeds in society and at times plays a very real role. As far as I know no serious sociological investigations have ever been conducted in the Soviet Union about this sector, so that its precise magnitude is not known. But every citizen one way or another bumps into it.

To this private sector belong the personal plots of collective farmers; the market-garden allotments of town-dwellers; the markets; the renting of accommodation in towns and resorts; private tailors, hairdressers, dentists and jewellers; private lessons, speculation in scarce goods; every kind of unlawful enterprise; the liberal professions; and much else that is permitted by law, forbidden by law or semi-illegal. In the country as a whole this amounts to a high order of magnitude. However, one must not exaggerate the role of this phenomenon. The proportion of it in the whole volume of activities of the population is relatively small. But the main point is that private enterprise in no way undermines the country's general social order. The majority of those who take part in the 'private sector' are in one way or another attached to primary collectives and are to some extent kept under surveillance by the authorities. The infringement of the norms of Communist society has here a purely criminal character.

Because of the fact that people in the private sector work better than their counterparts in the corresponding branches of the public sector all sorts of ideas arise about the expansion of the private sector within the framework of Communism. However, private enterprise has no prospects under Communism. It leads to the accumulation of wealth in the hands of people who do not occupy high social positions and this contravenes the general principles of distribution. Besides, private enterprise would enable a mass of people to escape communal control. So the authorities do not allow it anything more than moderate growth. And the basic mass of the population supports them in this.

THE LIFE OF THE PRIMARY COLLECTIVE

An abstract description of a primary Communist collective makes it look like something absolutely beyond reproach. Individuals go to work in it, hold a position in it that matches their training, work according to their ability and are remunerated in terms of their output. When they have done their duty in the primary collective individuals leave it and then lead their private lives in a manner which they can afford and which suits their private inclinations.

Of course, for some people life does turn out to look as idyllically futile as that. But for the vast majority of society's active members this abstract model has no sense at all. For them life is basically all that they do in the collective, for the collective and through the collective. This communal life is reflected in all the other bits and pieces of their lives; it dominates them; it paints them in its own colours. It has an overwhelming influence on the lives of the members of their families. And even afterwards when they do leave the collective and get their old-age pension, they bear the imprint of their former communal life to the very end of their days. For this vast majority, then, it is not the case that they go to work in a primary collective in order to earn the means to a genuine life when they have finished work. In the event, exactly the opposite turns out to be the case; life *outside* the collective is geared to life *inside* the collective. Collective life is their real life and life outside is only a condition of life inside. The collective takes not only the best out of them physically, it takes their soul as well. The commune takes people in their entirety, squeezes all the physical and spiritual juice out of them and chucks them out afterwards on to the street and into private life as exhausted, drained, bad-tempered, bored and empty husks.

At the level of the primary collective people not only work, they spend their time in the company of people they know well. They swap news, amuse themselves, do all kinds of things to preserve and improve their position, have contacts with people on whom their well-being depends, go to innumerable meetings, get sent on leave to rest homes, are given accommodation and sometimes supplementary food-products. As there are continual shortages of food stuffs, the last is very important. In the collective people raise their qualifications and get all sorts of titles certifying them. It is here that they go in for art and sport, not to speak of joining political education groups. Here they do their social work. Here they become involved in every kind of mass happening: demonstrations, turning out to wave to arriving and departing VIPs, processions on public holidays, recreational evenings, tourist trips and journeys. What you have in the commune is no simple materialization of an abstract model but life in the most exact sense of the word, with all its joys and griefs, successes and failures, passion and drama. It is precisely this real life which a scientific description of Communism must take into account at the outset. But in fact nearly everyone writing or speaking about Communism ignores it. They prefer to speak of things that make a bigger splash, such as repression and absence of civil rights, things which practically don't exist for people who are living at the level of the primary collective. If such questions do arise there, it is only in order that the collective may condemn dissidents and express support for the authorities.

The essence of life as it is lived in the primary collectives is that the abstract boons which we mentioned above are the subject of a ferocious struggle between individuals. These boons (if that is the right word for them) do not come of their own accord. Here it is a struggle to get even elementary justice. Moreover it is not just a one-off struggle. This justice has to be fought for constantly. A person only has to let his efforts weaken for a short time before he is, in one way or another, done down. Here everything which people have 'as of right' must be fought for tooth and nail. Despite this even the most elementary justice is attained only as an average tendency: i.e. via transgressions of and deviations from the norm. One individual rips off more than his due, another less. The same individual gains here and loses there; holidays, prizes, pay-rises, promotions, a place in a children's nursery, a flat, and so on: these are all of very real value. To get them there is a fierce battle of everyone against everyone else. And here the forces of communality are unleashed in their full strength. And to save themselves from these forces (which means to save themselves from themselves) people have worked out socially effective means of defence in the shape of a particular system of norms and organizations to see that they are observed. These norms are the norms of the allocation of work and of everything that has a value for people. The organizations are the Party organization and the trade-union organization and a series of others under their control, such as the *Komsomol*, the bank for mutual aid, the housing committees and others.

The most deeply ingrained and at the same time the most visible features of Communism are revealed where people work and acquire their means of subsistence: in the commune. The commune is, as a rule, an organization with a complex structure and a complex system of mutual relationships. For the casual observer it is very hard to make head or tail of the system of relationships. Indeed, it is almost impossible. It is as hard as it is sometimes for an ethnographer to analyse the behaviour and relationships in some primitive tribe. The members of the commune themselves (the workers) know their way about it very well. And this isn't surprising because their basic social profession is to be able to orientate themselves in this milieu and to be skilful enough to snatch from it as much as they can. Their productive activity is something secondary and incidental. The commune doesn't exist for its work. The work is tolerated and done inasmuch as it is the commune's *raison d'être*. Only a few enthusiasts are captivated by the work as a thing in itself and then only at times. Rewards, promotions, publicity, appointments and so on sooner or later reveal the social essence of their enthusiasm. The endless ululations in newspapers and on the radio and television about the enthusiasm of the working masses is either lying propaganda or a pure formality. The work people do in the commune is seen by them merely as their means of getting vital commodities in accordance with the actual laws of society and their means of preserving and improving their social position.

THE SYSTEM OF VALUES AND VALUE JUDGEMENTS

To the outsider it seems that almost nothing of interest happens in a commune. Everything appears to be superficial, trivial and insignificant. To notice anything meaningful one has got to live in it – and that then excludes all possibility of objective observation. In a commune everything lies on the surface and is known to everyone. But at the same time everything is hidden. Hidden because it is not clear what one must discover and identify as worthy of attention from the point of view of what is immanent in the life of the commune.

It is one thing when you are whirling around in the hurly-burly and quite another when you are looking at it from outside. Everything looks different. If you begin to look at a commune from the standpoint of a naturalist studying an ant-hill, a colony of monkeys or a population of rats, you will be struck at the outset by the apparent senselessness of most of the actions of the workers and by the disproportion between the events which occur and the workers' reaction to them. For instance, why does this crowd of exhausted people go to the assembly hall and suffer torments in it for hours when they know in advance that they will have no effect whatever on the proceedings, since everything will have been decided long before and endorsed by the appropriate authorities? Why does the chairman of the assembly put the matter to the vote when he knows in advance that the majority will scarcely manage to put up its hand before, without even a glance at the hall, he will declare that the decision is taken unanimously and that nobody will let out a squeak about it? Or here comes worker A. He looks as if the most terrible misfortune has befallen him. But what has happened? What has happened is that they gave worker B a Highly Recommended (another nonsensical piece of paper), while all that he, worker A, got was a vote of thanks recorded in the minutes (also a meaningless sentence in a meaningless piece of paper), although his services to the commune (what services?) exceeded those of worker B. And, my God, what a depressing spectacle people exhibit when it is a matter of money, trips, flats! What passions are ablaze! The perplexing question arises: surely a five-rouble pay rise isn't really worth all that emotional upset? What is the difference between being a pauper on a pittance and being a pauper on five roubles more? But there *is*, it seems, a difference, and a very serious one. For those who take part in this nonsense everything is much more serious than it is for people in the position of kings, ministers, millionaires, outstanding writers and scholars, artists and generals.

Each society has its own system of values and value judgements. What these values are is known to everyone from the cradle. You've eaten all your porridge: there's a good little fellow! You've broken a cup: naughty boy, you've misbehaved! But what is far from known to everybody is that there are certain general value systems that are universal for all societies, all spheres of life and for all individuals. We feel this intuitively in certain circumstances. If a tailor has made a bad suit of clothes, he has made a bad suit of clothes, whatever his intentions were. If a man sings badly then he's a bad singer, whether he's a night-watchman or a director. If a man has a speech impediment then he's a bad orator whether he is the head of state or the doorman.

One must distinguish between values and opinions. Opinions are subjective in the sense that there are no general uniform criteria regarding their expression. An opinion is not true or false. An opinion may be the result of the fact that someone likes some phenomenon, event or thing or does not. A value is objective in the sense that there are general criteria and rules by which it is established. Any individual who is guided by these criteria and rules can arrive at approximately the same evaluation of a given phenomenon. There are, of course, deviations from the norm, but that is not important. In the main the proposition holds. For example, different teachers in school mark their pupils' answers in more or less the same way. There are deviations of one or two marks. But if you take the bulk of the pupils and answers there is a reliable trend. The general principle of evaluation is grounded on the presence of such a tendency towards objectivity and its independence from subjective opinions. In everyday life, however, there are no general rules of evaluation which cover all phenomena. Values and opinions are mixed together. But none of this affects the concept of evaluation, nor removes in principle the possibility of there being general evaluative criteria for this or that individual case.

In Communist society a system of values prevails which is founded on the principle that there should be no general principles of evaluation. And this system of values is actually not a system. Here the value of the actions and ability of individuals is a function of the social position of individuals, of their intentions and the moods of those around them, and even of the specific nature of the type of situation in which the actions take place. For instance, the highest authority takes the decision to dig a canal from point A to point B and gives the order to start the work. According to the general principles of evaluation as well as those of a technical and economic order, the decision can be evaluated as idiotic in the extreme. But according to communal rules it is valued as a stroke of genius. This isn't propaganda. It is honest and sincere because the evaluation is seen as being a function of the *intentions* ('do it for the good of the people', 'expect no favours from Nature'); of the *social rank* of those taking the decision (the most senior civil servants who are by definition geniuses); and of the *particularities* of the situation (there is nothing to eat). The proposal of one ardent paranoiac to dig that canal, made a week earlier, was evaluated as harmful and even revisionist. For who was he to butt in with his plans without even clearing them beforehand with the leader of the planning group? But the intentions of the paranoiac happened to be the same: to do it for the good of the people; expect no favours. This kind of anti-evaluative system is worked out with the greatest care and introduced into all aspects of life, so there is nothing surprising in the fact that the citizens hail idiotic films, pictures and books as masterpieces, praise the quality of badly made suits and rotten potatoes to the skies, and elevate to the status of genius their staggeringly stupid leaders.

Beyond their everyday value, many of life's phenomena have a kind of symbolic meaning, and some of them *only* a symbolic meaning. For example, it is clear that pay rises have a practical meaning; but not only a practical one. They are also experienced by the individual as a symbol of the fact that he is respected, that his work is valued and that he is capable of advancing further. The expression of thanks in public has a purely symbolic value. However, we should not regard this symbolic event simply as having spiritual value. Symbolic valuations are the index of a person's position in society, of his prospects and of the recognition of this position and these prospects by society. That is why such strong passions are aroused by what appear to be absolutely trivial events. A prize is not just a sum of money (it is usually a small one) but the recognition of the security of an individual's position and of his career prospects. If a man is dropped from the presidium of the assembly, everyone knows that his position is not as strong as it was. Here every setback, however small, is an omen that things will get worse and every success is a hope that things will improve.

But since people live all the time in fear of things getting worse, every trifle is worth almost a fight to the death. In Communist society life is a permanent battle. If you slip in ahead of your turn you've won a victory. If someone slips in ahead of you it's a defeat. If you get a seat in the underground it's a victory. If others grab your seat, it's a defeat. If your colleague is praised, it's one in the eye for you. If he's bawled out, you go one ahead. Communal life is not the gentle simmering of mild cross-currents of disagreement, it is a seething cauldron of unbridled passion, but always about trifles. Life consists of millions of trifles requiring an enormous emotional and spiritual investment. There are only two means of avoiding this, but both are fictitious. The first is to get to the top. The second is to lower your sights. In both cases you deprive yourself of genuine human potential and turn yourself into an artificial being. Normal communal life is life lived in the quagmire of trivia.

Official ideology reflects this real-life position. It uses all its means of impinging on human consciousness to ennoble and idealize this quagmire, and on the other hand to preach something contradictory; the principle that one should be above everyday trivia. This principle was very popular in the Soviet Union at one time as a consolation for hopeless poverty and permanent difficulties. Now it has fewer and fewer supporters. But there are enough of them still, especially in the circles of the intelligentsia where a miserable standard of living and a primitive life-style are acquired at a specially high price. In so far as people are in the last resort powerless to extricate themselves from their own quagmire, they are glad enough to respond to the official ideology. And the latter does not tell lies; or rather it does not *only* tell lies; it does give people solace and diverts their attention into the narrow channels the ideology requires. One has to concede that from this ideological point of view the life of the collectives is admirably organized. All the relevant procedures have been perfected: meetings, bonuses, holidays, newspapers. Take, for instance, Soviet newspapers and films, read the typical books, look at artists' pictures. Everywhere there is the ordinary workman, doing his job well; all the same trivia of life are praised to the skies, trivia that form the impassable swamp of Soviet life. This doesn't mean that in the Soviet Union the ordinary worker and his concerns are the most respected of phenomena: Soviet propaganda and ideology are mendacious and hypocritical. What it *does* mean is that the ruling classes and organizations of society are pursuing the ideological processing of the population at the very base of its miserable existence.

People struggle for life's goods: that is the inescapable law of human existence. It is important to establish in concrete terms what these goods are in a given society for which people fight, how the battle is waged and who has the advantage in the struggle. The fight for lighter work, for a slight pay rise, for an extra metre of living-space: that is one thing. The fight for work that demands all a man's efforts and resources but offers a greater material reward in return, the fight for greater profits, for a higher quality of product, for new markets, that is quite another. In some cases the talented, educated and conscientious man has the advantage. In others it is the ungifted time-server and crook.

I do not make the general assertion that societies can be strictly distinguished by a set of all these indices. In any society you will find examples of them all. I only state that in every type of society something prevails, is perpetuated, is encouraged and has the advantage. Take Communist society. Which of life's goods are fought for in it? The things which are most essential and ordinary: food, shelter, clothing, rest, entertainment. In the struggle to acquire them what is the main weapon? It is social position, a place in the official hierarchy. Personal connections, acquaintances, mutual services, 'pull', bribes. Who has the advantage? Certainly not talent, certainly not the unselfish worker, but the intriguer, the careerist, the thief, the crook, the time-server, the informer, the dud, and the nondescript. Of course there are exceptions. In places one can still find opposite qualities prevailing, but on the whole things are as I say. It is not the slogans, the programmes and the other ideological gimmicks that define the basic features of communal society and its basic tendencies. They only formalize, whitewash, intensify and conserve Communist life's prosaic essence.

THE FORMS OF SOCIAL STRUGGLE

There are two types of struggle in which communal individuals engage. The first is competitive struggle. In the case of competitive struggle the individuals are independent of each other in regard to the activity in which they compete, and there are third parties independent of the competitors who decide who has won. The simplest and most obvious type of competitive struggle is the sporting contest when the competitors run or jump and don't prevent each other from doing so physically. And there are judges who see to it that rules are observed and decide who wins.

One can observe competitive struggle between social individuals in different types of society, whether between individual people or between whole collectives. Sometimes this type of struggle plays a huge role in society, as was the case in bourgeois societies of the recent past and even now makes itself felt in the West. In Communist countries, too, it is easy to come across competitive struggle. But here the conditions for this kind of competition are very much less favourable. Here it plays very much second fiddle; the chief part is played by the second form of competition. This consists of a struggle where the contestants are enmeshed in dependencies of a different kind which are bound up with the object of the struggle itself. We would obtain a graphic example of this kind of struggle if we could somehow attach competing runners to each other and give them the means of stopping each other from running. I call this form of struggle either 'obstructive' or 'preventative'.

Prevention is the main form of social struggle and it is conditioned by the whole order of life under Communism. At the same time it is one of the most important mechanisms for the preservation of Communist society and the operation of its laws. The aim of prevention is not to distinguish those who do best in a sector of activity from the rest of the population, as is the case under competition, but to prevent individuals from distinguishing themselves in this way and to reduce those who threaten to distinguish themselves to some average social level. Not only separate individuals but whole collectives have tremendous possibilities in this business of prevention. Moreover, they also have the means of masking its real essence by disguising it as evidence of social care, mutual aid and disinterested criticism.

The means of prevention are both overt and covert. The overt method is to detect shortcomings in the activities of distinguished individuals and so compromise them in public. The covert method is to denounce people in every way; to 'alert people to the fact that . . .', to write letters to governing bodies, to spread rumours and slander, to influence people who control the fate of the individuals in question and to produce forgeries. The most despicable forms of intrigue are used. One cannot draw a dividing line between overt and covert methods; they are closely related and merge into each other. What is important is that as soon as the surrounding people notice that an individual or a collective is beginning to rise above the average level then, without conspiring together, but in a very friendly way, they begin their systematic and relentless work to prevent the development of the distinction which they have noticed.

The experience of the Soviet Union shows that only when an outstanding individual is helped by the highest organs of power does he have the chance of rising for a fairly long time to a fairly high level. But the authorities rarely have enough power to exercise such a protection on behalf of many such people. Furthermore, they can't go too far with their protection, and therefore even distinguished individuals who *are* protected from above are brought down to the average level. In any case the majority of them do not usually succeed in distinguishing themselves very noticeably.

Moreover, the citizens themselves are quickly convinced that elevation above the average gives them little real advantage and indeed often brings extra unpleasantness in its wake. In the main the position of the rank and file of citizens and managers depends not on their superiority over others in a particular sphere of activity, but on other factors – including their ability *not* to distinguish themselves from the rest of society. Accordingly, people tend to be mediocre in all they do and fail even to try to raise quality and productivity.

Of course, these obstructive or preventative tendencies also have their advantages. Here either no one is defeated, or if they are defeated they don't suffer as a result, and at any rate they are not done for. Besides, one of the strongest preventative measures is mutual assistance and mutual rescue. Thanks to it the feeble are raised more or less to the average level. Not surprisingly mutual *assistance* and the *sharing of experience* are elements of so-called socialist *competition*. Those who are left behind in this society are as undesirable as those who distinguish themselves. But with them it is a simpler matter. All one has to do is lower the average social level sufficiently for the laggards to become the average. This is the cause of the tendency for the middling-mediocre level of everything produced in the society to sink even further.

The tendencies we have been examining coexist very happily with model individuals and collectives. In this aspect the Soviet Union has achieved outstanding successes. Here there are outstanding examples for foreigners, for the government, for demagogy and propaganda, for the needs of a certain section of society. There are 'demonstration-models' whose aim is to be models or 'beacons' for other phenomena of the same kind. There are model specialists and institutions who exist to meet particular requirements of the country, especially military needs. Sometimes they are the result of titanic efforts by individual enthusiasts. But all these exceptional cases merely underline the general mediocrity of the system upon which they exercise so little influence that one can leave them out of account. On the other hand they further the social tendency towards exhibitionist eye-wash, to organizational sham, to fake activities and to the substitution of genuine work by its imitation.

Obstructive activity affects not only the struggle between individuals and institutions of the same category but also that between different categories of institution. Its operations thus result in an established and sustained correspondence in level between different professions and branches of the economy and of culture. The difference in level between different spheres of human activity is conditioned by a series of causes that hide and modify the tendency towards mediocrity. For instance, the high level of sport, ballet and chess in the Soviet Union is maintained because these things have become elements of state prestige, weapons in the (as yet) peaceful conquest of the world by Communism. And the most curious thing is that these methods work. Not long ago I happened to be present among a number of fairly educated people. We were watching a television programme on sport in which Chinese gymnasts were performing. They were very good, and some of the spectators accepted this exhibition as evidence that life in China must be good. When I remarked that the sporting successes of the Soviet Union were perfectly compatible with a low living standard and mass repression, my companions reacted as if the idea were outrageous.

THE INTIMATE LIFE OF THE COLLECTIVE

The intimate life of the collective does not embrace only productive or official activity. It includes social activity as well (meetings, evenings, journeys), and also personal relations and activities emerging from these: gossip, visiting, love affairs, drinking orgies, local groups and mafias, collective guarantees, mutual services. It is the latter which give an intimate character to relations within the collective. They bind the collective together into one family. Not just in a figurative but almost in a literal sense. They bind it into something bigger than a family, that is into a sort of single personality: the super-personality of Communist society; into the kind of 'we' that has the right to regard itself as an 'I'.

This is very important if one wants to understand everything that goes on in Communist society. There, let me emphasize, the bearer of personality is from the start not the individual but the whole institution. The individual is only a bit of a personality, a feeble claim to personality, a protest against non-personality, is merely a memory of what personality used to be. It is not the individual who is the precious subject of law and morality in this society, but only the institution, itself separate, whole and autonomous in its activity; it is the only real individual. When the norms of law and morality, long enracinated in Western civilization, are transferred to Communist society the same amusing incidents arise which for decades have been the object of absolutely senseless conflict.

The intimate life of the collective consists of a vast number of actions and connections that are in most cases habitual, automatic, obscure, unnoticeable to outsiders but very real to the initiated. They amount to everything that makes a man 'one of us' in some part of the collective, and through that part, 'one of us' in the whole collective. Because of this there is nothing left in the intimate life of the man which is unknown to the collective, from the condition of his bowels to his love affairs. For a man to be recognized as a member of the collective he must possess a certain set of vices permitted by the collective in reality, although often they are officially censured. For example, drunkenness (provided of course that it is not so bad as to become a stain on the reputation of the institution or to make his wife complain), two-facedness, sycophancy, a quarrelsome disposition and absence of talent. A man is accepted by the collective even more if he has a lot of misfortune such as illness, trouble at home, lack of success with his children. The collective, for example, is willing out of sympathy to smother in kisses someone who has been burgled and had his fur coat stolen. The collective, in fact, is essentially a union of injured, pallid, unhappy creatures which compensates for their defects.

There are always some people in the collective who become the professional experts of its intimate life. They poke into all the details of the lives of colleagues, spread news, rumours and gossip, mobilize sympathy or censure. In a word, the collective of the institution in which a man works is his basic organic environment without which he simply cannot imagine himself as a person. And society for its part does not grant the status of full citizen to a man who is not either himself, or through members of his family, inscribed in and attached to some kind of institution, who doesn't as the saying goes, work anywhere. This is an objective fact of life. It is neither the propaganda of apologists nor the slander of enemies, but a fundamental fact of the whole social structure of society.

SPIRITUAL PROPINQUITY

One often hears complaints that in the West people live in spiritual isolation from each other, this isolation being contrasted with the nearness to one another which people experience in Communist countries, especially in the Soviet Union. I am not concerned here with people's isolation in the West. But I know very well what Soviet 'nearness' means. It is possible that it has its value. It almost certainly has – after all, it is the natural form of human relationship in conditions of communality. But the essence of this 'boon' is mutual coercion, mutual humiliation and mutual surveillance. All this is the manifestation of the Communist power of the collective over the individual. Moreover, the individual voluntarily submits to coercion by others because he himself takes part in the exercise of such coercion. In actual fact, the principle of these 'warm' and 'friendly' relations is this: 'we are all nonentities'. In such relationships people try to know everything there is to know about the lives of other people; they relish all the biographical details (usually dirty ones); they try to get inside the private thoughts and lives of other people, they jeer at each other behind their backs, they spread gossip and slander. In showing each other such attention people willingly or unwillingly try to 'land' each other 'in it' and to lower the tone of life to a level which is rather unpleasant. This is no achievement whatever as regards humanity's spiritual development. Rather it is a kind of promiscuity in the sphere of social and spiritual life in general.

I know of no more loathsome phenomenon in human relations than the intimate nearness of Soviet people. Imagine that you found yourself thrust into a situation in which your every step was watched and discussed by those around you. You sit down to eat and everyone looks at your mouth, tells you that one of your teeth is missing on the left-hand side, and that your teeth generally are rotten and everyone else's are better. Something like this happens in all human relations in Communist collectives. There the absence of all culture in human intercourse is elevated into a principle which presents itself as the highest achievement in this sphere.

Moreover, the intelligentsia not only does not lag behind the lowest and the highest in the land (who hardly differ from each other); it sets an example by going even further than them. Boorishness, mutual denigration and the vilification of everything in the world reaches truly monstrous dimensions in the intelligentsia. The mud slung by his neighbours has to stick all over a man if he is to fit into *this* milieu. Perhaps this mutual vulgarization is one of Communism's worst phenomena. The principle 'the interests of the collective come before the interests of the individual person' operates in practice as an attempt to turn everyone into nonentities fit for ridicule and contempt. 'Let's have no personalities!': that is the essence of it. And the 'personalities' who are inflated officially are just as much nonentities as the others. Every member of society knows this, especially the educated ones. Communism was conceived by the best of people in the past as an organization of human life in which people work together, enjoy their free time together, endure their difficulties together and share their triumphs. In this ideal society everything would be shared equally and justly. Everyone would live openly for all to see and be 'soulmates' together. They would care about each other, worry about each other, love each other: in short, live as one friendly family. But such a Communist cell is a pure abstraction if society is taken as a whole. It entails leaving out of account the question of successive generations, the family, bureaucracy, the hierarchy, the state, the Party and the organs of repression. Such an abstraction may sometimes exist in reality in the case of small groups in special conditions for a short time, but not in the normal life of society as a whole. It was no accident that the founders of Communist doctrine spoke about the withering away of the state and of the organs of suppression when Communism arrived: they sensed even then that their idea was an unreal fantasy and therefore furnished their fantasy with conditions that could never be realized.

COMMUNAL ENSLAVEMENT

Man in Soviet society acquires the minimum of vital goods, an uncomplicated life and minimum guarantees for the future at a dear price; the price of losing his personal independence, the price of subjection to a primary collective, the price of communal enslavement. I have in mind not only social control over how an individual performs his practical duties (this is exercised in all societies in which people work together). I am thinking of the attachment of the individual to the primary collective and his subjection to rules of communal behaviour within the framework of the collective and of society as a whole. This is the specific Communist form of enslavement.

In critical literature it has become a commonplace to compare Communist society with the concentration camp of Stalin's time or with the corrective-labour camp of the 'liberal' present (at best). Of course concentration camps do bear many similarities to Communist society: large masses of people are forced to live in them together according to the collective principle. But there is all the same a distinction in principle. In the concentration camp people are forced to live together by external forces and the type of society there is forced on them by normal 'free' society. Communist society, on the other hand, beyond the confines of the camps, is the product of natural, intrinsic human behaviour. At the outset it is produced, one may say, voluntarily, and only on this basis is it imposed on people as something given by nature. Moreover, it is imposed on them in quite a different way from that of the concentration camps (from birth, through family education, and by the whole of life's everyday experience). Man in Communist society is free in a sense in which he is *not* free in the concentration camp. The comparison of Communist society with the latter (it has become fashionable to talk about Communist society as one 'big' concentration camp) obscures the essence of that society and hinders our comprehension of it.

Moreover, concentration camps cannot serve as the model of Communist society as a whole, just as an isolated organ of a differentiated organism isn't the model of the organism as a whole. The concentration camp is a useful arena for observing the manifestations of the laws of communality. There they operate more openly than in 'free' society. But the camp as a whole is not the normal working cell of Communism. The administration and the security of the camp can be viewed as a Communist cell in special conditions. But the inmates, although they are put to some kind of use, are from the social point of view material for the camp administration in the same way that children in nursery schools and pupils in schools and institutes are material for educational workers and educational establishments. Invalids in hospitals are also people, but they are not colleagues of the staff of the hospital viewed as a working cell.

Although the number of prisoners in Communist society may assume vast proportions, it is not the camps which are the socio-economic basis of society. Under Communism prisoners are the product of the normal activity of that life. Concentration camps are the consequence of that society and lie outside its limits: they are not its basis or a particular example of it. I repeat: people in normal Communist society are free in a sense in which they are not free in corrective-labour camps, or in prison in general. To understand the type and degree of civic bondage in Communist society we must begin by understanding the type and degree of the citizen's freedom. All freedom is limited freedom. Two different questions, which are usually confused, arise in connection with this: 1) how free within the limits *are* people? 2) how stable and how narrow (or broad) are these limits?

For example, a man who wants to go to the West from the Soviet Union and is refused permission regards the refusal as a sign of the absence of freedom there, whereas to the man in the depths of the country who couldn't even conceive of making a trip to the West the opinion of his countryman seems absurd. 'Why doesn't he ask for the moon as well?!' To the pupil who has no hope of admittance to the Institute of International Relations, his exclusion seems a limitation of his freedom to choose his profession, whereas from another point of view the matter does not look like that at all. Not everyone can be a diplomat, and to prove that the above-mentioned pupil has a greater right to become a diplomat is impossible for the simple reason that there is no such right. In case there is any doubt about that, the regulations will see to it that the pupil won't get into the Institute: they will simply fail him in the exams or ask for a special character-reference from the regional committee of the *Komsomol*, which won't be forthcoming. To be a diplomat is a privilege of the ruling classes. But such privileged professions exist in all countries, and are not a speciality of Communism.

The nub of the matter is that people in Communist society, because of their education and the obvious conditions of their personal fate, have to accept whatever limitations apply to their behavioural freedom or un-freedom as something natural and self-evident. They are brought up to live within these limits and grow accustomed to them from childhood. They accept the form of life that is foisted upon them, having no other choice, and they themselves foist it on others. What happens when somebody tries to infringe the generally accepted bounds of freedom or un-freedom (they are the same thing) I shall describe later. The essence of communal enslavement is not its imposition by external force, but the population's acceptance of limitations to its freedom and its reproduction of these limitations in the normal process of its own life. The majority do not view their situation as enslavement at all. It is we who observe the society from outside who can allow ourselves to use such an expression as 'enslavement' when we compare the position of people in a specific society with certain real, or theoretically possible, alternatives.

The citizens in Communist society do not consider themselves un-free, living as they do within the framework of generally accepted and apparently quite natural limitations. Their consciousness is directed to something else: how to arrange their life to the best advantage within the framework of what is allowed. And we must admit that, for the majority, this is freedom enough. Limitations on the choice of profession, of where to live and work, on changes of domicile within the country and on journeys outside it are not as a rule regarded as the absence of freedom or freedoms. Usually people are either reconciled to this or find their own ways of getting round these limitations. For example, the limitations on residence in Moscow are circumvented by means of marriage or through bribes, through one's career, or through the exercise of one's talents. But not even the dissidents have yet thought of demanding the abolition of the residence permit system.

People live in all sorts of conditions under Communism. In one locality, for example, there will be no factories or special educational institutions; in another one factory and one technical college; in a third ten factories, two institutes and ten technical colleges. Thus the chances of educational and professional training and the choice of profession are not the same for all. Colleges and schools differ in educational level. Professions differ in terms of attraction and career prospects. People differ in terms of their natural inclinations, their family position and in many other ways. In practice it is impossible to destroy this diversity. And society finds the means to compel people to reconcile themselves to that fact to some extent. Such means amount to various limitations on personal freedom as regards choice of profession, place of work, educational establishment, choice of residence, travel.

In every society there are similar limitations. But in each society they have their own special character. In Communist society they are only an extension of the general principles of attachment of people to the commune and their distribution according to social position. For the reasons we have given, the limitations on the freedom of individuals under Communism become a conscious, compulsory administrative method of allocating people to communes geographically. A complex system of restrictions develops: passports, residence papers, problems with hotels and transport, problems with obtaining food supplies and arranging to work where you want. Peculiar norms of freedom come into being, chief among which is the system of privileges.

People discover the limits of freedom (or un-freedom) for themselves, but the latter are only experienced as such when people begin to transgress the written or unwritten laws of the Communist way of life. For example, if some people organize religious sects or political groups, try to publish something without the censor or to put on a demonstration that has not been authorized by the authorities, then they immediately discover that a whole series of freedoms is missing from this society, freedoms that are customary in the democratic countries of the West. How the authorities react to such initiatives is well known. What is more important is the fact that the authorities are merely expressing the reaction of the masses to deviations from the norm of Communist life. It isn't at all as if some evil rulers were deliberately depriving people of certain natural and generally recognized freedoms. No, the real fact is that Soviet society at its very foundations doesn't need freedoms of this kind and is even hostile towards them. To Soviet people these are alien phenomena. And the struggle against these 'alien' freedoms is conducted above all at the level of the primary collectives.

PERSONALITY AND FUNCTION

From the day he is born the individual in Communist society is subject to powerful formative influences which, with few exceptions, turn him into a 'new man' in accordance with the principles of that society. It must be admitted that the society does this particular dirty piece of work very well. It is by now clear that Communism is above all a society of people who behave badly. But the business of producing this shoddy product is going very nicely. To be good at producing rubbish, trivia, 'bullshit', to be expert in passing fiction off as fact, imitation as the real thing and the production of counterfeit goods as honest activity are the inalienable qualities of Communist society. And the remark is especially relevant to the most important production of all: the production of human beings. Here society's assembly-lines mass-produce marvellously made people, completely deprived of any social or moral foundation and ready for any abomination that circumstances might demand.

From the standpoint of human material Communist society is typically unable to contain on a large scale individuals who could be described as persons. This should not lead us to imagine that individuals cannot commit acts that are characteristic of persons. What it does mean is that if an individual does something characteristic of a person, then he is simply removed from the historical arena; he is either destroyed as a biological unit or forcibly isolated. A man may act once like a person; but this is too little to make a person, because a person is a social individual who accomplishes such actions more or less regularly. Of course, there are exceptional situations when a man wins the opportunity of being a person for some considerable time. But sooner or later Communist society, in one way or another, cleanses itself of such individuals. Besides, such individuals are very rare. They are not typical or characteristic of Communist society. What is typical of Communism is precisely the absence of such individuals or the destruction (including their exiling abroad) of individuals who by chance survived and had the impudence to dare to be persons. Communist society gravitates towards an absolutely homogeneous de-personalized state. That way there is peace and quiet. Everything is more orderly and everything is much easier for the government.

If a man in Communist society turns out to be a significant person or 'personality' who stands out against his environment, this does not mean that he has lived a virtuous life or that he should be canonized as a saint. If he really does try to live such a life, he is either speedily liquidated by every available means or he grows into a fighter against small injustices in his immediate environment. This type is in every way encouraged by the Soviet authorities and by Soviet propaganda. Such a fighter for truth battles with the housing authority to get leaking water-taps mended, fights to ban smoking in public places, mounts a campaign against the noise of transistor radios. Such a fighter is a buttress of Communism, and absolutely never reaches the point where he would oppose the whole Communist order of life. To oppose in that sense means really doing something; it means living for a fairly long time; it means thinking deeply. It means that for one reason or another, society itself has chosen you and pushed you right into the role. Of course traits of character, educational conditions and events in one's past life play a role in all this: sometimes a decisive one, but not always, and not always noticeably. The main thing is that such a man lives his own life normally, only gradually accumulating his exclusiveness. It is no accident, therefore, that in the Soviet Union there are sudden 'outbreaks' of personalities, when suddenly it seems that well-off and reliable citizens begin to rebel, protest, and try to insist on their own personal worth.

Once again this position is the consequence of the very form of life of the basic population. Because of their situation in the communes people do not perceive each other as whole, autonomous beings who contain in themselves all the world's values, but only as partial functions of the whole. So they easily change their lovers, their friends, their comrades-in-arms. They do it easily because in the commune it is only the function that matters, which any suitable individual can fulfil, and not some sovereign participant of interactions which only take place at the elevated level of autonomous individuals. The ruling principle in practice is this: no one is indispensable.

The difference between man-as-function and man-as-person doesn't depend on the respective levels of education and culture. Man-as-function can be very highly educated and cultured; man-as-person may be uncultured and illiterate. The distinction lies in the character of the human relationships and in the relations between individual people and the community. I am not expressing value-judgements here. To be a person is not necessarily a good thing, while to be just a partial function is not necessarily bad. The workers in the Soviet Union's collective and state farms, for instance, are better educated than Tsarist peasants, and on the whole live better than they did: but they are all partial functions of collective personalities, whereas even the poor peasants of the past gravitated towards the man-as-person type.

Besides the division of people according to their functions in the working life of the collective and their official social position there is an unofficial, but in reality no less important, division: the one corresponding with their unofficial functions in the collective. Here the concepts of free-will and compulsion do not apply. It is simply the case that certain people are suitable to play particular roles in the life of the collective. Such roles include: management spy, gossip, 'fighter for the truth', informant, 'decent bloke', 'reactionary' and genius. I have described many of these man-functions in my books, including the function of the 'decent bloke'. I will give a description here of the 'decent bloke' as a characteristic example of the *genre*. It is an interesting one and something of a supplementary stroke of the brush on the portrait of Communist man.

Communist society has contributed its own special chapter to general social progress by breeding its own type of individual, never seen before and never met with in societies of another type. This is the 'decent bloke'. It is not that there weren't or aren't decent blokes in other countries, but that isn't the point. Formerly there were more of them, and in contemporary societies of another type there are immeasurably more of them than in Communist countries. But that isn't the point either. The point is the special social role of individuals. Just as in any large stable social group there are always some people (usually one person) who take upon themselves the role of voluntary jester, in Communist social groups one or several (more often one) take on the role of 'decent bloke'. What sort of individuals are thrust into this role? Naturally the most useful and most suitable, who know how to extract from this honourable role a perceptible advantage. But that isn't the main point. What is important is to determine the visible actions which these people perform regularly, and their hidden social meaning. Usually the decent blokes themselves and those around them are not conscious of this and that they are not is one of the most important features of this hidden meaning. The decent bloke does all the same things that others do, but he does them in such a way that, against the background of the others, he looks like the incarnation of goodness, sensibility, honesty, bravery, fidelity to principle and other abstract virtues. By the very fact of his existence he seems to be saying to people: 'You can be virtuous and at the same time avoid suffering and even get your reward!' By taking part in different organizations and events he somehow ennobles them and masks their real essence. Indeed, it is the decent blokes who hide the most unpalatable phenomena of Communist life from the eyes of the general public. They are not only co-partners in crimes, they give the latter the mask of virtue, or sad necessity. Besides, they are dangerous. They deal you a blow at the most crucial moment; and quite unexpectedly, bcause you are relying on them and it never enters your head that they constitute the most vulnerable spot in your position.

The authorities take excellent account of the role which decent blokes really play; and within certain limits encourage them and even invent them if such people don't appear on the scene according to the natural laws of communal life. They are elected to every bureau, are rewarded with prizes, and are held up as examples. There are hardly any cases where decent blokes evolve into oppositionists. As soon as the authorities notice that a decent bloke is transgressing the limits of what is permitted, they quickly put him in his place or deprive him of his particular role.

I chose the example of the 'decent bloke' for a particular

reason that I wish to underline. In a society in which communality rules, even virtues are special functions of people and not innately noble qualities. Moreover, virtue often pays better than vice. And its hidden role is sometimes more disgusting than the open behaviour of evil men.

It is exactly the same with all the other social functions of the collective. I have already mentioned the functions of those who 'fight for the truth'. What is interesting here is that the average commune resembles the elements of one individual scattered among many different people. If you want to know what the potential of any one Communist is, you should carry out the following operation: take an average typical social institution, analyse its structure and the different functions of the people in it and then put them all together in your imagination to form a whole being, the character of one man. You will then get the being which Marx himself defined as the aggregate of social relations. Here the collective begets its members in its own form and likeness; and the members of the collective reproduce their community in keeping with their nature. The circle is closed, and there is no exit from inside it. We make our social life correspond with what we are. In Communist society an enormous mass of people are occupied professionally and semi-professionally with the task of bringing man down to the level of a certain small rodent. Their most powerful weapons in this business are their own insignificance, reptility and bestiality. This is their natural form of self-defence and self-preservation. So, to stop this frightful force, centuries are needed; and sacrifices.

THE RESPONSIBILITY OF THE COLLECTIVE

The communes are so placed in society *vis-à-vis* the authorities that it is they who bear the responsibility for the behaviour of their members. And if individual members of the commune do socially reprehensible things, then the rest of the members of the commune will suffer for it in one way or another. The situation is the same as it is in the army. For instance, a soldier goes into the town on a pass, gets drunk and breaks the place up. As a result many commanding officers get strips torn off them, moreover in hierarchical succession. The regimental commander gets his from the divisional commander, the battalion commander from the regimental commander, and so on down to the man in immediate command of the culprit. The political officers step up their educational activity. The whole platoon or even the whole company loses its leave passes for the next few days. Meetings are called; wall-newspapers are issued. In brief, everyone in the vicinity of the soldier is compelled to pass judgement on him. The reaction of the commune to the misdemeanours of its members is organized in exactly the same way. The administration of the commune is hauled before higher authority and receives a roasting. And this has its effect on people's position and careers. The collective suffers not only symbolic forms of punishment, (e.g. losing its position in a 'socialist competition') which in the last resort produce palpable effects (e.g. the loss of prizes), but also punishments that are immediately felt, such as time wasted in meetings and committees of all sorts, the reinforcement of work-discipline and vigilance towards other potentially disruptive elements. I have given a detailed description of this system which forces the commune to react to the behaviour of its members in my book *In the Ante-Chamber of Paradise*, in the chapter called 'The collective's responsibility for its members'. This system not only places power over the individual in the hands of the collective but makes the exercise of this power inescapable.

RENEGADES AND THE COLLECTIVE

The nature of the relationship between the individual and

the collective in Communist society becomes particularly apparent in the case of particular individuals who are known in the Soviet Union as renegades*. I describe the renegade in detail in my books *Notes of a Nightwatchman*, and *In the Ante-Chamber of Paradise*. Here I shall include only a few fragments of the description.

Every commune contains an active part, a passive part and a 'nonconformist' part. A comparatively small number of officials form the active part. They administer everything to do with the inner life of the collective: they pressurize the administration, the Party organizations and other social organizations. They form a peculiar mafia of their own, bound together by collective guarantee and mutual support. They are the carriers, the mouthpieces and the creators of public opinion within the collective. They are elected to the local trade union committee, to the housing committee, to the management of the mutual aid fund. They control the distribution of trips and loans and prizes. They spread rumours and gossip. They compile secret dossiers on every member of the collective.

Of course, not everything is in the power of this mafia. Besides, it usually fulfils the wishes of the official management of the collective, but it does have considerable power, especially as regards the lower ranks of the workers and the little things that make life bearable. The mafia isn't always homogeneous and unanimous. Sometimes it splits into warring factions and changes its composition. Sometimes it has its tail between its legs. But all in all its role remains stable: to snatch for itself everything that can be snatched at life's lowest level.

The overwhelming majority of the workers forms the passive section of the collective. People of higher rank also belong to the passive section; people who in some degree stand above the trivialities of collective life. They form a submissive and completely apathetic mass. Attention is only paid to them when one or other group is trying to seize the initiative and, for this, seeks to attract the mass to its side.

* *otshchepentsy*

The 'nonconformist' section is made up of a small number of people who, for one reason or another, stand outside the collective's intimate life. Usually they are people who have let themselves go to pieces or who are temporary workers in the institution. Nobody takes any notice of them: for the collective it is as if they didn't exist. But sometimes among the ranks of the nonconformists there are good workers who consciously try to preserve some independence and resist immersion in the petty intimate life of the institution. These people evoke unease and bad feeling. Efforts are made to squeeze them out, to compromise them and to destroy them.

The distinguishing feature of the nonconformist renegade is, above all, his non-participation in the intimate life of the collective. The members interpret this as opposition to it, as conceit and disengagement from the collective. And the fact that he is a good worker won't help him. If the collective feels that the man is a 'renegade', it will do everything it can to destroy his reputation as a good worker. The process will be made to appear like a genuine case of 'unmasking' or of 'bringing things to light'. Later the incident is usually presented in a way such as to suggest that this good, honest worker had in fact all the time been an enemy.

The collective doesn't dub a worker a 'renegade' all at once. Years go by, sometimes decades, before this happens. Indeed, the worker doesn't always become a loner all of a sudden, or if he does he is not always immediately aware of it. Sometimes he never becomes aware of it at all and falls into a state of extreme perplexity when the collective starts to settle accounts with him. In the beginning the collective will fight furiously to prevent the worker's cutting himself off from it and opposing himself to it. All possible measures are applied, from cajolery to threats and worse. And it is rarely that a man does not bow to the collective's onslaught. When a campaign against a worker is in progress, the collective may allow itself many things that would be inadmissible with regard to workers who are reliable. For instance, the collective may hide from the administration the fact that the worker has found himself in the sobering-up station and in that way lure him into closer relationships with trusted people in the collective.

As a rule workers do not try to become loners, and the collective itself sincerely tries to draw people into its own life. This is evidence of a fundamental law regarding the levelling of the individual and his attachment to the collective: both sides strive towards this end. And if a man does fall into the category of loner, then this is a deviation from a general norm. This deviation is not an accident because there are other laws which account for it. By virtue of the laws regarding the unity of the individual and the collective, the latter prefers not to expel the individual but to tame him by force and include him in the collective duly reformed. Therein lies the force of the principle 'become what we all are and then we will forgive you'. The loner is thrown out only in the extreme case when there is no hope left of taming him, or when the authorities order him out. Usually the two things coincide.

One of the most potent means with which the collective can pressurize an individual who defects from it or who tends to do so is slander. Slander existed in the past, but only in Communist society has slander become a normal social phenomenon that evokes no open censure and causes no pangs of conscience. Only here does it assume monstrous proportions and invade life at all levels. Of course, everything depends on whom it is directed at. If it is directed at one's own administration or (Heaven forbid!) at a higher one, then it is a criminal action. Slander goes unpunished only when its object is singled out by the collective, and endorsed by the administration, as an individual who is setting himself against the collective and society in general. Such an individual lives in an atmosphere of perpetual slander. In so far as people have no inner censors (such as fear of God, conscience, moral principles, good breeding) while all external restrictions have been removed, people are not sparing of their slander; moreover, they exhibit a wealth of invention. The talent of the population is to a large extent squandered on the slandering of one's neighbour.

Social skills in slander are highly developed and the habit of slander is developed from generation to generation so consistently and thoroughly that people do not even notice that they are engaged in slander. The capacity for slander is organically inherent in them as one of the nation's greatest historic achievements. Slander is a factor of everyday life at all levels. It is practically impossible to bring slander out into the open because everyone practises it and because its sources and initiators are never revealed. Outsiders are in no position to distinguish slander from truth, and any attempt to unmask it easily ends up as an apparently ridiculous fuss about nothing.

Nevertheless, what is striking is not that the collective settles accounts with loners but that it inevitably pressurizes one of its own members into that role. The loner is alien to this society, but he is alien in a way that makes him at the same time indispensable to the collective. To force a suitable contender into the role of loner; to try at the same time to make him its own; then to try to discredit and suppress him; finally to expel him from society: all these are necessary elements of a society's training in monolithic unity, and demonstrate that very unity both to itself and to others. They are a means of constantly conditioning society in a particular mould and of preserving that mould.

Enemies of society are not born. They are made. And they are made by the will and wish of society itself. The collective singles out a certain type of individual for future sacrifice, and involves him in its life in such a way that his projection into the role of enemy is an inevitable consequence. And the enemy is almost always fictitious and illusory. Very rarely is he real. Here we see a characteristic of this society manifested in the contradictory processes of incorporating individuals by first singling them out and of alienating individuals by seeking to incorporate them. It holds some deep meaning which escapes the participants and which is analogous to the meaning of ritual sacrifice in societies of the past that were not founded on legal, moral or Christian principles.

Candidates for the role of renegade have certain qualities. They will be people of originality. They will be daring, upright, of free and independent attitude and colourful. That is to say they will be those who are most defenceless in the social context; the most vulnerable and the most hateful to the grey mass of the workers of the collective. In the case of such people all the measures taken by the collective to incorporate the loner into its intimate life actually stimulate him to resist the collective and to stand apart from it as a sovereign person. This either results in the ruin of the individual on the level of the collective (he takes to drink, becomes apathetic or begins to take risks) or his actual expulsion from it which also means that society loses him. Very often it means the enforced physical isolation of the individual from society by its punitive organizations.

The behaviour of people who have attracted the close attention of the collective is not perceived objectively but is subject to interpretation. Essentially what happens is that others attribute to such behaviour whatever motives, objectives, causes or effects take their fancy, i.e. they attribute a particular meaning to it. And from there on people are dealing not with actions as such but with their interpretation of them. In so doing they fail to notice that they are interpreting the actions in a way which most suits the given situation and the dominant part of the collective. The members of the collective do this not because they do not know the underlying reasons, motives, aims and consequences of a certain person's actions but because their own interpretation is convenient to themselves. It affords them psychological justification, stimulates a particular disposition and gives them arguments for the punishment of the victim. They themselves are both judges and executioners. The collective itself is in the position of being responsible for the behaviour of its members. This is convenient. On the one hand the individual is released from responsibility for what is in fact the collective coercion of a neighbour. On the other, the collective is compelled to react spitefully to the dissident member and to deal with him without mercy.

The punishment of the victim proceeds according to definite rules. A whole system of organizations and officials see to it that these rules are observed and that the punishment is carried through to the end. All interested and responsible authorities must be convinced that the collective has reacted correctly in the 'emergency', that the collective is fundamentally sound, that the management will deal with the situation and take measures that will prevent a repetition of such cases. Otherwise these supervisors will have to explain their lapses in the matter, and so on until the wave of responsibility is exhausted in the depths of the social hierarchy. The fundamental principles of the ritual punishment are these: 1) denigrate the victim in every possible way; 2) express one's astonishment at his behaviour; 3) confess one's own fault in the sense that one has 'overlooked things', and 'displayed a liberal attitude' without 'paying due attention to certain signs and signals'; 4) punish those who are deemed guilty of having 'overlooked things'; 5) take prophylactic measures.

The purpose of punishment is to exact retribution from the person who has deviated from the generally accepted norms of behaviour and to serve as a lesson to others. Punishment is not a single act, but a continuous condition of the culprit for the rest of his life. Moreover, the convicted man loses the defence of the collective against hooligans, thieves, bandits, the militia and his neighbours. In a society in which the individual has no legal defence against the whims of local authorities, the collective is his only defence on that level. Without the collective man becomes the plaything of chance even when his punishment is relatively light.

INDIVIDUALISM AND COLLECTIVISM

The Communist collective reacts very sensitively to that phenomenon which is the polar opposite of its own form of conduct, psychology and ideology, that is, to individualism. I drew attention to this phenomenon extensively in my book *The Yellow House*. Here I shall limit myself to some brief remarks.

Individualism and collectivism are special types of behaviour which differ psychologically and ideologically. From the behavioural point of view the individualist prefers to act by himself, independently of other people. One must not confuse this attitude with the urge to secure a privileged position. The individualist is ready to forgo privileges and do heavier and less remunerative work if it provides him with some independence from the activities of other people. The collectivist prefers to act in a group and be in contact with other people doing the same thing as he does. The individualist avoids large assemblies and tries to separate himself from the crowd. The collectivist seeks the mob and seeks entry into groups, castes and parties. Situated in the mass, he acts according to mass laws and doesn't separate himself from it. One mustn't confuse this attitude with careerism or its absence, or with the urge to be boss. The collectivist is even more inclined to rise above his fellows and gravitate towards the leadership and a career than is the individualist, because for him his behaviour and role within the collective is precisely that, whereas for the individualist it is merely a means of separation from the collective. The individualist tries to make his way in life through his own abilities and by his own work; in other words, by his own endeavours. The collectivist advances together with the collective, by means of the collective and by means of his role within the collective.

From the psychological point of view individualism and collectivism are not to be confused with egoism, egocentricity, altruism, misanthropy, gregariousness, unsociability or other qualities of this type. The collectivist can be an egoist and egocentric, a misanthrope and a recluse. The individualist can be sociable, a lover of mankind and a man who avoids attracting attention to himself. The collectivist can be a self-seeker, ready to betray his collective for his own petty advantage. When it comes down to it there is no guarantee whatever that he will sacrifice his own interests for the sake of the collective. The individualist, on the other hand, may be devoted to the collective and may sacrifice his own interests for its sake. This is not at all the point. The individualist is psychologically self-sufficient, he feels himself to be a whole and sovereign personality, irrespective of his social position.

From the ideological point of view the individualist regards himself as an autonomous being of intrinsic worth, and recognizes other people as similarly sovereign beings. Moreover, the individualist even regards the collective as a being possessing equal rights. He rejects the principle the interests of the collective come before the interests of the individual. He accepts the principle the interests of the individual members of the collective and of the collective as a whole are of equal importance. The collectivist for his part regards himself as a function of some other sovereign entity, namely the collective. He accepts the principle the interests of the collective come before the interests of the individual. Individualism is the most vibrant manifestation of the social need for personal identity and collectivism the least. They differ only with respect to the issue of personal identity, not collective identity. For collectivism, references to the importance of the collective principle in society are only an argument in a debate, or material for self-justification. For the individualist, human society is a community of intrinsically sovereign 'I's, while for the collectivist only the unity itself is an 'I'; only 'we' is 'I'. The active individualist tries to be unique among his equals. The active collectivist tries to lower others to his own level, to raise himself above them and become the 'top dog'.

Collectivism makes the individual more adaptable to the complicated conditions of contemporary society than does individualism. The collectivist is more flexible, more agile, more wily than the individualist, and in the context of Communist society or islands of Communism in other societies, collectivism shows itself to be maximally adequate. For that reason it specially cultivates collectivists. Individuals who in other conditions could become individualist by virtue of their innate gifts are forced into the general norm, rather as born left-handers are forced to become right-handers. Society tries to prevent the appearance of individualists. But they still keep on appearing. Why? Partly through negligence on the part of those around them. But mainly because there are always types of activity in society which only individualists can handle. Generally these are kinds of creative activity in which the collective, either in principle or *de facto*, is unable in certain circumstances to replace the individual and in which the collective has no advantage over the individual. But the situation of the individual who survives or even flourishes is in the overwhelming majority of cases dramatic. The execution of the above-mentioned types of activity threatens to elevate the individual above other mortals, not because of the laws of society but in spite of them, and this creates tempting precedents. The individual threatens to corrupt the whole substance of society, i.e. of the human material forming that society. Therefore society tries to destroy those types of activity utterly or to reduce them to the minimum or to envelop them in a standardized collectivist environment in which the first victims will be the individualists.

Of course, Communist collectivism has its good points as well. It destroys the personal 'cocoon' of individuals which condemns them to spiritual isolation and brings people together. But what does this means of curing people of their loneliness really amount to? It is like a dirty communal pre-war Moscow flat in which five or six families huddle together, eternally quarrelling and eternally relapsing into a state of maudlin friendship.

POWER

Communist society is a voluntarist society to the highest, possibly to the maximum, degree. In it the power-system reaches monstrous dimensions and entangles the whole of society in such an all-pervading network that it is practically impossible to separate the rulers from the ruled. For this reason it is utterly absurd to hope that one can change the way of life in this or that Communist country by changing the form that power takes within it. Here one can change the form of power only by changing society as a whole; or, to be more precise, by destroying the country and building a society of another type from its ruins. But, as I said earlier, the possibilities of doing this are very limited.

What is power? The concept is rather vague. First of all power is the sum total of all the authorities in the country. And goodness, how many there are! In a country as large as the Soviet Union their number is so huge that together with the members of their families they form a whole state within a state. This statement is purely metaphorical, of course, because the authorities do not form a single unified whole but are distributed throughout the country among the mass of people under their control. Indeed, a huge number of bosses are themselves subordinate to other bosses and are less well-off than many representatives of the privileged classes who are not officials (for example, the ordinary university teacher may be better off than an officer of the militia). But from all this it doesn't follow that people regard the exercise of power as unpleasant and burdensome. There is a struggle for even the lowest positions in the power-system because they signify a rise in social position and offer relatively tangible privileges.

This huge army of officials is a particularly communal phenomenon. It is a direct result of the splitting of society into functional cells and beyond that into social and functional groups at different levels, into hierarchies of cells, and by the unification of all sorts of groups of people into complex groups and of these groups into a whole society. One can't get away from this phenomenon because it is governed by objective social laws which are as inevitable as the laws of nature. There are definite bounds within which the number of functionaries fluctuates in a contemporary society once it has reached a certain stage in its development. It cannot be less than a certain minimum dictated exclusively by the interests of government, and this number cannot be reduced by any kind of governmental decree.

One can reduce the number of officially recognized officials, but then more *de facto* officials will appear. They may not be officially recognized but they fulfil functions which accord completely with *social* laws. The number of actual officials may be curtailed by diminishing the numerical strength of a country's population, by cutting down the number of hierarchical levels in the social structure, by simplifying the system of management and by other means. But do many of these procedures match the tendencies of social evolution? As a matter of fact one of the reasons for the change from Stalinist procedures in the Soviet Union to the Khrushchev-Brezhnev type of regime was that a process of rapid diversification of the country's life had begun, and previous forms of control were no longer adequate.

Communist society has not invented power, but it enables the proliferation of power in society since the owner has been replaced by the official, who rules over something that he doesn't own. In addition, the official gains office not by virtue of tradition, custom, or inheritance but by virtue of relationships of supremacy and subordination as such.

Furthermore, Communist power is an aggregate of special organs of the social organism: the Party apparatus, the ministries and territorial authorities. Their task is to weld large groups of people into a single whole, and in the end into a whole country. These organs themselves have a complex structure. In the last analysis they too are composed of functional cells. Within these cells as well people are divided into the rulers and the ruled. These organs also have a complex structure on another plane: there is again the Party apparatus, but also an administrative-managerial apparatus and the state apparatus (in the Soviet Union, for example, the state is represented in the territorial *soviets*). Later I shall come back to examine what, from the sociological point of view, the basic properties of this rather cumbersome power-apparatus are.

Finally, power exists where any one person can exercise force in his relations with others. In Communist society power in this sense becomes especially potent. It consists above all in the power of the whole collective over the individual members of the collective, the power of individual members of the collective, the power of individual members of the collective over the rank and file, the power of any member of society over any other member who is at any time dependent on him. Relevant here are the countless occasions when people become the objects of other people's activities (for example the power of the shop-keeper over the customer, the power of the militia-man over the drunken member of the intelligentsia, the power of the taxi-driver over the client who is in a hurry and is desperate to catch a taxi). For ordinary citizens this power is so tangible that it often pushes all the other forms of power into the background.

In the narrow sense of the word, power is an aggregate of people employed in the governing apparatus of the state and its innumerable branches. In the Soviet Union this consists of *soviets* on different levels, ministries, committees, unions, the militia, the organs of state security and so on. And of course the Party apparatus, which unifies all these into one whole, stands at the head of the whole power-system and forms its core on all levels and in all branches.

The overwhelming majority of those who represent power are poorly paid civil servants. This results in the inevitable tendency for low pay to be augmented through the use of one's office. So there is nothing surprising in the fact that many of the low-paid representatives of power live a good deal better than their more highly paid fellow citizens. Thus power is materially attractive even at the lowest levels. The overwhelming majority of the powerful officially possess only a very small portion of power. This leads to the tendency to make up for one's inadequate power by exceeding one's official competence; and the possibilities of doing this are almost limitless. So it is also not surprising that in practice low officials in the power-apparatus dispose of a *large* amount of power.

This incidentally accounts for the hatred of the ordinary official for the higher-ranking scientific-technical intelligentsia and those working in the arts, a hatred directed by the law of compensation for impotence at the most defenceless and the poorest part of the creative intelligentsia. Hatred of the intelligentsia in general is an element in the ideology of mass power as a whole, if only because in the lowest sections power is held by the least educated and the least gifted part of the population, while in the upper reaches it is held by people who, from the point of view of education and talent, everywhere and always are inferior to their contemporaries who are scholars, painters, writers, or representatives of the performing arts.

Power in Communist society is at once omnipotent and impotent. It is *negatively* omnipotent, in its ability to do harm with impunity. It is positively impotent in that it is incapable of doing good gratuitously. Its potential is enormously destructive and minimally creative. The successes of the economy (and of business generally) are not due to power as such. As a rule these successes are, from the point of view of power, a necessary evil. This goes even more for successes in the field of culture. Such things are in general not the function of power. The illusion that they are the product of the exercise of power arises because decisions are taken, plans drawn up, instructions issued and reports completed about absolutely everything. But really these are only superimposed formalities: there is no nexus of cause and effect. Management of absolutely everything is merely a façade disguising the existence of power for its own sake.

This omnipotent power is incapable of carrying through even a well-prepared tiny reform on a national scale if that little reform is called for in order to improve social organization: i.e. if it is a positive reform. But with a mere wave of the hand it can destroy whole programmes of science and art, whole branches of the economy, centuries-old structures and even whole peoples. But it cannot defend even the smallest creative enterprise from the attacks of those around if the latter have the intention of grinding it to dust.

Power of the Communist type is in principle unreliable. It cannot carry out its promises for long enough and systematically enough. And this isn't because it is fraudulent. Power cannot keep its word because of the way it works. This applies of course in the first place to positive intentions

181

and only to some extent to negative ones. People who have promised something can easily be replaced by people who interpret that promise as a mistake (in order to discredit the people they have replaced). The general tendency for norms of life to shift, together with the tendency of the authorities to re-organize everything, can change the situation so much that previous promises lose their sense or are simply forgotten.

Unfulfilled official promises become the norm. Deep down nobody believes the authorities. They don't believe themselves either. When decisions are taken this disbelief is taken for granted as a matter of course. Not openly, of course, and, I repeat, only in matters concerning positive action. But as regards negative activity the signal has only to be given. It is much easier to be destructive than constructive.

In addition to everything else there is almost total irresponsibility with respect to the course of government business. Power grabs everything it can for itself. It then arranges its business in such a way that it bears no responsibility whatever for blunders and deficiencies. What makes this possible is an elaborate cover-up within the power apparatus.

Power in Communist societies is an element not of political relations but of other social relations, namely communal ones. It is power for its own sake and has no other basis than itself. Here power doesn't exist for society. On the contrary society only exists, is recognized and permitted to a degree necessary and sufficient for the production and functioning of power. Under Communism society, biologically speaking, is merely power's 'culture medium' and an arena for its own circuses.

All forms of power in Communist society and all the people who participate in power and possess some of it will stop at nothing – in other words they are capable of anything if it gives the desired result and isn't too severely punished. Communal considerations are the basis and essence of everyone and everything. Other phenomena in human relations derive from this basis and are subordinate to it. The state power of a Communist country as a whole is subject to this principle. If the government of the country considers that such and such an operation is necessary and comparatively safe, nothing from within the society is able to stop the government from carrying it out, however monstrously immoral or cruel the operation may seem. Communist power is limited in its arbitrariness only by external obstacles and by its own ability to overcome them.

POWER AT THE LEVEL OF THE CELL

The essence of power in Communist society is clearly revealed at the level of the primary collective. Of course in larger units (right up to the scale of the country itself) power assumes functions which it doesn't enjoy at the level of the cell. But it is in the cell that the roots of these functions are nonetheless to be found. The functions of power on a nation-wide scale are merely generalized, enlarged functions of power in the cells. For example, at the level of the cell there are no courts of justice or punitive organs, yet punishment functions are already part and parcel of the primary collective. The primary collective cannot give a worker permission to go abroad, but whether the worker can make that journey will depend on the collective no less than on the Ministry of Internal Affairs. In a very large number of cases the primary collective authorizes the instigation of criminal proceedings against its own workers and even takes the initiative in such matters.

In their own working cell citizens come up against administrative power (i.e. management); against Party power (including the *Komsomol*) and against the power of the collective (including the trade-union organization). The overwhelming majority of workers in the collective takes part in the exercise of this power in some way or other. And although the chief administrators are appointed from above and the Party management is selected and supported by the highest Party organs, power at the level of the primary collective is genuinely autonomous. For the majority of citizens life is limited to the level of the primary collective, so that for them everyday power is seen first in its aspect of local autonomy. At this level it isn't regarded as compulsion. Even the higher ranks of the leadership of the collective do not stand out against the rank and file in the way that happens in the case of owners of enterprises with hired labourers, or landowners with farm-hands or serfs. Here they are all members of the collective. They may have ambitions to rise higher and so stand out from the collective as something external and superior. But while they are in a particular collective, they are all comrades together. Power in Communist society is in the highest degree democratic at its own base, and this fact is expressed in the personal relationships between the rulers and the ruled. One of the tricks of the social system, to which I always draw attention, lies in the fact that a highly democratic power-base in the collective can give rise to the most undemocratic power on the scale of the regions, the provinces, the ministries and so on, not to speak of the country as a whole.

THE GOVERNMENT OF THE COMMUNE

The leader of the commune (the manager or director) is appointed by superior administrative organs. But it is the appropriate Party organ which gives the go-ahead for his appointment and often it takes the initiative in the choice of a suitable candidate. In the Soviet Union, the director of an institution, and often his deputies too, are the nominees of regional, town or higher Party organs. They form part of what in the Soviet Union is called the *nomenklatura*. Functionaries within the cell are also sometimes selected for less senior positions by the higher administrative and Party organs (this is *nomenklatura* at a lower level) and sometimes they are selected and appointed by the management of the cell, naturally with the go-ahead from the Party organization.

It would be wrong to think that the rank and file of the workers do not take part in the appointment of the management. Even the appointment of the senior managers of the collective often depends on the opinions and wishes of the workers in the institution. Both Party meetings and general meetings of the institution do play some role, as do workers' assemblies and other forms of democracy. Usually appointments to the lowest posts depend very definitely on the rank and file. It is hard to compute an accurate percentage, but probably the greater part of the directors of primary collectives comes from the rank and file.

I have already discussed the purely social aspect of management. Here I would like to draw attention to the following phenomena. The selection of people for power positions at cell level is something of an everyday procedure. It is uninterrupted; that is, it doesn't take place for all positions at once but happens continuously, as positions fall vacant or new ones appear. Sometimes the fiction of free elections is acted out (for example in the case of scientific staff). But this happens as an exception to the general rule.

The power system is renewed without interruption as a normal routine. There are some general rules for choosing people for office. Among them there are formal requirements (for instance an engineering diploma or a Doctor of Science degree), but in most cases it is unwritten laws which operate; i.e. the laws which underlie the operation of the relevant organs and collectives. To describe these laws or rules would be to describe the type of people who have the advantages in career terms, the type of people favoured by those who have the power to select and appoint. Of course, there are mistakes and miscalculations, but these are rare. Usually those who are doing the selecting have enough experience to choose someone suitable. When a candidate is being selected for a post his ideological, professional, moral and general human characteristics, such as his attitude to other people, are all taken into account. The candidate who has been chosen by means of these criteria turns out, as a rule, to be a reliable manager of average capacity. It is not true that the most cunning and cynical rogues are chosen for office. At the level of the primary collective they know people well enough and don't like such types. But if those respectable candidates who have been selected subsequently reveal all the characteristics of the toady, the cynic, the dodger and the thief, this is the effect of general communal laws from which only few manage to escape, and that rarely.

Of course, one mustn't imagine that a management appointed from above does not depend on its subordinates. The manager's security and career prospects depend on the efficacy of his subordinates' work. In primary collectives the manager is exposed to both open and hidden criticism. Open criticism takes place at meetings and works conferences. Hidden criticism takes the form of signed or unsigned denunciations, complaints to higher organs, rumours and slander. Sometimes the manager has to spend more time defending himself from this sort of criticism than he spends on the performance of his duties. Thus the picture which I sketched above appears harmonious only when it is abstracted from communality, which in real life is in full spate at the level of the primary collective, and poisons practically everyone's life, including the management's. Although people fight to become managers, their life is not one of unadulterated pleasure. Often it is fairly fatiguing. But people join management all the same, because for many it is the only way to tear themselves out of the quagmire of communality.

The power of the director of the commune over his subordinates is not unlimited. Besides being limited by the demands of the official business of the commune, it is also limited formally: by laws, by superior administration and Party authorities, by the Party and trade-union organization in the commune, by the authority of other management personnel in the commune. So at times the director is compelled to fight a long, exhausting battle in order to be able to dismiss someone and often he may not succeed. At times the sub-managers of the commune succeed in defending their own interests against the management. From the point of view of the organization of the commune's business there is little that the manager can alter. The work-activity of the commune is limited by its legal status and by plans, and the manager is obliged to work within their purview, so that even a small initiative costs managers of communes immense efforts, and quite often the result is a heart-attack. For this reason managers are more concerned with the showy side of communal life; about things which look good in accounts; about their personal relations with every kind of important and useful personage; about their formal authority. The lion's share of the efforts and talents of managers of communes is devoted to maintaining themselves in their posts and in creating a healthy set-up (which means that the authorities are content with the commune and that discontent within the commune is kept within bounds).

From the point of view of the internal life of the commune the director or manager has real power as regards the daily life of its members. Much depends on him: promotion, prizes, housing, pay-increases. But even in these areas he is not completely in charge. There too he is watched over by the social organizations and the rank and file of citizens who write complaints and anonymous letters to all sorts of organs and often criticize the managers openly. Thus the manager can only use his power for himself personally and his henchmen, toadies and those people who are his real assistants.

Naturally the managers of communes are constantly trying to exceed their authority and abuse their power. This is the norm of social life unless of course someone goes too far or a campaign is begun for which sacrificial victims are required.

Since individuals chosen to be communal managers are usually suitable, and as they undergo the appropriate training for the role, the managerial position as I have described it usually suits them admirably. The limit on initiative removes at the same time the risk of their losing their job through making their own mistakes. On the other hand the initiative which is circumscribed by the limits mentioned above is still sufficient. True, this remaining initiative, as a rule, is rarely directed at anything to do with the interest of the commune in terms of active progress. Managers are not interested in technical progress, in rationalizing production, in lower costs, in higher productivity or in anything like that: a fact which contributes to the general trend towards stagnation.

The managers of communes are working managers, engaged in production, direction and administration, and at the same time they are the representatives and plenipotentiaries of the Party in the governmental system of the state. It is at this point that the regulation of society carries over directly into the management of business. This fact is very important for an understanding of the nature of power in Communist society. There is another important function in the power system at the level of the commune which I will speak about later. But already enough has been said about commune managers for us to reject as nonsensical any idea of an opposition between Party power and managerial/governmental power. Power in this society is one and the same. And managerial/governmental power is only a function and branch of a single system of power, which appears as 'Party' power only in its extreme manifestations.

PARTY ORGANIZATION

Although the structure and role of the Party in a Communist society may seem to be completely obvious, incomprehension of the essence of the Party in the critical literature can in fact assume monstrous proportions. It is strange that former members of the Party and even people who have held posts in the Party apparatus are still as capable as others of talking utter rubbish on this subject. For instance, what value should be placed on the assertion made by one well-known critic of Soviet society that a kind of Partocracy is prevalent in it? Why does this happen?

There are many reasons for this, and I will refer to two of them. The first is purely psychological. Officially in the Soviet Union, and in other Communist countries, the Party is held to be the guiding and organizing force of society. If one believes that Soviet propaganda lies, then one will take this formula for a lie, although it is an absolutely justifiable statement. And although the role of the Party cannot be denied, the other extreme is the theory that power in the country belongs to those at the top of the Party hierarchy who suppress everyone else with the help of the KGB and the army. Incidentally, the expression 'the guiding and organizing force' does not necessarily mean that the Party is something very good. It is not a value-judgement. Even when Soviet propaganda affirms that the Party is the mind, the honour and conscience of Soviet society (and even of the whole era), it is telling the truth; but it doesn't follow from this affirmation itself that this mind, honour and conscience are of high quality.

The second reason concerns the distinction between knowledge and understanding. One can know a lot about a phenomenon without understanding anything of its essence. This applies precisely in the present case. The word 'Party' here is misleading. The Party in a Communist society is regarded by analogy with other political parties as a political phenomenon, whereas in reality the role of the Party in an established Communist society is qualitatively different from the role of political parties in non-Communist countries. Under Communism the Party is no longer a political phenomenon. And to understand what it really is requires that method of understanding about which I spoke earlier: we must first of all understand what the Party is at the micro-level of the primary collective, that is, at the very base of society. Only then can we explain those transformations of the Party which take place at the macro-level of society as a whole. It is only by taking this road that we can, for instance, understand why the very idea of a multi-party system in the framework of a Communist society is ludicrous.

In accordance with the philistine mode of thought only bad comes of bad; and if something is bad in society, then the reasons which have caused it are also bad. And, in general, in a bad society everything is bad. But in real life it is continually the case that good engenders evil, and evil good, and even in the worst society one can find something worthwhile. If a society exists for long enough and reconciles itself to some evil or other, then either something exists for the sake of which people will put up with that evil, or else people themselves are engendering the evil because they are not able, or perhaps even willing, to vanquish it.

So the position is that on the micro-level of the primary collective the Party is the embodiment of good. Here (and throughout the country in general) it is the one single force capable of somehow restraining the turbulent forces of communality and of defending people against themselves and ensuring some sort of progress.

The Party consists of people. Therefore our attempt to understand it must begin with the question of its membership. We must recognize as an indisputable fact that the membership of the Party is a voluntary matter. Why people enter the Party is clear to all. The main reason is that they have mercenary and career considerations in mind. But they do it voluntarily. To be a Party member is the desired aim of many. But not all are thus blessed. There are occasions when people are forced to enter the Party for work reasons. For example, it is virtually impossible for a non-Party man to work in the field of the humanities. But this does not affect the principle of volition. People voluntarily choose this sphere of activity for themselves, as a rule knowing in advance that they must gain entry to the Party. The managers of institutions are, as a rule, Party members. They engage in the struggle for managerial status of their own volition and enter the Party for that reason. Whoever says that he was forced to join the Party against his will is simply a hypocrite.

It can also happen that people who have entered the Party do not believe in its ideals, in the purity of its morals and conduct, and despise Party discipline, its demagogy and its meetings. There are very many of these. But this fact doesn't make any difference, once people conduct themselves formally as sincere Party members should. The important thing is their actual behaviour. There is nothing immoral in that because there is no possibility of revealing that someone is only pretending and is insincere as regards the programme, ideology and demagogy of the Party. Insincerity on entering the Party does not invalidate the principle of free choice: it affirms it. It shows even more that the act was committed on a basis of personal calculation and decision.

The free will aspect of Party membership is the basis of the whole state system. It is on this basis of absolute free will that the system develops its complete and unbridled power of coercion. Coercion is the resultant force of the free will of individuals and not the evil design of tyrants. Tyrants are as much the pawns in the hands of a power that has burgeoned of its own volition as are their victims. The unlimited power of the tyrant is an illusion which is born of a situation in which absolute power is vested in the victims of power.

The second principle of Party membership is the principle of selection. People enter the Party voluntarily, but not all are accepted into it. The selection takes place according to strictly defined principles. The selection also determines the direction in which the sum total of the free will of individual people will manifest itself as their collective power. Once set in its mould the system of selection for Party membership renews itself in stable fashion from day to day and from year to year, subject only to insignificant changes.

There is no complete coincidence between the structure of Party organizations and the structure of the primary collectives. One can find social groups in which there are no Party members. Sometimes a Party group is made up of Party members of different social groups (albeit of groups which are rather close to each other functionally). Sometimes the primary collective has so many Party members that the Party organ in charge of it acquires the rights of a regional Party committee (as, for example, the Party committee of Moscow University). But in the main the structure of the Party organization gravitates towards the official social structure of the primary collective, so that on any occasion one can regard the Party organization as an element of a social group.

THE PARTY IN THE COMMUNES

In the critical literature the image presented of the Party is persistently negative. For some the Party means power (a ruling Party élite); for others it is the road to a career, but on the whole it is the organ by which good non-Party people are persecuted by wicked Party people. It is undeniable that Party officials, starting at whatever level, are privileged people. The great majority of managers of all sorts are Party members. A vast number of vitally important functions in society are entrusted only to Party members. Many people make use of Party membership solely to further their career; and so on. And yet that does not entirely capture the essence of the Party. Essentially the Party was different in the beginning and it has become what it is largely as a consequence of other factors. Most Party members get very little for themselves out of their membership; for many the only reward is additional chores and unpleasantness (Party subscriptions, meetings, social work). Most members live the usual life of the non-Party masses, sharing with them all the burdens of their existence. The non-Party mass of the population does not in any way censure members of the Party for being members of the Party, but rather regards such a state of affairs as right and proper. In difficult situations of various kinds Party members do indeed take the lead, not all of them, of course, but those who do lead are usually members of the Party. Those who enter the Party are far from being the worst people; and from the point of view of the interest of the collective and of society they are the best. Non-Party people in one way or another have an influence on whether someone is elected to the Party by creating a certain opinion of him. Up till now the people call 'real Communists' not those who are Party careerists but the ones who are honest, modest, courageous and selfless. The Party is a mass, multi-million-strong organization of the population which forms not only the kernel of power but also the kernel of social life as a whole.

Before we do anything else we have to gain a truer insight into the relationship between the Party apparatus in its key role as part of the state apparatus and the mass of Party members who work in the primary collectives. From the outside it appears that there is a Party in the form of a monolithic organization, with a leadership which rules over society using the Party as a means to this end. The idea has even been voiced that the power-system in the Soviet Union should be regarded as a Partocracy. But the reality is different. The Party apparatus supervises the Party organization in the communes; it supervises the intake of citizens into the Party; it gives uniform directions to Party organizations; it takes into its own ranks the most suitable workers from among Party members. All this of course gives it additional means with which to govern society. But once established the Party apparatus preserves itself and renews itself independently of the mass of the rank and file of the membership of the primary Party organizations. In principle one can conceive of a situation in which a clearer division of them will come about, so that even the names will be different. It is possible that the formal renewal of the Party apparatus will take place without an electoral procedure which even in the Soviet Union is now recognized as semi-fictitious. Ordinary members of the Party as well as the primary organizations will be given nominally the role which they play in fact: a role that relates exclusively to the level of the primary communes and operates within them.

The Party organization in the primary collectives and the Party as a whole are not collections of people in the way that communes are. Within the primary collectives the members of the Party may still meet together, and this gives a certain illusion of unity. But the Party organizations even of neighbouring communes live quite independently of one another and form no kind of unity whatsoever. On the regional level there is a kind of union of Party organizations in that they elect delegates to the regional Party Conference (who are nominated for them by the regional Party committee), and these delegates elect its bureau. Moreover, candidates for this bureau and for the post of secretary are earmarked in advance. This electoral procedure is bogus. Were it to be abolished, nothing would be changed in substance. The important thing here is that the formation of the bureau of the regional Party committee (incidentally its large apparatus is not even ostensibly elected) does not amount in any way to the unification of separate Party organizations into a whole. They remain separate. They are even more separate at the level of the province and of the republic, and at the highest level the severance of the Party apparatus from the mass of the Party becomes absolute.

Even at the level of the primary collective the Party organization is not one social group among other subdivisions of the collective. Its unity is fictitious. The appearance of unity is achieved only because people who have entered the Party are obliged to observe certain rules of behaviour which apply to Party members. The observance of these rules gives them certain advantages. Failure to observe them would curtail and even destroy their chances of keeping their previous position. For a person entry to the Party is only one social act among many others that determine his social position. Moreover, it is not the most important one. What counts most is a person's position in the primary collective from the functional point of view. Membership of the Party is only one of the roads to a career. Even the Party managers at the level of the primary collective depend to a greater degree on the management of the collective than on the regional committee of the Party. They depend on the latter for their election and for their future career in some senses. But they are members of a collective and receive all their material benefits in and through the collective. Although the director of an institution, as a Party member (and usually as a member of the Party bureau), is subordinate to the secretary of the Party bureau, the latter rarely abuses his power. The director still remains the highest power in the institution, and by no means only in the managerial sense. The director of an institution is in fact the representative of Party power. He is the *protégé* of the Party apparatus, chosen for the position by the Party apparatus itself. And the Party bureau and the Party organization are his helpers. In some degree they supervise him. But even more they obscure the fact that in reality power is essentially a non-Party phenomenon.

The role of the Party organization in the primary collective is characterized by these most important conditions: 1) it represents the interests of the whole mass of the collective and speaks for it; 2) at the same time it is the representative of the organs of power of society as a whole in this given sector of society. The Party organization executes its first function in as far as its members are part of the general mass of the collective, are completely bound up with it, do not form a special privileged caste and do not cut themselves off from it. The Party organization executes its second function through its own leaders who are subordinated to the Party apparatus, as well as by constant supervision exercised by higher Party organs. Thus the Party organization in the primary collective exhibits both the power of the people and the limits of that power. It is at the same time a connecting link and a regulator of the relationship between the power of the people and the power of the state.

The role of the Party organization in the life of the primary commune is enormous. It is a gross error to imagine the population of a Communist country simply as obedient pawns who have no influence on the life of society. At the level of the primary collective the population displays a certain activity; and in the persons of its Party representatives it takes part in decisions about the institution's business and exercises control over many aspects of its activity. Criticism of the shortcomings in the life of the collective is a normal item in the work of the Party organization. The latter maintains a certain decent standard in the collective and does educational and cultural work. In short, all sides of communal life fall within the sphere of the Party organization's attention and influence.

The fact that the Party organization within the commune does not in practice influence wider communities or the life of the country as a whole is another matter. But that isn't part of its job as a specific social phenomenon. It is not a political organization, but only an element in the cellular structure of society, not of society as a whole. It is the Party apparatus which functions in society as a whole and is part of state-power. It too is not a political organization, but it is an organization of a quite different order to that of the primary Party organizations.

It should be clear from what has been said why a multi-party system is impossible in a Communist society. Firstly, even a single-party system is impossible in it because this society excludes parties in general in the sense of political organizations as they are found in the West. Under Communism any attempt to create political organizations is regarded as an attempt upon the prerogatives of state-power and is cut short with the silent agreement or even support of the general population. Secondly, there is simply nobody for many parties to represent. The population of Communist countries is grouped, structured and crystallized in such a way that each primary collective as a whole creates its own active representation in the system of power. This representation is the primary Party organization. In accordance with the general tendency towards standardization and subordination these organizations are also standardized and subordinated to the organs of power.

It isn't a question of nomenclature. Other organizations exist in society and continually appear which represent in one way or another the interests of different categories and groups of people: e.g. trade-unions, *Komsomol* organizations, sporting organizations and so on. But by virtue of the general principles of command and subordination they are all in one way or another under the control of the official system of power.

THE PRIMARY PARTY MANAGER

The question of secretaries of primary Party organizations and of Party organizers (who are the leaders of small Party groups) is part of the general question of the status of the Party in Communist society.

It is an error to think that primary Party managers are all villains in the way they are made to appear by the debunking tendencies of our times: that is to say, careerists, thieves, liars, cowards or time-servers. In almost all cases known to me they were far from being the worst citizens. Knowing the general situation in the Party I can affirm that this is a natural phenomenon. The explanation is as follows.

As I have already said more than once, we must distinguish the Party as a multitude of primary Party organizations in the communes from the Party seen as the aggregate of the professional workers of the Party apparatus: whether in regional, municipal, provincial and republic committees or in the Central (All-Union) Committee of the Party itself. These institutions are all directorates – and the most privileged ones. It is very important for an understanding of Communist society that we fix in our minds the distinction between the rank and file of Party members and elected primary Party functionaries on the one hand, and the Party apparatus seen as a hierarchy of Party committees professionally occupied in Party work on the other. Although the first phenomenon produces the second, nourishes and supports it, while the second grows from the first as an instrument for unifying it on a national scale, the second is isolated from the first as part of the privileged command structure of society. It knits well with all the rest of officialdom and becomes its crystallizing core. The first subdivision of the Party merges with the non-Party body of society and shares all its burdens. The second uses that body in every way for its own mercenary interests.

It would be erroneous to exclude all mercenary interests from the people who enter the Party, including primary Party managers. Almost the whole managerial section of society starts by joining the Party, so that in the overwhelming number of cases this is the careerist's route. But even those Party members who don't succeed in making a career have the potential for one, and at least Party membership is a means of self-assertion for them. The Party secretary is usually a fairly mediocre workman in his professional field. He instinctively prefers the job of Party activist to a career in his own profession. The secretary of the Party bureau, moreover, has power, and he likes that. When he says that he is sick of the job, he is being hypocritical. Of course to some degree he *is* sick of it, but he enjoys it more than he is sick of it. He likes chairing meetings, making speeches and having conversations with people. He would clearly love to move higher up the Party ladder, but for some reason avers that he's 'not keen'. Why? There are many Party secretaries but distinctly fewer places in the higher apparatus. Sometimes the reason is that he is a *good* secretary. He is not good from the point of view of a Party career but from the point of view of the immediate management of the institution's Party organization and of the Party management of the institution itself. He is rather like a political officer at the front who spends his time in the trenches with the rank and file, goes into the attack with them and perishes with them. That kind of political officer does not meet the requirements of a functionary in the political section of a division, an army or an army group. If the secretary hopes to get a flat that's about as much as he is likely to get. At times the important element in the behaviour of such people is not mercenary calculation but some natural human qualities which have nothing specifically to do with Marxist ideas on the Party programme. In certain people these qualities are simply the embodiment of certain general functions of the collective. The Party apparatus merely clothes these general human phenomena in the required garb and turns them to its own use.

The Party secretary almost never involves himself in a major conflict with the management of the institution or a higher Party authority. He is a reliable transmitter of the Party line. The regional committee of the Party and the management of the institution can rely on him absolutely. They have elected him for his reliability (and before that he has been earmarked and endorsed by the relevant authorities). But in any institution it is not just directives from above which count; the activities of the workers and their relationships play a part as well. It is important for the life of the institution which groups of workers the Party bureau relies upon when it comes to promoting the general Party line. Higher Party directives are realized in practice by the actions of the rank and file of the Party and via the lowest ranks of the Party leadership. On the other hand, the state of affairs in the lowest sphere of Party life has some influence on the general line of Party behaviour. Stalinism in its time was not only imposed from above, but also emerged from the grass roots of Party life and was stimulated by it. The 'liberalism' of Khrushchev-Brezhnev expressed a 'liberalism' which had been growing continually at grass-root level within the Party.

TRADE-UNION ORGANIZATION

Trade-unions in Communist society are one more example of how concepts, at one time devised to describe the life of Western countries, have acquired many meanings or have become meaningless, and of how the same words can erase the distinction between totally different phenomena.

The word 'trade-union' is used in connection with the phenomenon we will be speaking of here because of a certain historical continuity and a certain similarity of function as between the organizations we are examining and those of trade-unions in Capitalist countries. But the continuity is not inevitable and the similarity of function is not so great that we can regard them as qualitatively identical phenomena. The experience of Communist countries has shown that the existence of trade-unions in previous societies is not a necessary condition of their emergence in a new society. (We are going to have to use the word 'trade-union' while keeping in mind the sense which it has in Communist society.) In the Soviet Union, for example, there were no trade-unions at all in the great majority of places and institutions before the revolution. Now they are an indispensable element in people's lives in all parts of the country and in all institutions. And they arose in order to fulfil vitally important functions in citizens' collectives and in society as a whole.

It is entirely possible that the form which trade-unions take in the Soviet Union is mainly a tribute to Marxist teaching, tradition and propaganda. A gigantic trade-union apparatus has now evolved which struggles for its existence and demonstrates to everyone in every way possible that it is necessary to society in that form, and it is not so easy to reconstruct it in such a way as to reveal the nature of the social functions that this apparatus has taken upon itself. It is always possible that some kind of re-organization in that direction will actually happen. It is possible that the 'purest' apparatus of this type will be instituted in other countries straight away as a result of necessity. But nevertheless we can still isolate the social role of trade-unions in any Communist country in their 'pure aspect' whatever form the trade-unions might take and however they might be named.

All the members of the primary communes are members of the trade-union. Their membership is strictly formal: they pay membership dues. These dues go towards the upkeep of the trade-union apparatus (just as in the case of the Party), on journeys to rest homes and on all kinds of other things. Since every worker of the commune is a member of a trade-union the trade-union organization as a separate entity has no sense. Everything that a worker gets as a member of a trade-union he can have as a member of the commune, and all the elective trade-union organs could be simply elective organs of the collective. The payment of dues could be discounted in the pay-packet. All the functions of the trade-union apparatus (which is also independent of the primary trade-union organizations, and to an even greater extent than the Party apparatus is of the primary Party organizations) could be fulfilled by appropriate branches of the state power apparatus. However, once functions exist in the primary collectives which trade-union workers now fulfil, and in the country as a whole there are functions now fulfilled by the trade-union apparatus, then, because of the tendency of society to subdivide functions and embody them in the activities of special persons and organizations, formal structures equivalent to the present trade-unions would inevitably appear.

Their functions are indeed very real ones. The function of the primary trade-union organizations and of every kind of elected person and organ in them is to supervise on behalf of the mass of workers in the commune their conditions of work and day-to-day existence. The trade- unions have an influence on the hiring and firing of workers, the procedures for rewards and punishments and on promotion. They control wage-rises, the distribution of free trips to rest homes and to a significant degree the allocation of housing. They also control everyday details such as loans, the admission of children to nursery school, tourist journeys, mass cultural events and much else. At the level of the primary collective somebody has to deal with this, and it is the trade-unions which do so. Knowing this important role of the trade-unions, many workers who have no chance of improving their living conditions by other means, throw themselves very actively into trade- union work.

For many, trade-union work is one of the spheres of social work in which nearly all workers are obliged to take part. Many begin their Party and administrative career from the humblest posts in the trade-unions. Of course, this is a very limited sphere of popular activity, but for them it is extremely important. The functions of the trade-union apparatus are the standardization and supervision of the work of the primary trade-union organizations, together with the defence of their powers. The administrative powers tend to leave the workers' interests out of account in the most important sphere of their life, in the sphere of their working and living conditions. The trade-union organizations restrain this tendency. The trade-union organization protects that power. There are specific juridical norms regulating the position of the trade- unions. The whole activity of the trade-unions from top to bottom is under the general supervision of the Party apparatus.

Like the primary Party organizations, the primary trade-union organizations are not in fact amalgamated into large integral organizations. Their functions are limited exclusively by the framework of the primary communes. Westerners are often surprised by the fact that trade-unions in the Soviet Union do not fight for improvements in the working and living conditions of the workers, and in particular that they do not organize strikes. The reality is that the trade-unions do deal with these matters: they do fight for improvement in conditions and see to it that the relevant norms are observed, but only within the normative framework which is the same for the whole of society and is secured by legislation. In this society strikes are simply nonsensical, because the situation of the workers in the primary communes is determined by the general situation in the country as a whole and by identical laws for all citizens and not at all by special situations in a commune, in a region or in a sector of activity. Of course there are differences, but these are determined by conditions that are independent of the people living in one commune or another. Where infringements of norms do occur, the struggle to rectify them is a matter of administrative routine. In this the trade-unions play their part. It is, therefore, a mistake to explain the absence of strikes simply in terms of fear of punishment. There is also a deeper reason for it: strikes cannot effectively change the situation in the country. Of course events can occur (and do occur) in Communist countries which are similar to strikes in the West. But these are spontaneous rebellions against exceptionally difficult conditions. The trade-union organizations do not start them; on the contrary they oppose them. Such rebellions are rare, and usually end soon. It can happen, of course, that the authorities faced with a strike will take certain measures: for instance, they may order more bread to be delivered to a certain region or cancel an increased work-norm and so on. But they always punish the ring-leaders.

Trade-unions of the type found in Western countries are impossible and meaningless in Communist society, basically because of the way people's life and activity are structured and not because of the unwillingness of evil authorities to allow them. The authorities, of course, do not wish to allow them and indeed they will not allow them. But in forbidding them they are supported by an objective fact: the lack of interest of the population in trade-unions of the Western type and its inability to create anything of the sort on a large enough scale and in practical form. The so-called 'free trade-unions' in the Soviet Union, much spoken of in the West at one time, would have been like something out of comic opera, if the authorities had not persecuted their organizers. The existence of a few people who suffer a fate that is not normal for Soviet citizens in a country of 260 millions is not a sign that there is a trade-union movement of the Western type. After all, one can find a few hundred monarchists in the Soviet Union, but it would be absurd to regard that as a fight by the Soviet people for the restoration of the monarchy.

THE *KOMSOMOL* AND THE YOUNG

Komsomol (The Young Communist League) is in many ways like the Party. It has a similar structure and is entirely and completely subject to Party management and control. The great majority of Party members have their preparation and training in the Komsomol. Very many Party officials receive their basic training in the communes' Komsomol organizations and in the Komsomol apparatus. The Komsomol is an effective branch of the apparatus of power and plays its part in controlling, organizing and educating the population of the country in the necessary spirit by taking charge of the young, as opposed to the adult population and children. The Komsomol is a grandiose institution. Relatively few young people evade membership or are not admitted to it. The number of youngsters who are within its grasp is so vast that practically the whole of Soviet youth comes within its purview in one way or another. The fact that part of the youth is unorganized doesn't weaken the Komsomol but even raises its prestige. Exclusion from or non-admittance to the Komsomol is an act of punishment and education, and moreover, often a pretty serious one. People who reject the Komsomol also encounter unpleasantness. For example, it is harder for them to gain entry to the educational establishments they wish and to choose the occupation they wish. It is harder for them to arrange a type of work for themselves in institutions which carries some privileges. Usually it is impossible to start making a successful career. Society will only exceptionally make allowances for 'unorganized' youth, for instance in science, art, sport (when young talent is obvious and the Soviet Union needs it for some reason or other).

The characteristics of people of Komsomol age are well known. Here I want to dwell on only a few of them that have an immediate connection with the theme of this book. A person's fate in Communist society is determined during the period when he is eligible for Komsomol membership either in terms of his future social position or of the line his career will follow. While Communist society was being established in the Soviet Union, countless professions and jobs which were attractive to young people were coming into being. At that time the choice of profession, education and career seemed unlimited. But in the years since the war the situation has stabilized. Society now has its full complement of specialists and officials holding down posts which are attractive to the young. Indeed there are too many. The turnover of jobs follows the normal pattern: some people are pensioned off, some die and others are selected to fill their places. Of course, people's social possibilities continue to widen to some extent via the emergence of new professions or new enterprises. But this falls short of the former illusion of 'hundreds of paths and hundreds of roads'. Nothing remains of this illusion except hypocritical demagogic phrases, and now Soviet youth lives in a well-established Communist society, in which from the very start of its conscious life it is confronted by society's actual social structure and the problems engendered by it.

Although the social structure of Soviet youth is more

uniform than that of the adults, inequality of opportunity makes itself felt right at the beginning. School education differs in quality as between large and small towns, and between towns and country villages. Even the gifted pupil when he has finished school in the provinces (even more so if he has been to a village school) is less well prepared for entry into higher education than the mediocre pupil who has finished school in a large town. The level of school education differs in the towns as well. There are privileged schools which it is not simple for ordinary mortals to enter. There are special schools in which the teaching of certain selected disciplines is far superior to that in ordinary schools. The vast majority of educational establishments attractive to young people are in fact closed to the majority of those who want to go to them. In the privileged strata of society children can have the benefit of supplementary education at home which is denied to the families of workmen, peasants and petty functionaries. And the difference in the quality of school-teaching is very real, given that there is a significant gap between the school programme and the demands of higher educational establishments, and the fact that there is strong competition. Furthermore, there are privileged higher educational institutions, entry to which is restricted to the children of highly placed officials and to people who can pull strings. The children of parents with a high social position have a better chance of entry to institutes irrespective of their state of preparedness. The percentage of youth that is accepted for direct entry into institutes after school is not high. Preference is given to candidates with a work-record and with good Komsomol references. Children of privileged families have the advantage there as well. Moreover, special difficulties are made for young people coming from villages and small towns when they try to gain entry to institutes in large towns. (They are not given the necessary papers and are compelled to stay in their birth-place 'voluntarily'.)

In short, the multi-million army of youth is processed from the very beginning for the purposes of allocation, and is allocated to places of training for future work, not in accordance with the talents or wishes of young people themselves, but in accordance with the social laws of society. The distribution of young people among the cells of a social structure gives rise to inequality in any society. What is important is how this inequality is determined. In Communist society it depends in the first instance on the place in the social structure in which a person is born and grows to adulthood. Society cannot exist without workers, agricultural labourers, minor civil servants, soldiers, militiamen, salesmen, teachers and so on. This is a banal fact. The important thing is which part of the population is *obliged* to take such jobs and have that kind of social position. From this point of view the myth of Communist propaganda about the equal opportunities for young people to choose their path in life in Communist society has absolutely nothing to do with reality. Social laws in fact operate according to which the children of the privileged strata are kept safely in these strata, and downward mobility is rare. The great majority of the children of the representatives of the low strata either stay in them or drop down to an even lower stratum.

Young people under Communism know from the very beginning what social level fate has prepared for them in view of their family position, place of birth and schooling and their natural endowment. There are many examples of this kind before their eyes. Sometimes, of course, unexpected things happen. For example, a beautiful girl marries an officer with prospects and becomes a general's wife. An ungifted Komsomol activist from the provinces becomes an important official in the central apparatus of the Party. But these exceptions happen in any society, and do not alter the general tendency which I have described above. The structure of adult society is known to young people from the very start. And they perpetuate this structure, not only by their individual struggle for the best position, but through the preordained character of their success or failure in the battle. Most young people accept the situation as natural, just as most of the population in general accept their given situation in life as a matter of course.

Indeed, the naturalness of the way of life and its renewal from generation to generation creates an ideology of the justice of what happens. A feeling of social injustice in regard to the social order occurs only in individual young people and is experienced by them not as social injustice in general but as a personal injustice that has happened to *them*. Moreover, in reality it *is* just that, since from a social point of view there is need for only a limited number of writers, artists, professors, diplomats, Party workers and so on. Nature offers no absolute criteria for deciding why one young man rather than another should occupy a particular social position. The difference between people, when they are counted in millions, with respect to their natural gifts is not large. In society as a whole, viewed as a mass phenomenon, there is a rough kind of justice, but the mechanism of its realization has nothing whatever to do with a proclaimed doctrinaire harmony, being in fact a cruel struggle for the best positions in life in which no holds are barred.

In Communist society there are no problems of 'fathers and children' in the sense of a social problem. Young people gradually, one by one, occupy their position in life, replace the fathers and become fathers in turn. They have no chance of forming their own associations on a large scale outside the control of adults, the authorities and the social organizations (if one excludes criminal bands who are punished by law and receive no support from the population). Associations of young people in Communist society are defined by the general principles of the crystallization of the population into groups. Here there can be no question of specific youth movements such as are to be found in the West.

I will mention a few more features of Soviet youth that are important for the formation of the type of person who is suitable for Communist society. Because of the simplicity and the preordained character of Soviet life (by that I mean the very small range of choice and the lack of need to take real decisions) young people feel themselves young until thirty (the Komsomol's official age-limit is twenty-eight) and even until forty. Their chances of starting an independent life away from their parents are very limited, owing to lack of housing, low student grants and wages. This contributes to people's dependence on society and to their malleability. Furthermore, from the moment people go to school they start collecting the references on which their future depends. These references follow them everywhere, and young people take this into consideration and adapt their behaviour accordingly. The evaluation of their behaviour by society keeps them within certain bounds. This doesn't mean that youth is deprived of all freedom of behaviour; in the Soviet Union, for example, it considers itself fairly free in its life-style. It simply means that in young people's collectives and in collectives that deal with youth professionally the general principles of communal life operate normally. Young collectives seen as social groups copy adult collectives or indeed form part of them.

A sociological examination of youth in Soviet society could be the subject of a separate book. Here I will limit myself to what has been said. In my other books which I mentioned above, the reader may find, if he so wishes, extra information on this theme. In *The Yellow House* the main hero is a young man who has just left the Komsomol age-group.

Several years ago in the Soviet Union there began a special campaign under the slogan: 'towards a decisive turning-point in schools for the improvement in the training of young people for work in the sphere of material production!' What was this campaign all about? It was about the fact that society is being divided into privileged and underprivileged strata. Membership of them is becoming hereditary, and the measures taken in school contribute to this.

Their purpose is obvious: the children of workmen and peasants shall be workmen and peasants. The children of members of the *nomenklatura*, of generals, academicians, managers, writers, professors, will not enter the sphere of material production. For them there are special educational establishments, facilities for teaching at home, necessary connections. For the children of the unprivileged strata of society there is nothing of the kind. For them there is demagogy, reinforced by coercion. They are quite simply forced to enter the materially productive sector and are prevented in their attempts to enter higher and special intermediate educational establishments in the towns. Pressure is exerted on these youngsters through the Komsomol, and they are held to a level of education which debars them from competing with the children of the privileged groups. During the years of liberalism sociologists discovered that final-year students were not at all anxious to enter the material production sector. But that is clear enough even without sociology. Lessons learned about work at school and the pupils' work in workshops attached to schools produce a revulsion against physical labour. So the use of force on the part of the authorities is a fully natural reaction to the attempt on the part of young people to raise their own social position and improve their living conditions. It conflicts with the demagogy which proclaims the unlimited opportunities at youth's disposal. This demagogy is moving further and further away from reality; and the conditions of work at the lowest levels of society are far removed from propaganda ideals. This fact engenders particular manifestations in the milieu of the young which are not consistent with the norms of Soviet life such as the attempt by some young people to escape from the clutches of ideological control and to create their own unofficial associations and their own way of living.

COMMUNIST DEMOCRACY

Very many posts in Communist society are elective. Some of these are elective only in appearance. For instance, the deputies of the *soviets*, judges, Party officials, workers in scientific institutions. The candidate is usually pre-selected and the results of the elections are decided in advance. But even if the authorities allow an election with two or three or more candidates, the situation is still the same: the candidates will still have been selected and earmarked in advance.

Sometimes elections are genuine. But this happens only in trivial instances that have no influence on the fate of people or collectives. Such, for instance, are the elections of the trade-union organizers of groups, of cultural organizers, of members of the editorial board of wall-newspapers. There are occasions when the collective introduces amendments to the elections and to important bodies such as the Party bureau (at times the collective will reject a candidate standing for secretary put up by the regional committee of the Party). But even in those cases where elections are fictitious everything is done via a certain formal procedure without which the people who have been earmarked cannot fulfil their functions.

All this creates an atmosphere of a special kind of democracy, which is reinforced by events representing an important element in the life of citizens in Communist society such as meetings, consultations, conferences, congresses, rallies and other get-togethers notionally summoned for the purpose of solving problems collectively. I will use the general term 'assemblage' to describe them. Assemblages play such an important role in the life of society that a standard system has been instituted for them complete with ritual conduct. They especially affect people who take part in government. Here I cannot give a detailed account of this almost totally unstudied phenomenon. I shall examine only two types of assemblage: meetings on the communal level and management get-togethers.

Meetings on the level of the primary commune are general meetings of the workers, Party meetings, trade-union and *Komsomol* meetings. I shall present a generalized sketch of them, concentrating largely on Party meetings as being the most important and able to serve as a model for the others. Meetings in Communist society are the highest form of democracy for individuals who are on the lowest rung of the social ladder, and this democracy is restricted to the sphere of things that do not matter and the interests of the collective.

Meetings have various types and functions: the dissemination of information about decisions of the higher authorities, educational work, participation in running the commune's business, questions of organization. Readers can find a more detailed description of all this in *The Yawning Heights* and *The Yellow House*. It should not be supposed that Soviet people go to meetings only because they are forced to do so under threat of punishment. In most cases they go of their own free will. Those who try to avoid them do so in reality without being punished. Society turns a blind eye to these 'deviationists' because there is still a surplus of volunteers. Why should this be so? Because, for some, meetings are a stage on which they can show off in front of their colleagues; for others it is a means of attaining their practical ends; for a third group they form the arena in which they can attack their enemies; for a fourth group they are the place where they defend themselves against attack; for a fifth they are a talking-shop; for a sixth they provide a bit of theatre; for a seventh a place in which to fight for the 'good of the cause'. In brief, meetings in the primary communes fulfil an important function. They offer the maximum of what is to be gained in a positive sense by the broad mass of the population from participation in the management of society. Any attempts to go beyond that maximum can lead only to squabbles, chaos and time wasting. The population understands this very well: unlimited activity on the part of the masses is all right in abstract doctrine, not in reality. I think that the supporters of such doctrines would begin to doubt their validity if they went to a few meetings at which the managers lost control over the body of the hall.

Management assemblages vary enormously. Here I am singling out those which happen regularly and are a element in the power-structure: sessions of Party, trade-union and *Komsomol* bureaux, the bureaux of regional and provincial committees and so on right up to the plenum of the Central Committee of the Party and of Party congresses. I shall not be dealing with the activities of the corresponding organs consisting of many people fulfilling specific functions (the management, the Party bureau and so on). I shall single out only what is connected with the fact of assemblage itself, when people assemble physically, consider certain problems, and take collegiate decisions. In this connection only those in total ignorance of the real facts of the matter could imagine that such assemblages are pure fiction, with individual people taking all the decisions and the rest merely voting. Undoubtedly these assemblages are prepared in advance: this is an element in the very procedure relating to their activity. Everything may be agreed in advance and the assemblage may take purely formal decisions. But this isn't always so. Sometimes, indeed, there are real working discussions, disputes and conflicts. But even if the business was nothing but a rubber-stamping of decisions taken elsewhere, this function would not be superfluous or fictitious. The very fact that some proposal has been formally endorsed; the very fact that a decision has been adopted by a given assemblage plays a very important role: it confers legal force on the intentions of individual people or groups to take certain measures. This is indeed the formal role of assemblages which at first sight seems fictitious but is in reality their main social function. Discussion is only something secondary and derivative. This is a very important point about the power-system of Communist society and one which is rather hard to understand. I shall try to explain it in a somewhat paradoxical form.

I want to avoid using the words 'dictatorship' and 'democracy'. But in order to explain why they are inapplicable I still need to use them in a general sense, without claiming that they are scientific terms. One of the social functions of assemblages is to mask dictatorial power, that is the power that comes from above and meets no opposition from below. But dictatorial power itself is organized and operates in such a way as to counteract the dictatorial tendencies of individual people and groups, and at the the same time to remove from the real rulers personal responsibility for the results of their actions. Management assemblages are summoned not so much in order to give a democratic appearance to what is dictatorial power (that is a secondary matter) as to deprive that power in fact of its dictatorial character. Hence the tendency is not so much towards camouflage as towards collegiate government. So the concepts 'dictatorship' and 'democracy' become meaningless when applied to this form of power in their strictly scientific sense. In the Communist power-system there is a quasi-dictatorial tendency *and* a tendency which is quasi-democratic. But other terms are needed here. 'Centralization' and 'decentralization' do not fit either. Perhaps 'one-man management' and 'collegiality' are better. These two tendencies are complicated distillations of the general twin principles of government and subordination when we apply them to society as a complex whole. Even Stalin, the greatest of dictators, was not a dictator in the strict sociological sense of the term. He was a leader (*vozhd'*) whose power exceeded that of the dictator. The quasi-democratic tendency also has another nature. Sometimes it can develop a greater power than the one deriving from the first (dictatorial) tendency. The struggle between these two tendencies in government enables the formation of a ruling clique. The latter brings to prominence, as their own symbol and guarantee of formal legality, figures very like the dictators of the past but who are rarely dictators in fact. Only in exceptional circumstances do they actually become dictators. 'Dictatorship' is typical of the formative period of Communist society and of crisis situations but not of society in conditions of normal stability. Even Stalin was in part a fictitious dictator. Khrushchev's attempt to follow his example was a failure, while Brezhnev as dictator was pure fiction: he was, rather, a mockery of dictatorship.

PUBLIC OPINION

Is there such a thing in Communist society as public opinion? To answer the question one must define what public opinion means. Not everything that people think about a certain fact of social life is public opinion, even if masses of people are agreed about it. Millions of Soviet people thought that Khrushchev was an irresponsible buffoon and that his plan to grow maize everywhere was laughable. Millions of Soviet people thought that Brezhnev in his later years was senile and that his internal and external policies were dooming the country's population to suffering and pushing the world into catastrophe. But so what? What people think is not transformed into public opinion because it has no influence on the government's behaviour. More than that, in spite of what the population think, if the government demands it, it will openly express its approval of the government's policies. Public opinion operates as a real fact of social life when it exerts pressure on people's behaviour and on the behaviour of groups and organizations. In Communist society public opinion in the sense of a national factor influencing the behaviour of the government doesn't exist; or it exists to such a minimal degree that it is hardly noticeable. It exists only at the level of the commune. Moreover, at this level it is strong when it comes to influencing the behaviour of individual members of the commune, and rather weak (although still perceptible and at times significant) *vis-à-vis* the behaviour of the commune leadership. In short, public opinion in the Soviet Union may be described as the normal form of communal domination exercised by the collective over the individual. Hardly at all is it a means of defence against communality or a means of defending individual people or the collective itself against the authorities.

SELF-GOVERNMENT AND GOVERNMENT FROM ABOVE

Under Communism self-government in the commune in practice degenerates into a situation in which one part of the membership of the commune seizes power, and exploits and terrorizes the other members for whom life becomes a nightmare. The Soviet Union has had experience enough of this. It is enough for the higher authorities to relax their control somewhat over the actions of a commune for a state of affairs to come about which Soviet people call 'running your own pigsty', and other rude names. Communes like this begin to live according to the code of a band of gangsters. For this reason people prefer that a limit be set to self-government by the transfer of basic power-functions to a centralized body higher up, so that self-government in the commune is kept to a bare minimum (which I spoke of earlier). This gives the members of the commune protection against the use of force by their neighbours which would be more humiliating and more cruel than the use of force from above. Thus the principle of government 'from the top downwards' is not so much the result of aggression by the highest authorities and organs of power against the unfortunate population as the result of that population's voluntary acquiescence. It is the principle of government necessitated by the very conditions of communal life. In addition there are the purely 'technical' laws of administration. In Communist society every commune exists only as a part of a more complex whole, and government from above makes this a real fact. The idea of a confederation of self-governing communes is only possible in doctrine and on paper, not in reality. In reality it is possible only as an exception and in the short term. Even with supervision from above there is a constant tendency towards the infringement of the rules which bind together and to chaos.

As regards the business activities of the commune, self-government has no meaning. The remuneration of members of the commune depends very little on its productivity: most often it has nothing to do with it at all. The members of the commune are in real life indifferent to this aspect of the life of the commune as a whole. Very rarely do they feel 'patriotic' about their institutions; rarely do their 'hearts bleed' for its interests. Except for the top management of the commune, whose first duty it is, and for those who derive advantage from a bleeding heart in the form of prizes and promotion. From above the authorities try to stimulate productive activity, and encourage rationalizers, inventors, and instigators of every kind of campaign. However, in most cases all this is pure formality, eye-wash and window dressing. The members of the commune do not regard the business of the commune as a whole as their business. They regard it merely as the setting for carrying on their own small personal affairs. The main point is that the fate of the commune depends very little on whether the individual members of it do their work well or badly. The commune itself has a very weak degree of independence from other communes in terms of its own activity. Its functions, the quota and the character of the product produced, and where its products are destined to go are strictly determined from above. The commune cannot change its position with respect to other communes in the system. I will turn to this particular question later.

The members of the commune do not participate directly in the running of more complex entities such as regions, provinces, republics or the country as a whole. It is impossible that they should, for purely technical reasons. But the main point is that such participation can do little to change the conditions of the population, and the latter does not aspire to it. In this society people who seek to play a part in the power-system do this individually by participating in the professional government apparatus.

Ideas about 'Democratic Communism' (or Socialism) whereby broad sections of the population participate in the running of enterprises, regions, provinces, and the country as a whole, are asinine and ignore all the general rules of social organization and the specific laws of societies of the Communist type. In connection with this theme, I would like here to draw attention to one of the aspects of the 'power of the people' that is also usually lost from sight.

When people talk about the initiative of the masses, that doesn't mean that all members of the mass show initiative. In fact most people are passive. When they do get going it is thanks to the efforts of a small group of activists who stir them up. The presence of such activists is an element in the social structure of the masses. Activists collect evidence about certain members of the collective, compile 'dossiers', keep track of their behaviour, come forward at meetings and raise questions about the behaviour of certain individuals, send 'signals', write letters and take part in all kinds of investigative committees. Sometimes three or four of them determine the whole social and psychological atmosphere of the institution, and exercise control over all aspects of its life. This constitutes the genuine control of the mass over the life of society which is one of the levers of genuine 'people power'. An activist group of this kind is immeasurably more effective than people who are officially appointed. In order that it should exist and function well two conditions must be fulfilled: 1) the powers on high should protect it, give it their open support, and perceive that it is a support to them; 2) the activist group should have support and approval within the collective itself, i.e., among the masses: it must express the interests and the will of the collective at least as regards certain important aspects of life, and it must be an element of the real power of the collective as a whole over its individual members.

In Stalin's time there was a great blossoming of this aspect of the power of the people. At the moment it has somewhat weakened. The authorities are afraid of a return to Stalin's time (that is, to the genuine power of the people as we have described it) and so they are afraid of encouraging and supporting initiative-taking activists in the collective. Within the collectives themselves potential activists who would have the support and the confidence of the collective and who would fulfil their functions voluntarily and enthusiastically no longer emerge spontaneously. And this amounts to nothing other than a diminution of 'people power'. The real power of the collective over the individual has passed to the special organs and to officials, while the mass has renounced its own excessive power and become indifferent to it. We all know the type of people who thrust themselves forward for the role of activist in the primary collective. They are the dregs, the scoundrels, the informers, the *agents provocateurs*, the liars, the hacks, the dunces. Society no longer wishes to remain in their power.

The power of the people is reflected in a specific power-structure and is not something formless or unstructured. The characteristic figure under the conditions of people power is the omnipotent leader who is supported by the spontaneous action of the broad mass of the population and who relies on terror of the kind there was in Stalin's time. Under the power of the people, the popular mass develops a communal structure in which the laws of communality operate with a force which threatens the very existence of society. Our large modern society, with its complex culture and complex economy, comes into conflict with people power and excludes it, or at least ensures that it is reduced to the minimum, kept within the communes and restricted to the unimportant concerns of its members. One can repeat the Stalinist phenomenon only if one repeats the phenomenon of the unlimited power of the people.

THE SOCIAL STRUCTURE OF SOCIETY

Communist society is composed of a large number of primary working collectives: the communes. Of course, not everyone belongs to a commune. Invalids, old people, children and many individuals who, in one way or another, escape organization remain outside it. Nevertheless, the communes form the basis of the crystallization of society, and the majority of the population which is not directly included in communes is included in them indirectly as members of the families of persons who are attached to communes; or as the professional concern of special kinds of commune such as children's organizations, schools, hospitals and other special divisions of institutional authority. Thus the number of people who remain outside the influence of the commune is comparatively insignificant. Those who do are as a rule law-breakers of one kind or another.

Society is structured along other lines as well, although these have their basis in, and are determined by, the communal cell-structure. Here I would draw the reader's attention only to the most important ones: 1) the division of functions within industrial communes and the formation of a single system of production and allocation of goods; 2) the division of the social functions of the commune as a result of which individual functions become the speciality of special social organs. These special organs generalize and unify these special functions on the scale of society as a whole (or on the scale of one or other of its parts). These organs also have their cellular structure, and within their cells everything happens which we spoke of earlier; 3) the formation of a hierarchy of cells, thanks to which there arises a highly calibrated hierarchy of social positions on the scale of the whole society; 4) the distribution of the population into national and social groups dependent on people's social position, on parental and other non-social relationships, or territorial affiliations and other circumstances.

THE COMMUNES IN A UNIFORM SYSTEM

A Communist country may be divided into comparatively autonomous areas. However, what develops in the main is the formation of a unified social organism in which every commune is assigned a strictly defined role. A single army, transport system, postal system, financial system and other social institutions naturally weld society together into a whole, but the chief interlocking device is the commune's place among other communes and its dependence on them. The communes are the cells of the whole, not only in the sense in which we have regarded them above but also in the sense of the cells of a living body. They are parts of a whole with definite functions in relation to that whole.

The commune or cell under Communism differs from the feudal cell or fief in that the commune is not an independent economic whole; and from the capitalist cell (private enterprise) in that it is not incorporated in society as a whole via the market or competition with other enterprises. It is a unit in the distribution of the activity of society and carries out particular functions. By so doing it becomes a sort of autonomous whole on its own in the same sense as that in which the cell of a living organism does not merge with the mass of other cells. Of course, this social whole has to come to terms with the historically given conditions in which the commune developed. Here there is a process of mutual influence. But in a society which has set in its mould we can observe the following fact: each commune is assigned a particular character and scope; the same is true of all the other communes with which it has business relationships, from which, for example, it receives raw materials or to which it sends its own products.

The membership of the commune and its distribution according to profession and social rank is determined. All this is secured by a body of special legislation that lays down the status of communes and by a system which plans the activity of all communes, by defining the way in which a particular commune participates in the general plan, and the extent of its participation. This fixes the commune's industrial position and its professional and hierarchical composition. A plan is also given for the observance of norms of communal behaviour. The task of seeing that this uniform system functions throughout society belongs to communes of a special type which form the state apparatus. I will examine this matter later in the sections relating to the state.

THE HIERARCHY OF COMMUNAL CELLS

The basic social division of functions within communes is between business-functions and functions that control business-functions. Special cells are formed whose sole task is to exercise this control. In each individual person there is, if we regard him as a social being, a governing organ which directs his body and has a higher social rank than his body's other organs. It is like this in society where there is a directing cell similarly related to the other cells.

The governing cell has all the social qualities of any other working cell. From this point of view it is like the cells which it governs. But inasmuch as it has the function of governing the others, it is the governing organ of a new social whole, and it therefore reveals new social qualities. The most important of them lies in the fact that a group of people which in its turn governs others in a governing cell has a higher social rank than the highest people in the governed cells. Of course there are certain exceptions to this rule, but they don't alter its general force.

A second consideration which is very important here is the formation of a complex hierarchy of cells within government itself which stems from the primary governing cells. I emphasize this: the hierarchy of communal cells is not formed along the lines of the hierarchy of the majority of cells which are occupied with the commune's actual business (and are themselves governed by other similar cells) but according to the cells concerned with government itself. In other words, there is a mass of business cells which govern nobody else. These are grouped into aggregates of business cells which form a body that is governed by a special governing cell, namely a primary governing cell or cell of primary rank. Depending on the number of governed cells, there grows up a number of governing cells of primary rank that in their turn need to be governed, and this brings into being governing cells of secondary rank. This process extends to the point where it comprises the entire society. Moreover, there are statistical social laws regarding government and group formation according to which the whole grandiose hierarchy of commune-cells takes shape. Thus the social hierarchy of society is a strictly governmental hierarchy in just the same way as the whole aggregate of military officers of different ranks grows up on the base of a mass of private soldiers.

Of course, even those communal cells which don't govern anybody somehow develop their own hierarchy, but this happens in quite another spirit. For example, there are factories and institutes of higher and lower categories. The category determines many people's pay (for instance a worker in a first-category institute is paid more than a worker of the same rank in a second-category institute). However, the factory of the second category is not subordinate to the factory of the first category just as a regiment of the line is not subordinate to a guards regiment.

There is an absolutely natural consequence of the hierarchical system of commune-cells which we have been examining: it is that it creates a social ladder with many rungs, and that it converts the business of governing people and groups who are occupied in some real task into something much more important than the actual jobs which the governed people are doing. The officers, generals and marshals are not there for the sake of the soldiers. It is the soldiers who are there for the sake of the officers, generals and marshals. Moreover, the soldiers exist only as raw material for their activities.

RELATIONS BETWEEN GROUPS

Between groups of individuals we find the same relations as there are between individuals in groups: subordination (governing and being governed); co-ordination (or co-subordination); and co-operation (for practical ends). The first two relationships are constituted by the relations between governmental or managing groups. For example, the government of an institute forms a ruling group *vis-à-vis* a department of the institute, inasmuch as the head of the administration, the director, is the superior officer and the man in charge of the department is his subordinate. Besides, between groups there is an inclusive relationship; the institute contains a department and the department contains a section. Society as a whole contains a complex structure of groupings built up in this way.

The kind of existence which people have in the group has very little to do with how the group as a whole performs. There are exceptions, but in the case of the great majority of people and groups their circumstances even out. This principle that an individual's position has nothing to do with the efficiency of the group is a very real one: it makes people indifferent to the success of the group. Sometimes the management of a group and odd individual members of it are interested in achieving the best results. But even this is far from always being the case. On the other hand an individual's position may be materially affected by the rank of the group to which he or she belongs and by the number of privileges it enjoys. For example, the secretary of the director of an important institute of the first category has a higher salary and more perks than a secretary in a small institute of the second category.

Generally speaking, most principles which act strongly on society have a negative character. It is the same, too, with group-relations. Take two groups of the same rank. The management of one of them tries to see to it that the other group is not more successful; or at least that the other group's success should not be noticeable, should not attract publicity. The management of the other group, if it is experienced, knows that the same law applies to the relations of its group and so does not especially want to fall out of line. All the more so since the careers of managers depend only to a very insignificant degree on the performance of their institutions. They depend largely on the manager's relations with those people who have the power to decide his promotion up the official ladder. So the management in charge of a group will try to see to it that its group is no worse than others. Here the phenomenon of competition is excluded, for the fate of a group doesn't depend on the results of its work. The group gives something to society and receives something in return which is regulated by its position in society. Therefore it can well be that the workers in an enterprise employing out-of-date technical methods have exactly the same living standard as, or even a better one than, workers of a similar enterprise which uses advanced techniques. In short, communal relations in no way stimulate industrial progress.

THE HIERARCHY OF INDIVIDUALS AND THE DISTRIBUTION OF GOODS

Because of the just principle of the distribution of benefits according to social rank which is at the very basis of society, a hierarchical ladder with many rungs evolves in the distribution-system as well. Moreover, the difference in the share of benefits as between the top and bottom rungs is huge. The share of benefits at each level is determined not by laws of nature (there are no such things) but by what any person can snatch for himself at any given level, and by how much he can compel society to yield to him. In other words, his share is determined by social struggle and enshrined by law. This being so, the differentials have a tendency to grow to monstrous dimensions.

Critics of the way of life in Communist countries talk about all kinds of defects, but for some reason they are silent about the main question in people's lives: the allocation of the good things of life. The actual position is this: there is an official basic wage, and it is generally known that there is a huge wage-differential, amounting sometimes to a hundred-fold. Moreover, there are hidden forms of supplementary remuneration such as prizes, honoraria, handouts, money in envelopes, travel warrants, free stays in sanatoria. There are special shops with restricted access where prices are much lower than the official price. There is the legal or illegal kitty derived from personal resourcefulness; so-called gifts, bribes, personal influence, the black market, ordinary bazaars. Things are continually bought and sold on the official and semi-official market which indicate the existence of very well-to-do social strata. The fact is obvious: society is divided into layers in which people exhibit different levels of consumption. Moreover, at times the difference is so great that the contrasts of the past pale into insignificance.

Furthermore, it is generally known that the ruling élite

receives more and better goods than their subordinates, and that as people go up the ladder their share of the social product grows. Moreover, the higher they go the easier their work becomes, the fewer talents required and the greater their privileges. The authorities themselves, irrespective of type or rank, have no doubts about the justice of all this and safeguard and extend their privileges in every possible way. The ordinary people grumble but they too don't consider this to be unjust; it is normal that high-ups should get pickings. The 'intelligentsia' feels pinched and insulted, but not enough to rebel. It redoubles its efforts to compensate for its position by setting out to create its own distribution-hierarchy. As for the mass of the population, it acts in the way dictated by the objective social laws of communality, and above all by the principle of distribution of goods which is in actual operation.

The principle 'to each according to his social position' is the main and most basic principle for the distribution of the good things of life in Communist society. This principle is in effect the embodiment of the principle 'to each according to his work'. When there are big differences in the forms of social activity and where the general human laws of communality operate, the individual's social position is the only socially significant criterion by which both his contribution to the social product and his 'reasonable', i.e. socially acceptable, needs may be estimated. There are deviations from this principle in society but these deviations come about not through a non-observance of the principle but by an attempt to observe the principle. The most powerful and noticeable consequence of this principle is the tendency for the share of the social product progressively to increase or diminish in line with an increase or decrease in social rank. The result of this tendency is the polarization of consumption: an unusually high level of it at the top, and an unusually low one at the bottom.

When the investigator examines the hierarchy of distribution, he comes up against the following difficulty: the officially fixed index of consumption often does not correspond with the real index. For example, an official from the apparatus of the Central Committee receives a comparatively small salary. But his consumption-level is several times higher than that of an ordinary citizen with a higher salary, since he can obtain goods at derisory prices, or without payment at all, that are not accessible to ordinary mortals. The manager of a restaurant or a department store is paid less than a school teacher, but in fact he is much better off than a professor of an institute. He simply has another way of getting hold of the good things in life. The manager of a meat *Kombinat* has a third way. A fourth one will be at the disposal of a hairdresser or of a seller of beer or soda water. So, in order to arrive at an accurate description of the consumption levels of different social strata we have to introduce the concept of the social outlay on an individual's maintenance, i.e. the cost of his existence to society. For most individuals the size of this outlay coincides with the size of his needs as established by his real pay (with slight divergences).

But for the privileged classes there is no such coincidence. There are a good number of citizens who 'cost' two or three times more than the average. Sometimes it can amount to five-or sixfold. For a smaller group it can reach several tens of times, even a hundred or a thousand times. The 'social outlay' on the highest Party and State officials is incalculable. No king, no emperor, no millionaire has ever cost society so dear as a General Secretary in the USSR, a man who is supposed to express the interests of the working people and to be leading society in the direction of a just distribution of material and spiritual goods.

I am not speaking here about the countless squanderings of social assets through stupidity, wilfulness or obtuse vanity. Unfortunately it is not possible to obtain data about the personal estates of representatives of the various social strata. The comparative value of these estates would give an even more frightful picture. For instance, the total area of plots of land (and they are only plots) given over to the privileged, that is to the *nomenklatura* of all ranks, exceeds the area of a medium-sized European country, while the value of the private residences, flats and villas which they dispose of in one way or another surpasses the value of the palaces of the most extravagant sovereigns of the past. Add to this the outlay on medical institutions which are exclusively concerned with the health of the Soviet rulers and the cost of their glorification. You will be appalled. History has never known such contrasts between the numerous strata of society in the matter of expenditure and the distribution of goods as is found in what the demagogues call the just society of the Soviet Union. At the same time, of course, the system exhibits a picture of frightful dullness, mediocrity and vulgarity. But this doesn't change the essence of the matter.

The system of privilege built on the principle 'to each according to his social position' is grandiose. The consequence of the system is that the principle which we have mentioned, 'to each according to his work', comes to look like a deviation from the former principle and a violation of it.

If we reason in the abstract the situation looks like this. Citizens go to work in their communes, fulfil their duties and are remunerated according to the legal scale for their social position; and they exist on this pay. For example, a shop assistant in a grocery sells goods to other citizens and for this he receives a miserable hundred roubles per month for which he cannot buy even a decent suit. Then he runs round to other shops and joins the queues for food. The director of a song-and-dance ensemble chooses the girls who apply to him, teaches them to sing or dance, helps them and receives two hundred roubles or less. After work he goes back to his healthy Communist family and sleeps with his shrewish old wife. The manager of the housing section of the town council lives cosily in the flat allotted to him according to the established norm. . . .

Such is life in the abstract. The reality is entirely different. The salesman helps himself to the goods in his shop, and contrives to do so without paying and even to make a bit of money out of it too. He does his friends a 'bit of good' and they help him out in return. Salesmen in the meat sections in Moscow shops, for instance, are among the richest people, although their pay is miserable, not to mention the people who work in commission shops* and jewellery shops. Directors of the artistic ensembles force boys and girls to cohabit with them. People who have a hand in the allocation of flats are the best provided for of all, and are often very rich people.

In reality a social law operates whereby each individual tries to make the very most of his social position for his own ends. This is a natural law, and it cannot be changed by means of any 'high level of awareness' which the ideologues promise, or by way of any kind of threat. There is only one way to stop the law operating, and that is to give a person 'legally' everything which, in his position, he can get hold of anyway. But even this method isn't absolutely effective. Receiving something 'legally' isn't as satisfying, and so the individual will make use of his position in some other way. There have been innumerable cases in the Soviet Union in which the highest in the land, who are provided for beyond all measure, have nonetheless used their position in the most monstrous ways.

Social privilege is the advantage which individuals of a certain sort have over others because of their social position. Not every privilege is a social privilege. For example, people who live in regions where there are holiday resorts, and have the chance to make a fortune on account of the resorts, have an economic/geographical privilege rather than a social one. A young man from the family of a highly placed official has a whole series of advantages over a young man from the family of a poor creative intellectual. For example, the former, even with a mediocre performance at school, is guaranteed a place of his choice in higher education. In the main this happens by parental selection or from calculations of subsequent advantage, but not according to the principle 'from each according to his ability'. Even the most gifted young man who has no influence may find it hard not only to get into an institute

* Shops which sell items on behalf of private citizens on a commission basis.

appropriate to his gifts and inclinations but into any sort of institute at all – unless, of course, his parents have connections thanks to which the examiners can be given a secret instruction not to plough* him in the exams. But when we examine the privilege of the first young man in comparison with the second, who perhaps sat beside him at the same desk, we can see that the social privilege of the first young man is not his but his father's. Because of a privilege of birth he receives a social privilege, so that one can view the privilege as a potential social privilege. But I will not launch into these fine points.

Western societies also had and have a system of privilege. For instance, if Western parents have sufficient means they can buy their children an education suited to their talents and inclinations. Not everyone has such means; they constitute a privilege. But it is a privilege deriving from wealth, not from social position. How the riches are acquired is immaterial. They can be earned, they can be inherited or they can be the result of social privilege. But the fact itself of having enough money to acquire education is not a *social* privilege. Similarly, a man who has a large sum of money can make a journey abroad if he is the citizen of a Western country. Again, this is a privilege in the sense that to make the journey isn't open to everybody. But it isn't a *social* privilege. In the Soviet Union if one wants to make a journey abroad it is not enough to have money and to be a normal citizen. The opportunity to travel abroad is one of the most important social privileges, and as a rule such journeys are granted to privileged people free of charge.

There isn't such a thing as a society without privilege. The chief of a primitive tribe who took the first piece of meat from a slaughtered animal was a privileged person, and indeed for those times very privileged. It is important to establish what type of privilege we are talking about and what role it plays in the society in question. Soviet liberals who demand freedom of movement within the country and

* One way of limiting intakes into *vuzy* (institutions of higher education) is to 'fail' certain candidates, irrespective of their school performances or talents.

abroad, more freedom of expression, of the Press and in creative work, are attacking the very foundations of Soviet life: they are threatening its inherent system of privilege. Their desires derive from their reading about the past and about the West. They have heard all sorts of little conversations on this theme and perhaps have seen a certain amount of these things themselves. But all this is foreign to Soviet social realities.

Social privileges are divided into those which are official and which have the sanction of law and custom, and those which are unofficial. The latter are divided into punishable, or at least censurable, privileges and those that are not punishable or only mildly punishable. But there is no strict demarcation. For example, high pay, a good flat, a private car and a hidden source of provisions, free sanatoria for high officials are all legal privileges. On the other hand, the compulsion of subordinates to share one's bed, theft of their ideas, the foisting on them of co-authorship, the fixing of jobs and education on the old pals' network, are all *de facto* privileges without legal sanction. Officially they are reprehensible. But are many cases known where the officials who enjoy such unofficial privileges have suffered for them? These privileges are just as entrenched as the legal ones. There are many positions where *de facto*, non-legalized privileges are important sources of every kind of revenue. And they are sometimes even taken into account officially when pay is fixed so that official remuneration becomes a pure fiction. Take a walk, for example, in the areas around Moscow where there are country villas and make an estimate of what the villas are worth and how much their occupants are paid. You will see that in the great number of cases the occupants would have to put aside all their pay for tens of years in order to accumulate enough to buy a villa.

Thanks to the system of privilege that actually operates (including legal privileges) there comes about a supplementary distribution of goods. This means that the principle 'to each according to his social position' is converted into the principle 'each man grabs for himself everything that his social position enables him to get hold of'. His official salary forms part of the share of the social product that the individual grabs. This principle applies to everyone, but not everyone can operate it over and above their basic pay. The lowest strata also contrive to supplement their pay, for instance via extra earnings on the side or petty theft. In Communist society most crime is connected with attempts to make use of one's position in this way, which in the case of the lowest orders usually means breaking the law. But for the middle and highest classes things are much more favourable. From a strictly legal point of view, they too commit crimes, but it is very hard, if not impossible, to detect them in practice. Moreover, those in positions of power aren't interested in detecting them because they themselves are the first to make use of social privilege. In the Soviet Union to make use of one's office for private gain isn't really an abuse, but rather something quite natural. Abuse is seen as infringing a certain limit and going to 'noticeable extremes'. Whole regions of the country are infected with bribery, back-scratching and the arbitrary rule of officials, to such an extent that even the all-powerful organs of state-security are unable to deal with it. Besides, they too are sometimes involved and are even the ringleaders of gigantic social mafias which have their claws on whole regions, towns, provinces and even republics.

Every well-developed society engenders a social hierarchy and that inevitably begets a system of privilege. This law works in a way that is primitively simple. If a category of people has privileges in relation to another category of people which belongs to a lower level in the social hierarchy, then in order to safeguard its own privileges it is ready to make peace with categories of people who have a higher position and enjoy greater privileges. This law explains the fact that the staunchest defenders of the existing social establishment are not the upper or even the middle strata, but the strata that are slightly above the lowest. It is similar to the army where discipline is upheld not so much by senior officers and generals as by sergeants and junior officers. It is naïve to think that the sergeants and lieutenants of society act as they do only because of instructions from above and from fear of society's colonels and generals. Mainly they act of their own accord and in their own interest.

This law also applies to people on the *same* level. If an individual in a given category has even the slightest privilege in relation to his fellows he will on that account do everything he can to preserve and endorse the entire system of privilege. In every institution there are model workers from the rank and file who regularly receive prizes, official thanks, trips to rest homes, better living conditions. Any person in authority is surrounded by a host of toadies, lickspittles, informants and boon-companions, who fulfil their unofficial functions in a way that is far from being disinterested. All of them feel themselves to be participants of power, and hence of privilege. It is the petty officials and their voluntary aides on the lowest level who make up the toughest obstacle to the rank and file who wish to rise in life. The lower the rank of the primary official stratum, the harder it is to get through and the more cruel its attitude towards those below it. Only where there are protectors on a higher level or when someone exercises great resourcefulness can the obstacle be overcome.

The stratum of primary officials forms the basis and the core of the primary collective. If a member of the collective comes into conflict with it, the collective will very rarely support him. Usually the collective takes the side of the officials because its whole life is far more dependent on officialdom than it is on the individual in question. Thus the overwhelming majority of the population of the country does not fight its way through the relevant primary official strata and therefore does not attain a position from which an individual can oppose the highest powers of the state, that is oppose society as a whole and not merely his own miserable collective.

THE STRUCTURE OF THE POPULATION

According to official ideology, the population of the Soviet Union is divided into friendly classes of workers and peasants, and a working intelligentsia forming a stratum in between. Even many critics of Soviet society accept this scheme in general. But it is a totally senseless one. How on earth can the intelligentsia be a stratum between the workers and the peasants? A stratum in this case is something intermediate between worker and peasant. For example, it could be peasants who were partly workers or the other way round. If it is meant that Soviet intellectuals are from peasant or worker stock, that would have some meaning, but they are not a layer between the two.

But let us leave these captious objections on one side. Let us say that the intelligentsia does originate from the workers and peasants. This statement would have been appropriate after the revolution when the old intelligentsia was absolutely wiped out or expelled from the country and when people who were called *intelligentsia* out of habit did emerge from among the workers and peasants. But what happens when such people are producing their own like, in the second or third generation – i.e. when they are the issue of the issue of peasants and workers? How can they come from peasant or worker stock if they are produced from strata which did not even have a name in the past, for instance from Party officials? Furthermore, where shall we place the huge army of Party officials, KGB men, army officers and militia officers? One cannot ignore this category of people because it exceeds the intelligentsia in numbers. It clearly has no connection with peasants or workers, and to relate it to the intelligentsia is somehow awkward. In any case, they themselves do not want that, since for the most part they despise the intelligentsia. So one has to admit yet another special category of people: government servants. Is this a class or a stratum? Finally, townspeople differ from country people in their way of life, though from a sociological point of view this difference is not as substantial as that between governors and governed, which is the same for country and town. Officialdom is aware of this and now prefers to speak simply about workers and to ignore the real division of the country into different social categories. I am avoiding the word 'class' in order not to evoke unnecessary associations with Marxist ideas about classes and the classless society.

It is particularly laughable to hear Westerners talk about the intelligentsia, scientists, military and economic planners as special social categories. In all this, for some reason or another, they entirely lose sight of obvious facts: that among the 'scientists' there are low-paid workers, and the professors, the doctors, the academicians, the managers, the directors and other people who exist on different rungs of the hierarchical ladder. The difference in social position between them is sometimes so great that to put them in one category is like placing peasant serfs and land-owners into a category called 'farmer'. The ruling scientific stratum merely makes use of its scientific endeavours for its own social advantage. It has nothing to do with the function of learning or the discovery of truth.

The picture is exactly the same in other spheres of activity. Each has, of course, its professional distinguishing features. Everyone knows the military ones, for instance. Writers, although they have their own complex social structure and hierarchy, as a whole form a subdivision of society for the purpose of ideological work. But these are professional differences, not social ones. The concept of the 'intelligentsia' in the Soviet Union has lost so much of whatever meaning it might once have had that one cannot designate a profession, way of life, or level of education which could distinguish the intelligentsia from other strata as an identifiable social group.

The structure of Communist society really needs to be described in terms of another system of concepts. In the first place, society divides into primary work communes and people are divided into social categories according to their functions and position in those communes. One can thus construct a scale of these categories beginning with the lowest workers and ending with the top bosses of the regions, provinces, branches of the economy and of the country as a whole. Different methods of classification are possible. The crudest is the division into lower, middle and upper strata, while the most accurate is a division into officially established groups with a register of degrees, titles and ranks. In the latter case we obtain a more or less uninterrupted series which has little scientific value, especially since here we shall encounter difficulties in regard to many categories of people who in one sense should be included in one rank and in another sense in another. For example, the manager of a commission shop as regards pay is inferior to a junior worker in a research-institute. His official position is equal to that of the director of the laboratory in which the junior assistant works. But in terms of the means at his disposal and of his influence on society, he is superior to the director of the institute of which that laboratory is a part. Thus from the point of view of the sociologist a classification would be more interesting that took account of many different parameters. In real life people constantly take these parameters into account and spontaneously classify themselves accordingly – a classification that has nothing at all to do with the idiotic scheme 'workers, peasants, intelligentsia'. What is very close to the real sociological structure of society is the officially recognized division of people into categories according to their level in the *nomenklatura*; and for non-*nomenklatura* people by the official level of their position in the primary collectives.

The great majority of the population accepts this social hierarchy and considers it to be a just one. Here the situation resembles that in the army where the lance-corporal thinks the system of ranks is just inasmuch as it raises him just a little bit above his ordinary fellow soldiers, while the soldiers feel that if there were no order and no hierarchy their own situation would be worse. In conformity with the laws of communality they would be bound to form a social structure in any event, but one without the protection provided by an officially established order. The population accepts the social hierarchy because for many it gives some hope of getting clear of the masses and elevating themselves while for others it gives the sensation of being protected. People understand very well that without a social hierarchy there could be no economy of the contemporary type and that it would be impossible to conserve even that level of life and culture which *does* exist and which seems to them a very low one. Thus only an insignificant part of the population is interested in the destruction of the hierarchy and their attitude either derives from their own selfish interests or is unthinking, although these people often chatter on about how they are fighting for the public good. The many opposition movements in the West (especially those involving the Left and young people) are really fighting against the inevitable structure of contemporary society, although they usually enter the fray with slogans about the struggle against Capitalism and Imperialism. These movements are often anti-Communist in essence even if, because of historical conditions, they dress themselves up in Communist garb. This is yet another interesting historical paradox.

It is quite obvious that those people who have the chance of obtaining a higher position in the social hierarchy regard the hierarchy as a completely just one. Try suggesting to those who have spent many years of effort to become doctors, university teachers, generals, ministers and so on that they give up their titles, rank and level of security and then see how they respond to your proposal. But even in the case of students, young workers, soldiers, workmen, peasants and shop assistants thoughts about a programme of destruction of the social hierarchy do not enter their heads. People are upset by any deviations from the norm. The norms are relative and subjective, but officially recognized norms are not considered to be unjust.

People's most basic social relations come about through personal intercourse. People know each other personally and enter into immediate contact. Associations of people that are not formed by the laws of the state, namely, unofficial and informal ones, arise as a matter of course. They differ from official associations in that they do not have their own management, their own accountants, their Party men, their trade-unions or *Komsomol*, their own territory, their own legitimate business or any of the other attributes of official organizations. These unofficial associations are extremely diverse. They arise in the business collectives themselves, or in connection with business relationships but in a wider field (for example in a given field of culture) or independently of people's actual occupation (for example, family and national associations). There are various combinations. Some have one activity and are regular, some are continuous, some are not. They may be noticeable or not, encouraged or discouraged, tolerated or not tolerated, punishable or unpunishable. These associations arise on the basis of traditional ties, personal attachments, mutual help and advantage, and for self-defence. These groups and strata play an altogether more serious role in society than divisions of people into peasants, workers and intellectuals. I will not go into the super-primitive formula 'people versus authority' which is current among critics of Soviet society and among Russian émigrés in the West.

The whole population of the country can, moreover, be divided into the privileged and the unprivileged. This division does not follow the line which appears to demarcate the presence and absence of privilege in general. People can belong to the unprivileged part of society even if they occupy fairly high positions and thus have certain advantages laid down by law; for example, colonels, university teachers, professors, engineers, doctors and so forth. What we are talking about in this case are *special* privileges and specially exclusive people. The ranks of the privileged in this sense comprise the highest Party and state officials and a few especially eminent artists, painters and writers. Individual scientists belong too, but only in their capacity as powerful officials in their own field. Within the non-privileged part of society one can detect the formation of what I call 'clans', while within the privileged part in addition to the 'clan' one can also detect the formation of privileged strata. I will explain briefly the distinction between these structural elements of the population.

'Clans' are formed out of families, friends, neighbours and colleagues. These are rather amorphous formations but not so amorphous that one can leave them out of account. One 'clan' might comprise officers, engineers, civil servants, students, school pupils and cleaning ladies. All of them, despite their differences, live in a similar way. Such groups can have their own privileged persons who are the object of pride, hatred and other feelings on the part of the other members. Members of such groups know about each other's existence, they meet each other fairly often in different combinations, they are interested in what happens to each other and play some part in each other's fate. They are the people with whom and among whom the individual lives his life outside the primary collective and thus form the environment of his private life. These groups of people are guests and hosts, they correspond with each other, talk on the telephone, marry, produce children and make friends. The groups may change their composition and they are not always stable. But despite their shapelessness and variability people nevertheless are involved in them, they spend a good deal of their time in them, are interested in them and take them into account. For the great majority of the population these groups are a supplementary source of influence and an extra supervisor of their own behaviour. It is in these groups that public opinion operates, and there its power over people is immense.

It operates in two ways. On the one hand it compels people to act in consonance with the social laws to which all members of society are subject. On the other it establishes certain limits to behaviour by creating standards of decency, good order and honesty. People are forced to reckon with these standards of behaviour which are deemed by these 'clans' to be correct. If an individual infringes the accepted norms of behaviour, the 'clan' will censure him. At times it will exclude him and have him punished officially, so that when individual people in the Soviet Union enter into serious conflict with society (dissidents for example) they meet with condemnation not only in the primary collectives but in their own 'clans'. In particular, relatives and close friends as a rule condemn these dissidents. People in the West cannot understand these phenomena. But they are an absolutely normal affair for people who have experience of Soviet life. The point is that the clans work out standards for the correct behaviour of individuals, borrowing them from the primary collectives. The fact is that a significant part of the membership of the clan (in any case the most influential part of it) are members of working communes, and for them the clan is only an extension of the working commune. Conflicts, of course, arise between working communes and clans, but they have no meaning in principle; they do not split the life of the population into two different lives: the communal and the private. Most of the conflicts are such that they can be ascribed to the behaviour of some individual who has infringed some behavioural norm in a collective.

Groups which are analogous to 'clans' are formed also in the privileged part of society. Everything that has already been said applies to them too, but something new arises here that is not accessible on the lower levels: there are broader possibilities of intercourse; a consciousness of a common prestige; the solidarity to be found among privileged people and other phenomena that unite the representatives of that part of society into wider groups and even strata. Even potential membership of such a group can be enough. For instance, it is enough for a privileged writer to know of the existence of a privileged painter or a minister for them to become members of a potential group to which he attaches himself. For these people the main point is that acquaintanceship with each other is possible in principle. They can render each other services and count on this in advance. Their children can go to the same privileged educational establishments and marry each other. Their villas are comparable and may even be in the same neighbourhood. In short, something is established that is similar to that which exists among the ruling classes in non-Communist society. Moreover, a special hierarchy of strata emerges which only partly coincides with the official hierarchy of middle and higher officials.

The social strata which I am speaking about here exert even greater pressure on their members than the 'clans' because the consciousness of belonging to the population's ruling class also operates. Although in this society the exploitation of some people by others as it is found in Capitalist society is absent, a more insidious form of exploitation occurs in the Soviet Union where the exploiting agent is not the individual but a whole social stratum. Members of the privileged classes feel themselves to be partners in exploitation and value this position. The existing Communist order is their way of life and it suits them because it is only thanks to it that they have the special position that raises them above the mass of the people. Therefore the members of the privileged strata deal rather harshly and mercilessly with those who infringe the accepted code of behaviour. However, such cases happen rather rarely.

Of course 'concepts' such as 'worker' and 'peasant' have not yet entirely lost their meaning and will retain some of it in the future. But they have lost their sociological sense as concepts that can categorize real-life Communist society. Already many people engaged in the industrial sector at the lowest level can no longer be designated simply by the word 'worker'. They are skilled men like mechanics, or instrument-fitters, and so on. The word 'peasant', too, has a very vague meaning even for people who live in the country. They prefer to be called 'tractor-driver', 'combine-harvester driver', 'agronomist' or 'livestock specialist'. Quite often 'peasant' is used only for the least qualified members of the population of the village.

In brief, a complex sociological investigation using all the methods of modern science is needed if an accurate description of the structure of the multi-million-strong population of a Communist country is to be obtained.

THE NATIONAL QUESTION

I am not going to examine the division of the population into nationalities and tribes. I will only remark that the Communist regime deals successfully with national problems, as Soviet experience has shown. In particular, it has been extremely effective in raising the educational, cultural and living standards of the more backward peoples and groups of the population to a comparatively high level. These peoples become a bulwark of the new society. Certain national minorities occupy a privileged position and are converted into groups which can hardly be distinguished from bands of gangsters. In the Soviet Union whole republics at times occupy this position such as Georgia and Azerbaidjan. Under Communism organized social life can very easily be converted into gangster-like social organizations and from this point of view control by the central government is in some places the only means of restraining this tendency.

In Communist society there is a very strong tendency towards destroying national barriers and levelling out national differences. There is a tendency to form a community of people beyond nationality, i.e. a tendency towards a generalized communality. It follows that any expectation that conflicts between nationalities will cause the ruin of the Soviet Empire derives from a total misconception of the real situation in the country in this regard.

THE TENDENCY TOWARDS SLAVERY

I want especially to identify one tendency in Communist society: the tendency to create a category of people whose status is very near to that of the slave. They are the convicts. In Stalin's time the army of convicts in the Soviet

Union was reckoned to be fifteen million. At the present time there is reason to believe that the figure stands at four or five million. This figure isn't enough to satisfy Communist society's real need for workers of this type, a need which is temporarily satisfied by making use of town workers, especially young people, as forced labour for harvesting and on building-sites and by using the army. The position of these people is very near to slavery inasmuch as they are adults who are torn from their usual milieu and their normal working collective, who do not procreate in captivity, who receive a pittance for their work, and who are not free to choose their abode or the kind of work they do.

The only thing the authorities don't do with these people is sell them, and the reason for that is that there is nobody to sell them to and nobody to buy them from. This army of slaves is topped up as a rule by law-breakers who are always in good supply in this society. The number of prisoners does not depend on the ability of the authorities to detect crime, but on the punishments imposed by the authorities and on the 'through-put' capacity of the organs of justice. The need for an army of slaves arises in those sectors where normal people have no wish to work (for example, industries with a high record of injuries or industrially related illness, factories in an unpleasant climate, and especially secret enterprises). This tendency to form an army of slaves derives from the fact that work in Communist society is compulsory, and from the power of the government to create such an army without the opposition of the population. Most people view the phenomenon with indifference or encourage it inasmuch as it cleanses society of thieves, bandits and burglars and other socially dangerous elements. But the authorities do not confine themselves to sanitary measures: they also 'recruit' as convicts the labour which is needed in the places mentioned above. It is easy enough to do this because in principle huge numbers of the normal population are vulnerable in relation to the courts of justice. As far as I have been able to establish, the prevalent type of Soviet prisoner in the last decades has not been the professional criminal at all but the ordinary man who has committed a crime either accidentally or because of his living conditions.

THE PREVALENT EVOLUTIONARY TREND

Social evolution does not take account of people's beautiful ideals and intentions. However deplorable it may be, we have to recognize the fact that the prevalent social tendency in Communist society and in Communism in the modern world is to organize the whole life of the popular mass as one organic whole: i.e. with complex internal differentials between people, with their attachment to one cellular unit which is their place of work and with their allocation to different levels of the social hierarchy. All this inevitably generates an irresistible trend towards inequality of status and rights. This is covered up hypocritically by everyone, but fully recognized in fact by the most active and effective part of the population. In its early days ideological Communism borrowed its ideals of equality and justice from the ideology of Western countries. These ideals came into glaring contradiction with the real-life historical fate of Communism as a type of society and as a general tendency of humanity. It is not impossible that in the future a struggle to legalize ideals of inequality of status and rights will play a no less important role in history than obsolescent ideals of equality.

THE STATE

In society the communal cells are hierarchized. At the same time a series of vitally important functions of the cells are converted into functions of certain organs of a special kind. These organs express the functions of large communities of people and of society as a whole. Through this process the huge aggregate of heterogeneous cells and the mass of humanity in which they are submerged form an integral social organism. The aggregate of these organs forms what one can call the state apparatus, which fulfils the functions of government and acts as a cohesive force in the regions, the departments, the provinces, the republics and the country as a whole. It has a very complex formation, a description of which would require several weighty volumes. I will limit myself to the more important points concerning its structure and functions.

The Marxist theory of the state is well known. According to it the state arises with the rise of antagonistic classes. It arises as the weapon of the dominant classes which is used by them to keep the exploited classes in check. When the exploiting classes are destroyed, the state will wither away. I do not want to discuss how the state arose originally, but from the sociological point of view the Marxist theory of the role of the state in society and of its future in the 'classless' society (by which is meant a society without landowners and capitalists) is obviously absurd. The theory is in fact a purely ideological phenomenon intended for the most primitive intellectual level of the popular mass. The ideologists of established Communist society obviously find this part of Marxism extremely awkward. So they have to resort to no less idiotic ideas about the fading away of the state via its strengthening and about the waging of class-war in the sphere of international relations between Communist and non-Communist countries. Soviet ideologies used to see the signs of the fading away of the state in 'People's Patrols' (which are formations of workers from various institutions that help the militia), in 'Comrades' Courts', in administrative committees attached to the local organs of power and in other supposedly voluntary organizations that fulfil a very secondary role in the power-system, without remuneration and in people's free time. Once I asked an ideologue of this sort when it would become possible for the ordinary citizen to fulfil the functions of General Secretary of the Central Committee of the Communist Party of the Soviet

Union, voluntarily and without remuneration. At first he was slightly perplexed, but then he found a way out: 'The General Secretary,' he explained, 'is no longer a state-phenomenon in the Marxist sense of "state".' This was still the case until the General Secretary in the Soviet Union began to merge his own functions with that of the Head of State. On one point this ideologue was right, without suspecting it. The state in the Marxist sense (i.e. the organ used by the dominant class after society has been split into antagonistic classes) actually no longer does exist in the Soviet Union. But, alas, the state as such continues to exist all right, and will collapse only with the destruction of the society as a whole.

The state apparatus of Communist society consists of a core apparatus and of a whole network of other apparatuses, subordinate to the core and acting as its branches and extensions. These are not different forms of power but elements of one single power apparatus. In the Soviet Union the core of the state apparatus is called the *Party apparatus*. It visibly binds itself to the Party, regards itself as the Party apparatus although its actual position is rather different. The branches and the extensions of the core apparatus are the soviets, the ministries, the trade-unions, the punitive organs, the ideological apparatus, the military and sporting institutions and so on.

When critics of Soviet society differentiate between the Party and economic and military powers-that-be, and even read conflicts into their mutual relations, then it is clear that they understand nothing at all about the structure and essence of power in Communist society. In that society there are no different forms of power but only different functions of one single power. Of course, conflicts do occur as in every collectivity of people or institutions. But they are in no way conflicts between forms of power but phenomena of another kind. They do not split society into warring factions and they rarely express the important requirements of the population as a whole. More often they are episodes in the struggle for power and complete control in the ruling group, whose members will use particular problems facing the country as a front behind which to make their power-plays.

In any case the conflicting groups do not represent, in their own conflict, the broad masses of the population because this cannot be so for strictly structural reasons. Expressions such as 'military', 'economic' and so on are often used in connection with a situation in the Soviet Union in a way that is completely devoid of sense, for the simple reason that no such social units exist. In the army, in science, in industry and in the other sectors of life there is to be found one standard social structure as described above. This divides people into social categories in such a way that there can be no question of there being representations of separate interests in a given sphere. The generals have more interests in common with academicians and managers of factories than they have with the soldiers. But in this respect they do not form associations distinct from the others. Talk about conflicts between ideologues and economists, politicians and the military is nothing other than a projection of conceptions of mutual relationships that exist in Western power-structures upon a phenomenon of a totally different order: power in Communist society. Of course, all forms of power have certain general features, but they are not these.

The spine of the state apparatus has the following specific quality. First, it has a hierarchical structure from the summit to the smallest territorial unit: the region. The regional committee of the Party is the core of power in the region, the provincial one in the province and so on up to the top. But notice that at the level of the cell the core of power is no longer the *Party bureau* or the *Party committee* but the *management* of the institution. Although the Party bureau watches over management, nevertheless their relationship is of a different order from the relationship between the regional Party committee and the other organs of power. Here the relationship is more like the relationship of the different sections of power at the highest level, since here we find an aggregation of a greater number of cells and an isolation of a series of their functions in the shape of functions of special organizations and thus an isolation of the different functions of power. Here, at the level of regional power, we have a divide in the Party structure which demonstrates the qualitative difference between the Party *apparatus of power* and the Party seen as a multitude of *ordinary Party members*.

A second peculiarity of the power-core of the state apparatus is that it contains within itself in concentrated form all the most important functions and potential of the state apparatus in general. These functions are broken down in detail into the whole aggregate of special institutions in the different branches of the state apparatus. It is from this point that the illusion is created that the Party apparatus duplicates the governmental apparatus in industry, agriculture, science, the army and the other sectors of society. It does duplicate it, but in such a way that only the roots and the nerves are strengthened; the roots and nerves of branches that develop into what are to some extent autonomous organs.

Reproaches levelled at Communist society regarding the exaggerated growth of the state apparatus have become commonplace in the critical literature about Communism. Of course the apparatus is huge, but its dimensions in Communist society are established by social laws, according to which society is crystallized. There are minimal dimensions below which simplification just cannot go because of the laws of social organization. The upper limits are more mobile, which does at times enable the apparatus to grow beyond an acceptable level. It would be possible to reduce and simplify the governmental apparatus below the minimal-normal line only if the population itself were reduced and its whole economic and cultural systems simplified – i.e. if life were made more primitive. There is indeed a tendency in Communist society to primitivize the whole of the structure of life, but nevertheless that tendency does *not* lead to a simplification of the state apparatus. This is another example of those strange social phenomena I spoke of earlier.

The position of the state apparatus in society is twofold. On the one hand it consists of cellular communes whose activity is subordinated to the general laws of communal life (which mean that what happens in them also happens in other communes). Of course, there are some modifications, but they do not change the communality of life in such cells. On the other hand the state apparatus is the governing organ of society as a whole regarded as an individual, and from this point of view the activity of the apparatus is like the activity of the governing organs of individuals of lower rank right down to the level of the individual person. But the complexity of the body that is governed, society itself, and the peculiarities of the behaviour of its gigantic body set in its environment condition some of the principles of state activity and cause them to spread downwards. That is to say, they are disseminated among the governing organs of the lower ranks. This is an example of the fact that two sources of influence are ceaselessly interacting both in the formation of society and during its existence, namely the influence of low-level cells on those above and vice versa.

I will draw attention to one more peculiarity of Communist power in a Communist society and that is its colossal network. What does this mean? The Party power apparatus is built on the territorial principle: it embraces the regions, the cities, the districts, the provinces and the republics. At the same time the communes which are situated on the above territories (primary territorial units from the point of view of Party power) have their own system of functional subordination. The communes enter into the fabric and the organs of a different, non-territorial, cross-section of society which extend beyond the frontiers of these territorial units. The fabric and the organs are subjected to Party power at a higher level in the territorial hierarchy (right up to the scale of the country as a whole). So there is a multiple interweaving of the network of power. It can be presented in this form:

1) *first level*: Party power in its primary territorial unit, with its network of antennae locked into the institutions that are in the jurisdiction of or actively supervised by Party power: institutions which are subordinated to higher organs via professional subordination;

2) *the second and higher levels*: This is Party power in the higher territorial units with its antennae which extend to Party power below and to the institutions under its direct control as well as higher-ranking institutions within its purview;
3) *the level of the country as a whole*;
4) *special and extraordinary conditions*.

Thus any attempt to tear the network of power from the social body of necessity entails tearing from it bits of its flesh and bones, which is tantamount to destroying society as a living organism.

TERRITORIAL POWER

In the Soviet Union territorial power is vested in village, regional, district, provincial and republican councils and in the Supreme Soviet for the whole country. But the word 'councils' (*soviety*) is immaterial because the essence and the functions of this locus of power are the same in all Communist countries.

In outward form territorial power appears to be freely elected. But what passes for an election here has long been an object of ridicule. However the ridicule has not been altogether justified because an election does indeed take place: the Party organs really do elect suitable candidates to be deputies. It is only from the point of view of voting citizens that the whole thing appears as a complete fiction. But that is beside the point. The official election of the deputies to the councils is the least significant feature of territorial power. The essential fact before anything else is that these councils are stable organizations (collectives) in which people work on a uniform basis. They are selected for work in these organizations individually although the selection is, of course, biased: not everybody is accepted who wants to enter them. But the selection of suitable people also takes place in other institutions which do *not* form part of the power-system. The important point is that people go to work in these institutions and participate in the power-system by fulfilling routine functions that often have nothing to do with power as such. And it is with these workers in the apparatus of power that the ordinary citizen generally has to deal, not with the fictitiously elected deputies in the councils. Most people never bump into a deputy or do so only in exceptional circumstances. The role of deputies is in general fictitious: they only vote on decisions which other people invite them to take. The directors of these organs of power are chosen formally like the other deputies, but in fact they are selected for their posts by the Party organs and work there more or less all the time. They make their career there or are transferred to other posts. But in this respect there is no difference at all between them and the directors of other institutions.

Territorial power remains root and branch under the control of the Party. In the Soviet Union this situation is graphically demonstrated by the fact that the head of the Party has become the head of the State as well. But this was the result of concrete historical conditions (state-visits, state-receptions and treaties, and the personal ambitions of the head of the Party), and there is nothing obligatory about it in principle. There is no such unity of power-functions at the lower levels; the only obligatory thing is that the directors of territorial power are selected and in fact appointed by the Party organs. They themselves are members of the Party's power apparatus, being members of the bureaux of the regional and provincial committees of the Party or members of the Central committees of the Party. Territorial power is only a branch of the general power-system, at the core of which is the Party apparatus.

For the ordinary citizen in Communist society, territorial power means the regional council with all its subdivisions: the militia, institutions for children, schools, social security, justice, the housing section and so on. And naturally the ordinary person is continually coming into contact with them in one way or another. If the citizen makes no claim to anything special and leads a normal life, he will hardly be aware of territorial power as such. Of course, there too one finds everything characteristic of Communist institutions such as red-tape and bribery, but in the main the citizens, in return for their own efforts, get their 'rights', that is, what they are entitled to by law. And at least they can fight for these rights. The important point here is that in relation to this territorial power the citizens are objects of the authorities' activity. The one party does not enter into *communal* relations with the other.

For the active part of the population territorial power plays a much less important role than the system of power in which they find themselves in the primary collective. But this doesn't mean that the role of territorial power does not matter. In principle a situation is conceivable in which the rank and file comes into contact with territorial power only via their own primary collective; or even in which the territorial power is swallowed up in the administrative, economic or industrial power. But despite all this there remain certain power-functions that will be fulfilled by certain elements in the power structure of the collective and by groups of them. This fact doesn't change the essence of power.

POLITICS

The word 'politics' is used in different senses. The behaviour of individual people is called political, as is that of groups, parties, governments, working to attain their goals. 'Politics' is a name for the sphere of activity of state-power and for that of people and organizations who affect the interests of the State. There is the well-known saying that politics is about power. But the question of power isn't always a political question. When people want to seize power and try to do so, then the question of power is a political question. But if power has been seized, then the power question in Communist society ceases to be political. In addition politics is not just a matter of power. But let us define the concept of politics in order to be able to speak about it more accurately. This is not, of course, a question of words. However, it is the case that a terminology that was invented by Western civilization for the purpose of describing its own phenomena is regularly applied to the Soviet Union, and the term 'politics' is included in it. But such an application forces one to look at Communist society in a light thrown upon it by a foreign conceptual system; and this does little to help one understand it.

There are differing relationships between social individuals, whether they are separate people, groups of people or whole countries. Earlier we were examining the relationships of command and subordination and the relation between subordinates. We can now add to them the relationships of coercion and games. The games are not to be viewed as anything amusing, but as something serious in which some players lose something and others gain something. In social life the stakes can be the fate of people, classes, parties and whole nations. Political relations can be included among these games.

Of course, in real life different forms of social relations are interwoven, so that it is hard to separate them. The command relationship may include both coercion and game-elements. A coercive relationship often contains an element of voluntary submission, but it is useful to distinguish these relationships in order to help us investigate the complex phenomena of social life. I have already said enough about the relationships mentioned above, with the exception of the game-element, about which I will now make a few observations.

The game-relationship between communal individuals arises in a particular situation in which individuals are compelled to come into contact, in particular when they form a single whole. But it is a relationship between individuals in which there is neither superordination, subordination or co-ordination. To some extent people here are independent, not subject to control and enjoy freedom of will and choice. Their influence upon each other is not determined by law, force or custom. Of course, people here have their own rules of behaviour, their own experience, their own skills when it comes to behaving advantageously for themselves. But these determine the behavioural procedures as such and not the relationship itself. Partners in a game-relationship try to extract maximum advantage for themselves and achieve their own ends.

The partners are not necessarily equally matched. One player may have a great advantage over the others but that does not stop him from entering the game because he as the stronger may elect not to apply direct force, i.e. a force which would obviate the need for the game in the first place. Not all the players will play actively; some may be passive. Moreover, one of the partners in the game may not regard himself as a player and may just be an object of the games of the others. For example, after the Russian revolution masses of peasants remained beyond the control of the new power-system. The latter applied force to the peasants. But the measures were inadequate and at times dangerous. Then the new power began to play its own peculiar game with the peasantry, which took the form of certain propaganda slogans, certain legislation and operations with industrial goods. By means of this game the authorities managed to divide the peasants, attaching some to itself and suppressing the discontented ones. Thus the peasantry went down the road desired by the authorities.

Political relationships are a special instance of social game-relationships. Their specific feature is that they are in one way or another connected with the power problem. Participants in political relations within the country are the following: 1) the organs of power and groups of people who are to some extent independent of power who try to acquire or conserve this independence; 2) different groups of people who have a political relationship with the authorities who seek either unity in this relationship or separation or domination and who thus either come into conflict or do a deal with them. In the first case the political relationships are direct, in the second indirect. The authorities in different countries are participants in political relations between countries, as are groups of people in different countries who have political relations with their own authorities. These groups also have relationships with the authorities of other countries. The sphere of politics is constituted by the activities of powers and groups which are carried out in connection with political relations. The state power of one or other country, or several countries, is an indispensable partner in political relations or an objective of these relations, either directly or indirectly. The aims of political activity within a country can be described as follows. There are those people without power who try to win some independence from the powers-that-be, to preserve this independence and to enter into a relationship with the authorities on the basis of this independence. Furthermore, they try to get their group a share of power, to dominate the power group, or to seize complete power. The people who are in power try to prevent the appearance of independent groups, to impose their own will on groups independent of themselves and to liquidate, or at least limit, that independence. The first try to achieve the possibility of political relations, and by using them, abolish them. The second try to disallow political relations, but if there are any, use them in order to liquidate them. The picture becomes more complex if one takes into account the struggles that go on within both groups. The main point in all this mish-mash of social influence and activity is that political relations are the least constant of social relations. They appear in order to disappear. The whole purpose of political activity comes down to this: that political relations should come into being and then be liquidated. While they last, the political game is played, according to well-known rules which at times arouse the loathing even of the professional politicians themselves.

If one examines state power in Communist society from the point of view of its internal position in the country and the relationships between people and the authorities, and with each other as regards their own relations with the authorities, then one can state it as a fact that here state power has lost all its political character; that the role of political relations in society has become minuscule and in principle has even disappeared, so that the political sphere has withered away just as the Marxist classics prophesied. All this has withered, not in the sense that the state has withered or the prisons or the punitive organs – on the contrary they have grown and been strengthened – but in the sense that they have lost their political character in the narrow sense we established above.

THE SPECIFIC FUNCTIONS OF THE COMMUNIST STATE

The Communist state fulfils several functions in society. Among them are functions shared with states in non-Communist societies, e.g. the maintenance of public order, the battle against thieves, hooligans and bandits, the realization of justice, the detention of criminals, relations with other countries. However, it is not these functions which determine essentially the form the state apparatus takes in a Communist country.

As I said earlier, in Communist society every commune has a position in the country which is strictly defined, as are its work-functions, its relations with other communes, its internal structure, its share of national production and the remuneration it receives. It is the state apparatus that lays all this down and controls the commune's activity. What constitutes the fundamental and specific role of the state in Communist society is this: to ensure that the whole of society acts as a single organism. The whole legislative and administrative activity of the state is geared to precisely this end. Without the state society would be like the body of an animal that has no brain or nervous system. It is on this basis that the other functions of the state grow up: organization for educating the young and allocating them to professions and places of work, the care of the old, medical services, sport, art and so on. In capitalist countries the state also undertakes these things to some extent: this is one of the elements of Communism in non-Communist societies. But only in Communist societies does the state seize these functions in their entirety and execute them indivisibly and as its main business.

PLANNING

The specific activity of the Communist state consists in the laying down of strict obligations for the communes which it governs and for all the complex aggregates of these and in the planning of their activities. So much is said and written about planning under Communism that there is really nothing of value to add. Apologists extol the planned character of the economy to the skies and regard plans as stages in the movement towards 'full Communism'. Critics make ironic remarks about the fictitious character of the plans, their actual non-fulfilment and the cruel measures used to try to fulfil them. They point out the elements of planning in bourgeois countries and the elements of chaos in Communist ones. But both parties miss the essential point of planning. It is true that there is much stupidity in the plans, that they are largely fictitious and propaganda-serving, that they are often not fulfilled and that something else happens instead of what was planned. However, none of this contradicts the fact that planning is an irremovable attribute of Communist society. The point is that the role of planning is by no means merely to provide a blueprint by which society is to be guided on its road towards its shining ideals. Planning is used by the state to preserve the unity of the social organism by means of compulsory activity. It is a purely Communist means of limiting the forces of communality in society. The real life of society, despite everything, gravitates towards plans and some kind of ideal or norm. The state's compulsion of communes to fulfil their plan is the only means of avoiding chaos and maintaining some kind of order.

The plan, I repeat, defines the status of the commune in society as a whole. The fulfilment of the plan is the index of the commune's activity. Here the deciding factor is not competitiveness, not the purely economic norm of profit, but simply the relationship between the plan and the commune's actual activity. The authorities at all levels make a sustained, systematic effort, therefore, to ensure that the communes operate within the framework of their plan. From a purely economic point of view the commune may well run at a loss, but this doesn't lead to its liquidation. It provides a livelihood for a certain number of people and produces its required product. This is enough to justify its existence. And the state, which forces the commune to act within its established framework, guarantees the commune a means of existence for its members, material for its activity and markets for its product. The commune is granted autonomy only within the framework of the plan. All kinds of rationalizations, initiatives, innovations, movements for over-producing the plan, for fulfilling it ahead of time, for making economies and so on are really only the means of keeping the commune within the framework of the plan, of driving it on to reach the plan's targets, of compensating for the unfulfilled plans of some by the over-fulfilled plans of others. Of course, all this is at the same time a means of influencing the masses through ideology.

The actual position in society is not so harmonious as it appears on paper and in propaganda. In reality 'harmony' is achieved at a very high price, at the cost of huge losses and absurdities, and it is only the dominating tendency among a mass of others that push society towards chaos and ungovernability. Moreover, the very system of planning creates a tendency exactly opposite to that which the whole ideal of planning is supposed to create. Thanks to planning, the fate of most, if not all, citizens and institutions does not depend on the marketability of their products. Their task is merely to produce enough to satisfy the accountants. The communes and their members invent different means of deceiving the authorities and different types of general eye-wash. There is a constant growth of fictitious plan-fulfilment in a context of factual non-fulfilment. In addition there are constant difficulties into which the central government lands the country and which necessitate a revision of the plan and the switching of resources to unplanned expenditure. The Soviet Union, for example, is chronically subject to economic difficulties, and it is only the population's habit of enduring a low standard of living and its submissiveness, together with the rich natural resources and aid from satellite countries, which deliver the state authorities from bankruptcy. The Communist state, which has taken into its own hands the direction of the country's production and attached it to a planning system, at the same time ceaselessly creates the conditions in which its own plans are undermined and creates a tendency towards economic uncontrollability and sheer chaos.

The problem of the relationship between centralization and decentralization of government is one of the most important in the existence of a Communist country.

Centralized government has its own major defects. It causes lack of initiative, wastefulness, senseless loss of assets, a brake on productivity and many other negative phenomena which are well known and enable one to affirm that the Communist countries cannot 'pursue and overtake' the leading capitalist countries either economically or in business in general. However, a centralized government has its advantages, which are just as well known. In particular, it is only by centralization that grandiose structures such as existed and are still being developed in the Soviet Union are made possible. The advantages for the development of the military industry and the creation of the armed forces are generally recognized. But the real point isn't the balance of advantage and disadvantage as between centralization and decentralization of government. Social life is not a search for some optimum academic solution. Communist society's centralized system of government is adequate for that and is better adapted to it than any other. And if it causes evil, that still isn't a reason why the governing organs should renounce any of their prerogatives. They have the power to keep them for themselves, the more so because it is doubtful how much good decentralization would do. Improvements would be noticeable on a small scale, but on the scale of society as a whole decentralization could lead to even worse difficulties than the ones that arise without it. Besides, experiments conducted in this field in the Soviet Union have not been successful.

PERSONAL AND NOMINAL POWER

Every manager, once he has obtained a post, tries to create an apparatus of personal power. To this end he gets rid of some people and replaces them with others who are personally known to him or who he thinks are personally devoted to him and wins over the rest to his side. All those not attracted by his 'magnetism', or who oppose him, he will try to isolate, neutralize or discredit. This is completely natural, because management has to rely on teamwork based on the personal contacts of its members. On average the apparatus of personal power that the manager creates is no worse than the power apparatus that might be installed according to 'just' laws: after all, there are no laws more just than the ones that work in real life, despite the wishes of people to escape from them. This apparatus at least has the advantage that it comes nearer to the ideal of the team than the nominal or official apparatus. Moreover, it is normally only necessary to remove a few people and put others in their place for a new set-up acceptable to the new manager to begin to form naturally. It won't be long before new lackeys will appear bent on betraying their former boss.

The apparatus of personal power doesn't wholly coincide with the nominal apparatus. Some people who occupy important positions do not belong to the nominal apparatus. Some who formally are in second-grade posts begin to play a more important role. The manager surrounds himself with a whole system of toadies and lickspittles, informers, intriguers and fixers who, together with all those supporters of the manager with official posts, form a ruling mafia. This happens at all levels of power, beginning with the primary communes. Even within the framework of the primary communes there are more or less powerful subdivisions which gravitate towards the same model.

Sometimes the apparatus of personal power assumes such strength that it ceases to take account of the norms of normal power. The mafia becomes the sovereign ruler and rules according to its own communal laws, virtually ignoring the limitations imposed by formal laws. In Stalin's time the system gripped the whole country: whole republics, provinces, districts, regions and institutions. It takes a lot of time and effort to overcome such excessive personal power and to keep it within tolerable bounds. But in general personal power is the normal system in Communist society. A large number of people gain a great deal from this system and rely on it in order to rule over others.

There is a definite technique of establishing personal power which is inherited and handed down from generation to generation. Besides, even the most mediocre managers very quickly grasp all its niceties and begin to conduct themselves like born intriguers and politicians. The occasions when the new manager suffers a fiasco are very rare. Higher authority and the whole of the power apparatus in one way or another do everything they can to ensure stability and the rapid adaptation of the new manager to the milieu and of the milieu to the new manager.

The greater part of the activity of the personal power apparatus, i.e. of the *de facto* apparatus of power, consists of personal communications, oral instructions, requests for favours, hints and other means which do not appear in official documents. The official documents are drawn up in a way that only people with experience of power and competent specialists can read between the lines and arrive at an understanding of the real state of affairs. Thus the secretive character of the activity of the powers-that-be, which strikes many observers, is their natural quality. It is to be found throughout the system from top to bottom and there is nothing specially evil about it. Secrecy is admittedly used consciously and on an immense scale on various rungs of the ladder of power and in respect of particular aims of the authorities. But the possibility of it springs from the very foundations of power.

For the reasons we have indicated, any group of people exercising power needs to be able to trust people on a personal level, needs reliable confederates and needs a system of mutual rescue and mutual support in time of trouble. None of this excludes the action of communal laws in the milieu, but they are limited by special conditions created by the ruling mafia. Of course, there is no absolute harmony here either. Here too there are actual and potential traitors, denouncers, wreckers, working against the interest of the mafia. Indeed, they are one of the means of limiting the mafia itself and of its control by the higher authorities and by the environment as a whole.

ONE-MAN MANAGEMENT AND COLLEGIALITY

Already at the level of the commune there are two tendencies in management: one towards solo command and the other towards collegiality. The first tendency arises from the natural necessity for unity in any management team. A bifurcation of management is unhealthy in the same way as a split consciousness is an illness in the case of the individual. It makes itself felt throughout the whole of communal life or at least throughout its more active part. Society doesn't encourage such phenomena and tries to limit them. The second tendency, towards collegiality, springs from the natural necessity that the various subdivisions of the commune should be represented in management and influence management activities from the point of view of the interests of these subdivisions.

Solo command is represented by the leader of the management team, i.e. by the leader of a special social group in the constitution of the commune. It is this managing group as a whole and not the ruler of the group who is the ruler of the commune. The ruler of the management group is only considered to be the ruler of the whole commune because such an exaggeration of his role is one component of the reward due to his social position. Moreover, the other members of the management are members of the commune who in their day-to-day routine in the estimation of the people look like elements of the general mass, which is itself on the opposite side of the fence *vis-à-vis* the leader of the commune. In the commune's external relations it is mainly the head of its managing body who represents it.

Exactly the same picture holds for the larger units right up to the country as a whole. This is why it seemed to the outsider that first Stalin, then Khrushchev, then Brezhnev ruled the whole of the USSR. That is a false impression. The role of these and other rulers of Communist countries is not so large as it seems from the outside, nor from the inside if one takes account of the government apparatus which is the actual ruler of the country. The ruler can be a complete nobody and irresponsible, while the impression is given that he is a dictator with unlimited powers. The impression is usually greatly strengthened by the fact that the 'ruler' creates for himself an apparatus of personal power which does not coincide with the normal power apparatus, and in particular because a cult of the ruler arises. At times this cult assumes vast proportions, as was the case with Stalin, Mao Tse-Tung, Kim-il-Sung, Tito, Brezhnev and others. The rulers themselves usually do everything they can to exaggerate their role and to diminish the role of others so as to appear as the top personality. In Communist society the personal vanity of the rulers coincides with the objective structure of power and with the wishes of the mass of people employed in the power system. In addition this vanity is encouraged by the ruler's whole entourage, which derives no small advantage from it. In fact, the ruler becomes merely the symbol and focus of the ruling mafia. He can effectively exercise a huge personal power over the fate of individual people, which also very much heightens the illusion that he is the all-powerful ruler over the whole life of the country. In reality this is a grandiose piece of deceit and self-deceit. Even Stalin was not in reality what historians, writers and politicians have hitherto imagined. For instance, processes in the country's life such as industrialization and collectivization were not thought out by him and foisted on society. Even the mass repressions were the work of a large number of people and not merely the personal invention and initiative of Stalin.

The collegiality of the leadership in Communist society is not something thought up by propaganda: it is a real fact. I have already remarked on its source. It fulfils a number of different functions besides. Let us note first of all that collegiality is not simply participation in management. Collegiality happens when decisions depend on the members of the governing body, such as, for example, the members of the management of research institutes, members of the Academic Councils, members of the bureaux of regional and district committees of the Party, members of the Politburo of the Central Committee. The basic functions of such organs are to limit the arbitrary actions of the single ruler, to give his actions their legal sanction and at the same time to remove from the ruler personal responsibility for important decisions. Collegial leadership is merely the means used by the 'sole ruler' for the purposes of self-defence and self-control. When the rulers who come to power take measures to place their own people everywhere and surround themselves with obedient servants, they are thereby merely asserting the natural principle of solo command which is to create for itself a suitable college. It is a piece of typical illiterate nonsense to say that collegiality is the leadership of a peer group who take decisions together. Collegiality is only an element of one-man rule that appears in the ruler's special apparatus of personal power. If one couples 'one-manmanagement' with 'collegiality' the second isn't even a partner with equal rights. The illusion that one can have a constant collegiate leadership arises because after a change of leadership the new leader has not yet got into his stride and has not yet set up his own apparatus, has not yet placed his own men everywhere, is still taking account of the comrades who have brought him to prominence, is still dealing with them. At the end of this transitional period it at first seems to his comrades that a lot of good norms have been destroyed. (Actually there are no such things.) But soon the situation becomes stabilized and everyone takes up his natural place in the *de facto* collegiate leadership. One must recognize that these people do function to a great extent in consonance with the ideals of power, as far as the routine business of the ruling body is concerned. The limits of collegiality are revealed only in exceptional cases when especially important matters come up for decision or when the personal fate of the ruler is at stake.

THE FORMAL OPERATION OF POWER

Power as it operates formally in Communist society presents a complex picture, not to say, a confused one. The picture also contains contradictions, since it seems to include completely incompatible styles of behaviour. I will isolate two important ones: the routine-bureaucratic and the voluntarist. For the second the expression 'creative-volitional' would be appropriate, provided that one did not necessarily associate anything positive with the word 'creative'. In the first case we are speaking of the everyday activity of the power apparatus in which people's behaviour is determined by laws, instructions, traditions and skills. Here little depends on the people themselves, if we leave out of account the ubiquitous and never-ending struggle waged according to the laws of communality. If, for example, you need the most innocent piece of information or certificate in the most run-down office, where they make you go several times and wait for hours, although the manager is dreaming away in an empty office, or if you are made to humble yourself ('who do you think you are?'), this is a normal situation for the citizen of a Communist country and an indispensable element of the authorities' work routine. If you have had to give a bribe or write a complaint, this is also in the order of things. From the point of view of the way power functions this is normal routine. Of course, even in this aspect of power unexpected and exceptional things happen, when the government is compelled to use its wits and take non-standard decisions. But these are exceptions which affect only rather unimportant matters. The authorities find some sort of solution fairly easily. Not necessarily a positive one. Not necessarily a good one. The main thing is that they have taken a decision of some kind. Here the important administrative principle is to harm itself as little as possible if it cannot get anything out of it and to take as little risk as possible if it must take any risk at all. In the second, voluntarist, case we are concerned with matters that have not been foreseen in directives, with extraordinary and very important events which place a very heavy responsibility on the authorities as regards their response. Here some intellectual effort and will-power are needed, and there is a risk that the consequences of the decisions taken might be unpleasant and even catastrophic.

In the Soviet Union in Stalin's time the voluntarist type of administration was the prevalent one inasmuch as the new society had only just been formed and even problems such as the receipt of an order for a stool or a pair of trousers required some voluntarist creative initiative. During that time a routine-type administration which owed much to the rich experience of the Russian Empire was also being established and it is this routine type of government which is prevalent in the Soviet Union today. But even in the most peaceful and successful years extraordinary situations are continually arising which give constant nourishment for the voluntarist approach. There is every ground for regarding such situations as the constant *sputnik* of Communist society, in which crisis-management is the norm of everyday life. This is of the utmost convenience to the government. All their governmental defects can be attributed to external difficulties, the arrival of the promised Communist plenty can be postponed indefinitely and opposition elements can be suppressed. From the point of view of government behaviour the voluntarist style has its great merits, which tempt countless officials to repeat the golden Stalinist years: golden, that is, from the point of view of the unruly exercise of power.

DECISION-TAKING

The decision-taking situation in which the top man finds himself in the course of his work is a complex phenomenon. It includes the substance of the problem, the reasons why it was formulated, the means at hand to take and execute decisions, the stuff of the decision (what does it apply to?), the receipt and evaluation of information, the weighing of the decision and its consequences, and the act of will itself. All of this can be embodied in one person, in a group of persons, in a complex institution, or in a system of institutions. The situation is not some kind of academic task in which a man can be replaced by a machine. What we have here is the real life of real people with all its attributes, and people will never relinquish it to machines. This life is more real for them than all the other aspects of their activity. They use machines but only as auxiliaries and not as deputies. Real life makes itself felt especially in those cases where the decision-taking situation involves a group of people, which is most characteristic for Communism. In these cases some people supply information which they can present in such a way that it can actually influence the decision in a direction desired by a particular category of people. Experts and advisers form another category of people – people, not gods. Moreover, they are people who value their positions and are afraid of risking them or of being dragged into some kind of intrigue. A third category of persons takes the decisions, and a fourth executes them, interpreting them in their own way. The decision-takers may have complicated relationships among themselves that can end up in conflict. Each participant in the decision-taking situation tries to avoid risks and to get some advantage out of the situation for himself. Amendments to the intentions of the deciders and the executants will be introduced by those at whom the decision is directed. To put it briefly: in the whole business there is a Gordian knot of complex mutual relationships which can either be cut by the sword of a voluntarist decision or untied according to the rules of this type of situation. These rules are very well known to the participants. Some of them are general rules of communal behaviour, some of them are specifically connected with decision-taking. A part of the rules is handed down from generation to generation as a body of unwritten professional rules; a part of them is entrenched in the system of instructions. There are special rules for the voluntarist form of decision-taking.

INSTRUCTIONS

The vast majority of the actions of the authorities are carried out according to instructions which are worked out to the smallest detail and apply to all of life's eventualities. The speed and pedantry with which the problem of devising such instructions was decided in the Soviet Union is simply amazing. These instructions simplify in the extreme the intellectual activity of people in positions of power and remove from them personal responsibility for the consequences of their actions. But no one, I repeat, can be replaced by a calculating machine. Firstly, the instructions are drawn up in such a way that people in power have a considerable freedom in their decision-taking. Secondly, these people decide how the instructions are to be applied to actual individuals and circumstances. In response to one and the same instruction a man may drag out the solution of a problem and frustrate it, or he can speed up the process and make the decision positive.

An instructional system is not a specifically Communist instrument of power. It is merely developed under Communism to monstrous dimensions and becomes very supple in relation to the interests of the people in power and of power as a whole. Besides, in Communist society instructions can easily be cancelled and replaced by others, depending on what seems to be in the best interests of those on high. The grandiose system of oral and written instructions makes the whole instruction system fairly indeterminate, so that cases where the powers-that-be freely disregard their own instructions are just as common as cases in which they follow them pedantically.

DIRECTIVES

The instructional apparatus is supplemented by the specifically Communist instrument of the directive. The directive is a special kind of decision by the organs of power which obliges subordinate organs of power or any particular group of subordinates as such to execute a certain number of measures in accordance with the directive imposed. It acts as a signal. The concrete measures that subordinates are obliged to take are not indicated. The executants themselves are given the possibility of deciding which actions will satisfy the directive and which not, and have enough experience to understand the essence of the directive and to follow it.

Let us take, for example, a directive to improve youth training in the sector of material production which we spoke of earlier. No matter how the directive is formulated, its meaning is clear to a huge apparatus of officials of all sorts: 'use all means to prevent young people leaving the villages'; 'young people in the towns without privileges or connections should be compelled to do the kind of work they are extremely reluctant to do of their own free will'. This directive is implemented by countless actions of the authorities, each of which would be normal on its own but which, taken together, express an important social governmental line. Directives of this kind are continually issued from above in all important sectors of social life. The whole official press is full of them as well as radio and television. Things which from the outside are regarded as nonsense or just propaganda in reality express in a special language, understood by everyone in power, directives which are coming from the highest authorities. Besides, many important directives are distributed without publicity in the form of secret written or verbal orders. In conjunction with the standardized experience of the rulers and with the instructions to which we have referred, this system of directives secures a uniform and conformist behaviour on the part of all the links in the power chain and of everyone who executes that power.

In case of necessity a directive may be easily cancelled or superseded by another directive, and the power apparatus will react quickly to this change. The directive leaves its executants a loop-hole so that they may get round it and at the same time pretend to follow it. In exactly the same way, a cancellation of a directive leaves the executants the chance to carry on the old line to some degree. So the appearance of a directive and a modification of it do not infringe the laws of fluidity in social processes. The directive allows the executants to act with due regard to concrete conditions in their sphere. Of course, in the myriad actions of those executants 'mistakes', 'miscalculations' and so on are normal phenomena. But usually they do not have catastrophic consequences and are gradually smoothed out in the course of life. The higher authorities are rid of the responsibility for any undesirable consequences of the implementation of the directive, for they can always represent them as consequences of faulty implementation and not of the directive itself. The latter is always formulated as an intention to make improvements in a particular sector of social life.

The force of the directive lies in the fact that it doesn't presuppose any serious scientific forecasting or calculation. It emerges from the decision-making organ of the social organism. It is an internal directive applicable to any conceivable situation in which the social organism might find itself. In relation to things that are going on it is *a priori*, worked out exclusively with regard to some general strategy of behaviour. For the Soviet government this strategy is the state ideology, i.e. Marxism-Leninism. Critics of Communism, sovietologists and Western politicians are very sceptical in their attitude and very ironical about Marxist ideology, but the fact remains that this ideology has been worked up into a Soviet state ideology and is more than adequate for the purpose of producing a definite system of *a priori* directives.

Of course, some kind of information from outside is needed as the basis of a directive; and some kind of elaboration and evaluation, some kind of recommendations. But in all this the *a priori*-directional aspect predominates. This has indisputable advantages for the powers-that-be. It excludes mistakes and miscalculations because the concept of *mistake* cannot be applied to it. The directive expresses the aim, the wish, the will to attain what is wanted at any price. Here the concept of *success* can be applied. If a sufficiently firm implementation is given to a directive it will somehow or other meet with some kind of success. This is very convenient in complicated situations when it is scientifically impossible to foresee the future. In these cases the directive justifies the actions of the authorities and provides them with some kind of orientation and confidence. The authorities can always interpret any successful results of their blind actions *post factum* as the implementation of some rational intention and in one way or another make use of any results in their own interests.

Some directives remain operative for a long time and form the 'general Party line' at a given stage in social life. An example which still remains in effect in the Soviet Union is the directive about the country's industrialization and militarization. Other directives have the character of short-term campaigns and are the customary form of Soviet life.

Not every social system, country or group of countries has the means to create special-purpose directives as an organized form of behaviour and to follow them for a fairly long time. The Communist system is not only able to do this, it cannot last long without such behaviour. If the Communist system lacks a purposeful directive, it will be at a loss. If this goes on for long enough, the system will begin to go downhill and even fall apart. The purposeful directive is an objective element in the organization of society.

Short-term directives can be occasional, adventuristic and futile (remember, for instance, the maize directive of Khrushchev's time). But long-term, general directives are a serious matter. They flow from society's objective tendencies and are introduced into life via a complex system of people and institutions, and in especially important cases by the whole organization of social life. In such cases directives gain the force of social inertia. When this happens only extraordinary obstacles can stop the movement of society in the direction laid down by the directive and cancel or weaken it. In principle it is possible to distinguish between long-term and short-term directives and as a result predict the possible actions of the Soviet government fairly convincingly. The invasion of Afghanistan by the Soviet army, for example, could have been foretold by anyone who was paying attention to the foreign policy of the Soviet Union and who knew the situation in Afghanistan. Although this task was primitive in its simplicity, the Soviet intervention took the West unawares; and one of the reasons for this is an inability to regard the behaviour of the Soviet government in terms of an appropriate and adequate system of concepts, in particular an inability to understand the directive as an integral form of behaviour on the part of Communist power.

It is a mistake to think of the directive in terms of the purposes which individual people or groups have when they agree and co-ordinate a plan of action. The directives are indeed elaborated by individual people and individual people secure their acceptance as guides to action. But at the same time a social mechanism is working whereby individual people are selected by the force of circumstances as representatives and exponents of the directive, which for them is a compulsory force emanating from the social whole. It is a matter of chance that the choice should fall on one person rather than another; but that certain people will be cast in the role of representatives and exponents of the directive one way or another is not a matter of chance. Social problems which beget directives are usually so obvious in their manifestations that even simple-minded people can see them. In this case the intellect of the rulers is more than up to the task.

TOWARDS A CONSENSUS

No matter what form the behaviour of the authorities might take, in instances deemed sufficiently important (and this will be determined in each specific case by experience) a principle operates whereby decisions have to be ratified by higher authority, or if there is no higher authority, agreed by the various sectors of the apparatus which, for whatever reason, have been connected with the issue at hand. The essence of agreement is not the discovery of the best variant from an abstract point of view, but in a resolution of the problem of the relationships between people in power in the situation in question. Of course, the intrinsic interests connected with the matter in hand do play a role and it would be a mistake to dismiss them entirely. But the issue itself merely provides the context in which people have to solve their social problems; i.e. decide how to preserve or strengthen their social positions, avoid danger, harm their colleagues and so on. For this reason ratification is often a fairly long and painful process. Its essence is especially graphically revealed when candidates are elected for responsible positions. For example, for many years there were no heads of certain divisions in the Central Committee of the CPSU: their functions were carried out by deputies. Often the choice of the director of an institution can take years, although there are more than enough competent aspirants. The point is that in circumstances like these the interests of many important people and organizations intersect and an agreement cannot be found that satisfies everybody's requirements. At the highest levels the problem of getting decisions agreed is only too familiar. At times the struggle takes such sharp form that the voluntarist methods of Stalinism begin to seem beneficial. Even in ultra-important matters the agreement procedure drags out the decision-taking for long periods, so that the decisions lose all sense or are obliterated. So it is no accident that, in such a seemingly careful system of power as the Soviet one, impulsive actions produce an impression of blindness or personal whim. These are the occasions which witness a voluntarist breach of the hopelessly dragged-out agreement procedures. Then the authorities drop their 'gradualist' directive behaviour and dull bureaucratic routine and become outright adventurers.

THE SYSTEM OF SECRECY AND DISINFORMATION

The system of secrecy is one of the essential features of Communist power. It penetrates the whole life of society. Closed sessions, meetings, directives, councils and deliberations, signed statements about non-disclosure, passes, rights of entry. The functions of secrecy are fairly transparent. The first aim is to hide what happens from strangers and from one's own people and to reduce to a minimum the extent to which people are informed. The badly-informed individual is easier to rule and manipulate. Further, secrecy renders demagogy as well as disinformation and the lies of propaganda less open to attack. It confers more significance on the powers-that-be in the eyes of the uninformed mass. Secret decisions work more powerfully on the masses. Rumours of them get about in one way or another anyway, and are sometimes spread on purpose by the authorities. In conditions of secrecy and of exclusivity and with the operation of a pass-system one can call people to justice on charges of 'divulging state secrets', 'slander' and 'collecting information'. People live under the threat of such actions, which is more effective than the actions themselves, for the latter quickly reveal their absurdity and the absurdity of the whole system of secrecy.

The system of secrecy is supplemented by a system of disinformation which is carried through so completely that even its instigators can no longer draw a line between fact and fiction. Here it is interesting to note that it is not so much intentional deceit that is at work as an inability to know the truth because of the social conditions in which information functions and of the state of affairs to which information refers. Besides, a standardized attitude towards events, an orientation of people's attention, a system of evaluating information, a use of language evolve in such a way that disinformation and deceit, including self-deceit, are an inevitable consequence even when people are trying to establish the truth. In this milieu they lie even to the advantage of the enemy and to their own disadvantage. In my books referred to earlier I look into this problem in considerable detail.

BUREAUCRACY

Bureaucracy is not necessarily an evil, and absence of it is not necessarily a blessing. The apparatus of government and power is not in itself a bureaucratic apparatus. People and organizations who compose a bureaucracy are divided into two groups: those who deal immediately with people, and those who deal with paper: that is laws, decrees, instructions, certificates, reports, directives. The director of a factory or an institute, the head of section in a factory, a divisional commander, the secretary of the regional committee of the Party are not bureaucrats, although they are officials of the power and government apparatus. The bureaucratic apparatus in the proper sense of the word is formed by people and organizations connected with the second of the groups I have just mentioned. One must put the question in this way: what place in the Communist system of power and government does the bureaucratic apparatus occupy? One usually associates with the word 'bureaucracy' some sort of red-tape and paper-games, conducted, moreover, for their own sake and without reference to the living people who, in theory, the functionaries should be serving. In this sense of the word, bureaucracy has always been a subject for the mockery of writers, artists, journalists and even politicians. However, bureaucracy is an indispensable element in the life of any well-developed society. The interests of living people can be ignored without bureaucracy. In the Soviet Union, for example, millions of people were at one time subjected to the most inhuman oppression without the slightest bureaucratic red-tape. Bureaucracy is not a specific characteristic of Communist society, and it is not an important actor in it. The important role in the power and government system is played by the people and organs of the first group. They act in accordance with communal principles and with the principles of their profession, about which we spoke earlier. Therefore every kind of instruction and regulating document is usually ignored or else interpreted in the light of how it corresponds with this or that directive currently in force.

Communist society is not a society based on the rule of law. It is nearer in its nature to a voluntarist system, i.e. a non-statutory system of power and government, and the form of execution appropriate to it is the directive. Bureaucracy is really a social form better suited to countries which have democracy of the Western type. Although it brings with it a whole series of negative phenomena repugnant to most members of society it is nevertheless the sign of a juridical society. Thus one should not regard the Communist system as a bureaucratic one, although its bureaucratic apparatus is enormous. Red-tape and formalism (bureaucratism) are greatly developed in Communist society; they do not derive from the bureaucratic apparatus but from the general system of power and organization of the government of society. What is absent from this system is personal interest in the speediest and best solutions of problems: what is present is the personal effort to avoid risk and responsibility.

COMMUNIST ADAPTIVITY

I will mention one more quality of Communist power: its most unusual adaptivity to circumstances. This adaptivity is of a special kind. It is not only found in the ready ability to change course in the light of circumstance. It is also the capacity to interpret and turn to good account any consequences of its own unwavering, directive-guided path. Adaptivity re-rationalizes the consequences of its activity in such a way that it begins to seem as if they are the results of a previously thought-out plan; it accentuates what is advantageous and can be interpreted as a success. Moreover, it is not only restricted to the world of words, thoughts and propaganda. The activity of power itself is stressed in this way so that people become bound to a particular way of life. And this is normal, because under Communism the initiative in social activity lies with the government. A society that is ruled by such a power is like a solitary traveller who can regard only movement forward as correct since it adds up to some kind of progress. For such a government the only important fact is that it governs, even though it pretends that it is leading society to 'full Communism'. The fictitious character of the 'final' goal is no accident. For power the only important thing is to remain intact as power and to play a role. It therefore adapts to circumstances by making them adapt to it and not the other way round; consequently it expects no favours, either from nature or from society, or from the human being. It is the crown of creation and the centre of the universe. Everything else must adapt to it and be subject to its will.

This quality of Communist society, alongside others (including its effort to penetrate to all places in space) allows one to regard it as a malignant growth on the body of civilization. Communism spreads and moves along the line of least resistance. Absolutely everything that happens with and to it is its own success. It knows neither mistakes nor defeats. The ideology of this society justifies any behaviour on the part of its leadership. No one suffers from the pangs of conscience, because phenomena such as conscience and other elements of morality are quite absent from the nature of Communism.

THE PUNITIVE ORGANS

The functions of the punitive organs seem obvious. There is a very large literature about them and their activities in Communist countries, and I do not wish to repeat what has been said elsewhere. I would only remark that one finds in these descriptions much exaggeration and a distortion of their social status. This is explicable: the victims have had immediate contact with punitive organs and project all their hatred upon them, just as soldiers associate all the burdens of army life with sergeants and petty officers and not with officers and generals. The punitive organs themselves are concerned to inflate their own importance. The real rulers of society, whose executive arm these organs are, also have an interest in inflating their importance for well-known reasons: to exculpate themselves from their 'dirty work' and to place the blame on others, as well as to inspire fear in the population.

The punitive organs are only the punitive functions and powers of the commune, alienated from them and generalized on the scale of society as a whole. It is not the punitive organs which force the citizens into a certain form of behaviour. It is rather communal relations which beget the punitive organs and give them the force which then appears to be a mystical and evil force proceeding from somewhere 'above'. The evil of the punitive organs is only the quintessence of good imparted by none other than the citizens of Communist society.

LAW

Communist society does not live under the rule of law. This doesn't mean that arbitrariness or lawlessness reigns there or that there are no norms whatsoever regulating human behaviour. There may be more norms in Communist society than in other societies, for it is indeed a normative society. It has its own order and its own legality. But not everything that is normative or legal is a sign of the rule of law. Legal norms are only a particular case of the norm. In general norms are authorizations, vetoes and obligations to do something or not to do something, and their negations. But all this can take place in a form that has nothing to do with the rule of law.

A society under the rule of law is characterized by the existence of a code of law, or aggregate of legal norms, which embraces all the spheres of the life of that society. This code does not exist only on paper, it actually operates. This means that citizens arrange their lives within the framework of this code and in their actions take account of it in advance. They preserve the code and defend it from those who wish to destroy it. There are special institutions and persons who bring about its execution and see to it that it is observed. Society itself is interested in the code of law and is capable of following it to some degree or other. A society may have a beautiful code of law on paper but neither the wish nor the strength to observe it in practice. Such a society does not have the rule of law. A society without the rule of law is not necessarily one in which legal norms are infringed. It may be a society in which there are simply no conditions in which legal norms can function: they are deprived of sense. For example, if there are no capitalists in a society, a law which regulates the relationship between capitalists and the workers they hire is deprived of sense. These laws are not broken: they are simply devoid of meaning. Something similar happens to codes of law in general in Communist society, whatever form they might take. But let us establish what we have in mind when we speak about legal norms.

The term 'law' has more than one meaning. People often call any old law of society 'law' (for instance the legislative compulsion to do work in Communist society is considered to be a legal norm) and even customs, such as 'the right of the first night'. But here I am giving the term 'law' only to that aggregate of norms of behaviour that are consolidated in the form of laws and those means of applying them that satisfy the following conditions: 1) Real law knows no exceptions; 2) A law which permits somebody to break laws is not a norm of law; 3) Law knows no privileges: before it all citizens are equal; 4) Law is indifferent as to its object: whether that be an individual person, a group of people, representatives of the authorities or the organs of power; 5) Law as such gives no preference to any of these; 6) Law allows no false rumours and no variety of interpretation. It is literal; 7) Law does not permit equivocation; 8) Even if the observance of law brings harm to society, that is not a basis for rejecting it or for failing to observe its norms; 9) The organs of jurisprudence are independent of power. In a sense they stand above society. There are other tokens of law, but I will limit myself to what has been said. Of course, in real life the principles of law are nowhere and never observed in their entirety, but in a society under law there is at least an appreciable tendency to obey the law; there is a possibility of fighting for its observance.

What is the position with respect to the fundamental principles of law in Communist society? The principle that the interests of the collective are higher than the interests of the individual is an obvious form of non-legality, however good it may seem to some people. Those in positions of power are brought before the courts for their crimes only in exceptional cases and have advantages over ordinary mortals. Different criteria are applied to different categories of people. One and the same crime is evaluated differently according to who committed it. The representatives of the privileged classes can always slide out of the application of any law which is binding on the non-privileged classes. For example, in real life neither the law about universal military service nor the one about compulsory work-service before entering an institute applies to the children of high officials. Laws allow of different interpretations. They are surrounded with a system of supplementary instructions and explanations, thanks to which their application becomes a matter of judicial arbitrariness. In a huge number of cases the powers authorize, or forbid, the bringing to trial of accused people. Moreover, they tell the judges in advance what the punishment is to be. The formal legal proceedings themselves are instituted in such a way that the principles of law can be destroyed with impunity at any point. In short, it is hard to name any element in the practice of law which would not be destroyed in the Communist system. And, most important of all, there are simply no significant groups of people in the country who are interested in the creation of a genuinely juridical environment.

One cannot say that, in Communist society, a person is completely defenceless *vis-à-vis* the authorities, other people or the collective. Indeed an individual *has* the means of defence. But his means of defence are such that he is badly defended precisely against these means of defence. This isn't a play on words. History knows many examples of town-dwellers and whole regions being the victims of the violence of friendly armies which have been invited to defend the citizens against the violence of other people. It is merely that in the very complex Communist society this sort of conversion of defenders into violators happens in very indirect ways.

Of course, it is true that on very many occasions something operates in Communist society that resembles the rule of law, but these are insignificant cases seen from the point of view of the social structure of society. But as soon as something touches serious matters, considerations and activities come into play which have absolutely nothing to do with legal ones. Soviet life and the life of other Communist countries have given so many glaring examples of this, that I need not say anything more on this subject.

The non-legal character of Communist society is conditioned by the most basic principles of its existence and of the nature of its power. Norms which regulate people's behaviour do not function within the framework of legal principles but within another framework: that of the principles of state expediency, the interests of the collectives and of the country. Moreover, the powers usurp the functions of supreme judge when they establish this framework and when they evaluate people's behaviour from this point of view. Special norms, skills and traditions regarding the application of written norms to people's behaviour are worked out: i.e. secondary norms of behaviour.

The general scheme goes something like this: 1) there are some written laws; 2) there are definite norms of applying them depending on the actual people who fall within the scope of these laws, on the interests of the collective or of wider entities, right up to the scale of the country as a whole; on the directive operating at any given moment or the ideological campaign running at the time or simply on actual circumstances. Whereas the norms of the first category still remind one of legal norms, the second are clearly of a different order altogether. Moreover, the very existence of norms of the second category bears witness to the fact that a system of 'legality' is indeed in operation, and not anarchy; but that the system is a specifically Communist legality and not law.

IDEOLOGY

Ideology plays such a significant role in Communist society that the society itself can be regarded as an ideological society. Here everyone is subjected to the influence of ideology from birth to death, systematically and with a strikingly pedantic consistency. The number of people employed professionally in the ideological field is enormous. The number of people who in one way or another are forced to carry out bits of ideological work is innumerable. Every official is one way or another the transmitter of ideology. In nursery schools, in schools, institutes, universities, technical schools, colleges and other institutions people are given specialized ideological teaching. Millions of people who have finished their education and are working in their own speciality, study in special Universities of Marxism-Leninism. Even more people attend every kind of ideological circle, seminar and lecture. Ideology penetrates all sectors of culture including even the specialist sciences and sport. The flood of ideological texts is virtually inestimable. If one could measure all the social resources allocated to ideology one would reach a sum fully comparable with expenditure on the military or on industry. Many people, at times even the ideological workers themselves, consider these ideological dimensions unjustified, and that the expenditure is senseless.

However, the unbelievable proliferation of ideology in Communist society is not something temporary or artificially inflated. It happens because of inevitable internal mechanisms within the life of the society, and because of its social instinct for self-preservation. From the point of view of the integrity and strength of the society the expenditure on ideology is fully justified. Moreover, it has a constant tendency to grow. Again this is no accident. As the cultural level of a society rises, as living conditions improve, as people become more educated, as an opposition develops and other phenomena that directly or indirectly threaten society's monolithic ideology, there is need for more effort and more ideology, which is unthinkable without an increase in expenditure.

But it isn't only a matter of the quantitative expression of the ideology: the problem is the qualitative role of ideology in society, and from this angle Communist society is an *ideological society*. A whole series of problems arises in connection with this. Numerous circumstantial investigations are needed to solve each one of them, which this book does not in any sense claim to do. I will confine myself to the examination of the most basic of these problems, and in general outline at that. I will not enter into the concrete details regarding the content of ideology and its mode of operation.

The problems are these: 1) what is ideology as distinct from science, religion and morality? 2) the particular features of ideology and its formation in Communist society; 3) Marxism as an ideology; 4) other ideological phenomena; 5) the ideological apparatus; 6) what happens when people are ideologically brainwashed.

I have given a lot of attention to ideological questions in my literary works and in my book *Without Illusions*, to which I refer the reader who wishes to acquaint himself with my ideas on this subject in greater detail.

The term 'ideology' has several meanings. I shall use it here in the following sense. Ideology is a definite teaching, about the world, about human society, about mankind and about the vitally important features of people's lives. A special system of persons and institutions exists (the ideological apparatus) whose task is to preserve this teaching, to adapt it to people's current lives and to impose it on the population of the country, i.e. to compel the population to make the doctrine its own doctrine, to accept it and in some way manifest it in its own behaviour. The population accepts this teaching, not because it believes in its truth or its proofs or that its propositions are supported by experience, but because of social considerations and because it is compelled to accept it.

The task of ideology is the organization and standardization of people's consciousness and control over people by means of the formation of a definite type of consciousness that is useful to their rulers. The ideological apparatus teaches and compels people in certain situations which are vitally important in the life of society, to think, speak and behave alike and in a way desired by their rulers. Here I have in mind behaviour that depends to some degree or other on consciousness. People are 'programmed' to think and act in a particular way. People's acceptance of ideology is expressed by the fact that they will act as society demands, in the form approved by it. A person who has been prepared ideologically and conditioned, i.e. educated in the

Communist spirit, knows how to behave without a prompter and without higher signals from higher up. Finally, ideology justifies, of course, the kind of behaviour which is demanded of people by the leadership.

It is a matter of historical fact that the basis and core of the ideology of Communist movements world-wide and the state ideologies of Communist countries was Marxism, together with various amendments and additions depending on the particular conditions of the different countries (Leninism in the Soviet Union, Maoism in China). There was nothing, however, preordained about this choice of ideology. But since it *has* happened like that it is a fact which has to be taken into account, and henceforth when I speak about the ideology of society I shall have in mind Marxist ideology. It is the most significant form of ideology in human history. When it is taken as an example, the properties of ideology as a whole become most clearly visible. Of course, there is not a complete coincidence between Marxism and Communist ideology. Not everything from Marxism enters the ideology of Communist society as it exists; and not everything that helps form this ideology is derived from Marxism. But we can neglect this discrepancy in our examination.

In order to determine the specific nature of ideology one must distinguish it from science and religion. This is necessary because Communist ideology bears a resemblance to both science and religion. It claims to be a science; and it seeks also to oust religion from people's minds and take its place, i.e. it seeks to persuade people to believe in the truth of the ideology and its teaching about the future paradise in Communist society.

Of course, in real life there are no absolutely pure forms. Religion may fulfil, and usually does fulfil, ideological functions, and it may even contain assertions which are supported by evidence in the same way that scientific assertions are. Such fragments of science can fulfil ideological functions. Ideology can be felt to be something like religion (to this day many people equate Marxist assertions with the Gospel truth). It may also contain scientific concepts and statements. An ideology may develop with scientific pretensions, as was the case with Marxism, and it may adopt a scientific stance, make use of scientific data and even embody such data. But all the same these three categories, ideology, science and religion, are in principle distinct.

When I assert that Communist doctrine, Marxism, *isn't* science and *is* ideology, I am not insinuating anything defamatory against Marxism or demeaning it. Ideology is no better and no worse than science. It is simply a different phenomenon, with different aims, different laws of operation and formation, different mechanisms of self-preservation and a different way of impinging on people's consciousness. When I state that Communist Marxism is an anti- religious ideology I do not wish either to praise or to condemn it. I am merely stating a fact about the difference in principle between ideology and religion which has become noticeable only recently with the emergence of anti-religious ideologies. Besides Marxism one could mention in this regard National Socialism in Germany. This fact forces us to distinguish between *ideological* and genuinely *religious* functions in the religions of the past.

IDEOLOGICAL WORK

Ideology is not only doctrine. An ideology is kept alive by the everyday activity of people in the ideological field. As I have said, a powerful ideological apparatus is soon installed in Communist society which penetrates the whole of society and reaches with its tentacles into the consciousness of each individual person. The activity of this apparatus is not a matter of this or that campaign, although there are ceaseless ideological campaigns at national level and at the lower levels right down to the primary collectives. It is never-ending, humdrum, routine work. Party organs at every level jealously see to it that the work is systematically carried out, because it is one of the most important, if not *the* most important, aspects of Party work in general. With rare exceptions, all ideological work is done by members of the Party and by the *Komsomol*, who have gone through a special training in it and who are particularly reliable. There are times when non-Party people are brought into it, but this is only for specific purposes and under the control of Party members. Usually they are people who are being prepared for entry into the Party and are being coached in the ideology.

What are the functions and activities of the ideological apparatus? Leaving aside its workers and the professional ideologues and their personal ambitions, the apparatus as a whole fulfils the following functions. The first is to acquaint the citizens with officially recognized ideological doctrine, to force them to acquire at least the basics of the doctrine and to force them to accept it. The doctrine in its essential features is set in its mould and isn't subject to serious changes. Nevertheless, certain changes are made in it, sometimes fairly considerable ones, as for example happened when the slogan 'dictatorship of the proletariat' was annulled. Important Party decisions are taken which become part of the ideology for some or other period of time. The leaders make long speeches with the intention of leaving their mark on the ideology. Important events happen in the world which are reflected in ideological teaching one way or another, if only as fresh illustrations of stale old truths. So the theorists have ceaselessly to renew the teaching and the citizens have ceaselessly to assimilate it in its renewed forms.

The means of compelling citizens to adopt the doctrine are very simple: exams, participation in seminars, written work, every possible kind of test such as 'Lenin's test', the *Leninskiye zachyoty*. And whatever people think of ideology they are forced to adopt it and memorize it for practically their whole life. The acceptance of ideology is not simply a 'once-and-for-all' event where someone promises to accept it, it is rather a continual readiness on his part to let people around him *know* that he has accepted it. Just as in the army the soldier clicks his heels, straightens his back and so on to show his readiness to obey his commander, the citizen in

Communist society must from time to time carry out his ideological heel-clicking so that those around him, and the ideological powers in particular, may know that this citizen is in agreement with the ideology.

The second function of ideology is to watch over everything which is produced in the field of culture: in literature, original art, science, the press and so on. It must suppress everything which does not agree with the ideology and encourage everything that does. Ideology considers everything that doesn't agree with it as hostile and as a threat to its own supremacy and even to its existence. This ideological intolerance makes ideology a close relative of religion. Instances of ideological intolerance in the Soviet Union in Stalin's time are generally known. At the moment there seems to have been some relaxation. But this is only in appearance. In reality the present Soviet ideologues have become suppler and wilier than Stalin's were. Besides, this 'relaxation' only applies to the theoretical 'high ground', not to the mass of ideological workers, and it has had even less effect on the position of the ideologically conditioned rank and file of citizens.

The third function of ideology is to interpret everything that happens in the world, including major political events, discoveries in science and technology, events within the country, according to the fundamental tenets of the ideology. Everything that happens in the world must support the doctrine and happen, so to speak, with its knowledge. To outside observers this kind of interpretation looks like sheer lying for propaganda purposes, although in fact prevarication is not the purpose. The deceit comes as a consequence and then only from the point of view of the external spectator. As far as the conditioned mass of the population is concerned what is taking place is simply a natural selection of information and its interpretation in the light of the generally recognized ideology.

The opinion is widely held that Soviet people are badly informed about what is happening in the world and that they are falsely informed. This, I repeat, is not necessarily the case. It is only a certain point of view about a certain type of information. In fact Soviet people are no worse informed than Westerners about what is happening but they are informed about everything in a certain ideological light. The first task of ideology is to orientate people's consciousness in a definite standard way, to strengthen this orientation systematically and to nourish it with specially predigested food. But this orientation of consciousness is in no way a routine deceit thought up by a band of evil-intentioned people who live in this society and for that society's preservation.

The fourth function of ideology is to force the citizens to be not simply passive observers with a correctly structured consciousness, but active participants in a pantomime organized in a definite way. The pantomime is acted out on many thousands of stages, large and small, beginning with the summit of power and ending in the smallest social groups. Therefore in Communist society people do not merely live, they masquerade, and the task of ideology is to teach them to masquerade seriously and with deep feeling. To accomplish this task ideology has one road to success: that is to release the social forces and direct them into an ideologically controlled channel.

One mustn't think that through the influence of ideology people become oblivious to such a degree that they don't see what they are doing. They are perfectly aware of the character of the pantomimes being enacted, and they *never* forget the fundamental social rules. They play their part seriously and with feeling in situations when the ideological ritual requires them to do so. In the intervals between ideological orgies they are ordinary people and even allow themselves to make ironic remarks about their behaviour and to complain of the rotten conditions which force them to be swine. These lapses are fully compatible with the moments of sulphurous incantations in the official shows: they are indeed a statutory element in ideological behaviour.

I have already said that it is a mistake to regard the ideological conditioning of the population as something artificial. That which seems absurd in relation to the behaviour of an individual person is rational from the point of view of those who regulate the behaviour of large masses of people. The historical paradox consists in this: ideology arises as a socially significant means of bridling the uncontrolled forces of communality, of limiting them by organizing people's consciousness in a certain way. But in practice this bridling process is realized as an unleashing of these communal forces on which the ideology then has to rely for its existence.

IDEOLOGY AND RELIGION

Like religion, Communist ideology aspires to the role of spiritual pastor. But it is, I repeat, different from religion in principle. The psychological foundation of religion is faith, that of ideology is its formal acceptance. I cannot describe the status of religion in detail here, but I will make one brief remark. The phenomenon of faith is a primary psychic state in the individual which presupposes no logical proofs or empirical verifications of the things in which that individual believes, and which does not presuppose external compulsion. It is an inner predisposition to 'recognize' something as really existing, true and necessary. I have put the word 'recognize' in inverted commas because here the important factor is the inner state of an individual and not its external symptoms. Faith is a capacity of man which permits a religious development of the psyche and religious forms of behaviour. The formal acceptance of ideology, on the other hand, does not necessarily presuppose faith in the truth of the postulates and promises, although it is possible to have such faith (as is borne out by the facts). Acceptance can leave people cold and indifferent to what they have accepted. Ideology is something accepted by the mind and through conscious or unconscious calculation of the consequences of one's behaviour and of how to acquire the best things in life. In extreme cases it is accepted in order to avoid the worst. Religion penetrates people's souls and is manifest in their behaviour. Ideology is a purely external element in people's behaviour and not behaviour itself. Their behaviour is determined by other forces, by the laws of communality. Ideology gives them direction and justification, but does not enter people's souls. There is no inner demand for ideology. If the powers-that-be did not insist on the recognition of ideology and on the confirmation of this recognition, people would soon forget about ideology. But they would begin to invent religion spontaneously, and facts of this kind can be observed even in the Soviet Union. This is not a failure of ideology, nor is it a sign of merit. Religion also has its apparatus similar to that of ideology, namely the church. But it was the need for religion that brought the church into being. In the case of ideology things happen the other way round: it is the ideological apparatus that foists ideology on the people as an element in their behaviour and as a means of solemnizing the conformity of the individual with society.

Communist society is an anti-religious society. In itself, I repeat, this is neither a good thing nor a bad thing. What is important is something else: why is this so? Can one explain the phenomenon solely in terms of the evil intentions of nasty godless people who have taken power?

First, one shouldn't idealize religion. There is no abstract religion as such: there are religions in concrete form. In Russia, for example, religion took the form of Orthodoxy, Islam and some others, and it would be in the highest degree unjust to deny the positive side of the anti-religious activities of Soviet power in past years. These activities liberated many millions of people from the snares and entanglements of religious obscurantism. This had a vast enlightening significance. Anti-religious activity has met and still meets with success among the masses, primarily because the above-mentioned forms of religion have proved to be inadequate to the mentality of contemporary man and to his position in society, and not because of compulsion. Force has been applied in the past and continues to be applied in this connection, as in many others, but it is not the basis.

The actual forms of religion with which Communist

regimes come into conflict are only suited to a population with a comparatively low cultural level. Intellectual depths and heights as they exist in religious doctrines are not accessible to the broad masses. Besides, it takes a lot of effort and a large measure of hypocrisy to make these depths and heights appear as such. Communist society can claim virtually one hundred per cent literacy. Almost half of the population, perhaps more, has had general or specialized secondary education. Many millions of people have higher education, many millions are occupied professionally in the sphere of culture. There is a comprehensive network of education and cultural institutions. Propaganda about scientific and technical achievements is widespread. People are continually reading literature which leaves no place in their souls for religious ideas. People lead a dynamic life, constantly moving around in collectives made up of people like themselves. They are compelled to do a number of things in their everyday life that are incompatible with religion as it actually operates, and it is not difficult to show that, in the case of the majority of believers, their religiosity is in practice hypocritical. In short, in the Soviet Union the historical religions are supported neither by the spiritual nor by the material life of the population. Therefore, even if the powers-that-be decided to implant these forms of religion by force, the religions would suffer bankruptcy.

What is more suited to the mentality and to the way of life in Communist society is ideology of the type which is prevalent in the Soviet Union and in other Communist countries (I don't know about ideology in China). I have already told how ideology is foisted on people. Naturally religion which is not encouraged and even at times persecuted in Communist countries cannot compete with ideology which is foisted upon people since birth by a powerful ideological apparatus. And that ideology is essentially anti-religious. Although it does not rely on faith, it uses all the achievements of science and technology and all the means of art and propaganda in its own interests. It is concerned with the same problems as religion, but in the eyes of contemporary man in the Soviet Union it possesses a clear superiority in its treatment of them.

Certain signs can be observed in Communist societies which allow some critics of Communism to speak about a religious revival. The most powerful example of this was the recent events in Poland in connection with the visit of the Pope and in general the position of religion in Poland. I will not deal with the special character of Polish religion. As for a 'religious revival' in Russia, there it is mainly an inadequate form of the expression of social discontent, and also a tribute to fashion, especially in the circles of the intelligentsia. Only in part is it the expression of a psychological need for something like religion. As yet we do not have enough evidence to be able to answer the question whether there can arise from this phenomenon new forms of religion or an adaptation of old forms to the conditions of Communist society. In any case, the fate of religion will depend on its fate in non-Communist countries, and on the fate of those same countries in the struggle with Communism. Experience in the Soviet Union has shown that religion can be allowed in Communist countries if it doesn't enter into appreciable conflict with the Communist order, is content with a very secondary role and lives according to the general laws of Communist institutions.

In brief, ideology in Communist society has the advantage over religion inasmuch as it provides a doctrine about the world, about society and about man that accords better with the type of culture and cultural level of contemporary human beings; inasmuch as it highlights clearly the forms of behaviour without which man cannot live in this society; and inasmuch as it makes man more adaptable from the point of view of the government which manipulates him. The religious individual is unsuited to function in this society both in relation to his neighbours and as regards his own ability to survive. That is why the state supports ideology and converts it into a devastating instrument of power.

Of course, as the population becomes more educated

and as knowledge about the achievements of science spreads, as experience of life in Communist conditions accumulates and is handed down from generation to generation, a discrepancy between the ideological doctrine and the general intellectual and psychological state of the population will increasingly arise. The doctrine is still working but it no longer commands the necessary respect. Just as people long for an improvement in housing, dress, food and recreation, they also long for less oppressive forms of ideology that would not debase their own human qualities and opinions and would even provide some kind of satisfaction. Ideology submits to such demands with the greatest reluctance because of the conservatism of every large and durable system. But, all the same, such a submission is taking place. A significant 'thaw' did occur in the Soviet Union in post-Stalin times and led as a direct result to a reduction in the gap between ideology and the real situation in the country.

IDEOLOGY AND SCIENCE

Communist ideology makes claims to be regarded as a science, to have a scientific basis, to generalize scientific data and to illumine the road ahead for science. As to the reference to illumination, there isn't a problem because ideology is an element in the government of society. But as for the other claims, they are to be explained in terms of the historic circumstances in which Marxist ideology arose, its original form, the spirit of our times, the role of science and technology in our times, the high degree of education and by the whole way of life of the population. Besides, society is not ruled in the name of God, which has become out of date, but in the name of the laws of nature and society, which is very convenient. Nevertheless, Marxist ideology is not a science.

Science and ideology are qualitatively different phenomena. Science presupposes precision, intelligence, accuracy and consistency of terminology. Ideology presupposes forms of language that are meaningless, fuzzy or that are open to several interpretations. The terminology of science does not require sensibility and interpretation. Ideological phraseology requires interpretation, analogy and amplification. Scientific assertions are statements that can be upheld or invalidated, or, in extreme cases, they can be established as being unprovable. One can't invalidate or uphold ideological propositions because they have no meaning. They are nonsense. The expression 'scientific ideology' designates the kind of ideology which sucks the juice from science and adopts science as a mask. But as science ideology is nonsense; it has quite different origins and purposes than those of the cognition of reality. Only when it is compared with some other form of ideology can ideology look like a product of knowledge and instruction. But this status quickly disappears.

To understand scientific literature one must have undergone a long special training and possess a special professional language. Science is confined to a narrow circle of specialists. Ideological texts are for the whole population irrespective of its occupation or level of education. No special training is required to 'understand' them, which really means adopt them. Everything that is unclear is clarified by reference to the same old examples.

The relationship of ideology to reality cannot be categorized in terms of truth and falsehood, but in terms of the extent to which that ideology serves the purpose of conditioning people's consciousness in the desired direction, how far it corresponds to people's general culture and way of life, whether people are adopting the ideology and what effect it is having on their behaviour. From this point of view Marxism is fully adequate for Soviet society. But the main thing is that Marxism is convenient to the authorities as a means of governing the many-million-strong popular mass.

I see no necessity to analyse here the concepts and statements of Marxism from the point of view of the criteria applicable to the concepts and statements of science. A huge literature exists on this score, and I have given numerous examples in my own books. It is not a complex matter to criticize Marxism on this level. But Marxism is not shaken by this kind of criticism any more than it is shaken by the disbelief of the population, and even of the rulers, in Communism's earthly paradise. One cannot invalidate ideology. One can only weaken or strengthen it by weakening or strengthening its influence on people.

THE IDEOLOGICAL FUNCTIONS OF SCIENCE AND THE ARTS

Marxism forms the basis, core and dominant content of the ideology of Communist society. This doctrinal core is enveloped in ideological formations of another kind. It coexists with them and enters into differing relationships with them. The most important of these formations is contemporary science. The point is that science has been converted from being a specialist phenomenon into being the most ordinary mass phenomenon. It is the occupation of many millions of people united into groups and communes that are subjected to the influence of the general laws of communality, even more so than other groups and communes. I described all this in *The Yawning Heights* as follows:

> Contemporary science is not a sphere of human activity in which the participants are concerned only with the search for truth. Science comprises not only learning as such, which is not at all like science in the generally accepted sense, but also anti-science, which is very harmful to true science but manages to appear more scientific than science itself. Science produces abstractions, anti-science destroys them on the pretext that they fail to take acount of this and that. Science establishes strict concepts, anti-science gives them many meanings on the pretext that in this way they will capture the true complexity of reality. Science avoids the use of means which it

can do without. Anti-science tries to include everything it can include on one pretext or another. Science seeks to discover the simple and clear in the complex and the confused. Anti-science tries to complicate what is simple and to present as clear that which is intrinsically hard to grasp. Science tries to establish as ordinary everything that seems extraordinary. Anti-science aims at sensationalism, to impart to ordinary phenomena the character of riddles and secrets.

Moreover, science and anti-science (under other names, of course) may at first be regarded as equally legitimate aspects of one and the same science. But then anti-science gets on top just as weeds choke all cultural growths unless they are weeded out. Within the framework of science, true science is relegated to a rather miserable kind of role. It is tolerated to the extent that anti-science can live at its expense. The tendency is to try to banish it from science altogether because true science is a reproach to the guilty conscience. So when people express the hope that science will play its role in the progress of civilization, they are making a big mistake. Science is a mass phenomenon that is governed absolutely and totally by the laws of communality. Only to a very small degree does it contain genuine science as such. Where communality reigns the element of genuine science approaches zero.

The consciousness of the average educated person of today is informed by a vast quantity of scientific data. He receives it through countless channels (radio, cinema, newspapers, popular scientific literature, science-fiction). Without any question this raises the level of people's education. But all this leads to faith in the omnipotence of science, and science itself acquires features which are far removed from its academic normality. When scientific information penetrates people's consciousness it does not fall on empty ground nor in the form in which it was first given. The man of today has the capacity which history has foisted on him to re-work information he has received into an ideological form whereby an ideological effect is inevitable. The upshot is that science only supplies phraseology, ideas and themes. But how this material will be used by that part of the system concerned with the ideological processing of the human consciousness does not depend on science alone.

One merely has to point out that science is a professional activity; that its results are meaningful and accessible to scrutiny only in a special language. If they are for wide consumption then they must be transposed into common parlance by means of simplifications and clarifications which create an illusory clarity, but as a rule have nothing in common with the material that is being clarified. The achievements of science are presented to people via a special class of intermediaries, the theoreticians of the science in question, popularizers, philosophers and even journalists. They make up a huge social group with their own social tasks, skills and traditions. So the achievements of science enter the heads of ordinary mortals in such a professionally predigested form that only a certain verbal resemblance to the original material reminds one of its scientific origin. And their role has become something different. So, strictly speaking, what we have is the formation of a strange series of twin concepts and scientific statements. Some part of these twins becomes an element of ideology for some or other length of time. In contrast with the concepts and statements of science which tend towards particularity and verifiability, their ideological twins are undefined, ambiguous, unprovable, and irrefutable. From a scientific point of view they are without meaning.

Society exerts pressure on people and compels them to voice respect for science's ideological twins. For instance, many of the propositions of the theory of relativity, which at one time were persecuted as heretical, are now, in their ideological reincarnation, on the point of canonization. An attempt to express anything apparently in contradiction with them meets with a rebuff from socially influential forces in Communist society.

Not all scientific truths are deemed worthy of the honour of having their ideological twin; only those which are suited to an ideological purpose. Thus a certain theorem concerning the incompleteness of formal systems of a certain type which has a meaning in logic finds itself converted into a banal truth, or truism, about the impossibility of fully formalizing science. It becomes extremely fashionable, while another truth about the existence of problems that cannot be solved in principle escapes the public concern, although far greater edification can be derived from it. In this area theorems are demoted and promoted, rehabilitated and advanced. All these appear to be genuine scientific events. In such circumstances ideology desperately wants to be taken for science.

Something similar takes place in the world of art, especially in the theatre, in the cinema, in literature, that is in those forms of art that have the greatest influence on the consciousness of the broad masses. I do not wish to repeat what I have said above, for the general laws of communality make themselves felt with implacable force in this sector of society as well. I will merely formulate a general statement that applies to the whole cultural sphere. It is wrong to imagine that under Communism science, literature, the theatre, the cinema and other areas of culture are under the yoke of the authorities and of the ideology, and that if the latter were absent there would be an abrupt change leading to an evolution towards Western models. True, there is governmental supervision and control over every department of culture, especially via ideological pressure. However, there is only a handful of victims. The fundamental mass of people engaged in the fields of science and art (in the field of culture as a whole) are themselves elements and mechanisms in society's ideological apparatus of power. Art in Communist society, and science too, is governed by official Marxist ideology, and is itself the transmitter of this ideology and its continuation. Art begets its own ideological phenomena which at first glance contradict official ideology but in actual fact coexist with it quite harmoniously. These phenomena (together with similar phenomena arising from science) are even advantageous to the authorities inasmuch as they mask the ideological oppression that actually exists and give an illusion of freedom. Critical works of literature are an example of this: recently they have been produced in plenty in the Soviet Union.

THE STRUCTURE OF IDEOLOGY

Marxism is the core of Communist ideology. But the latter cannot be reduced to Marxism. In Marxism itself one may distinguish a general part and a specific part. The latter is connected with the peculiarities of the new age and of the country in which Marxism becomes the ruling ideology. In the Soviet Union this is Leninism. I spoke earlier about ideological phenomena that have arisen in science and art which are not included in Marxism.

Besides, one can make a distinction between nominal and practical ideology. The first manifests itself in the hypocritical guise of virtue, the latter is utterly cynical. The first is directed towards propaganda and bamboozling people, the second to practical uses. In addition to all this there are numerous ideological groups which arise in very different ways and on very different grounds. The reader can read about them in my books *The Yawning Heights* and *In the Ante-Chamber of Paradise*. Official ideology tolerates such groups as long as they do not threaten it, demonstrate their loyalty to it or adequately conceal their disloyalty. At times officialdom even encourages these groups inasmuch as they distract people's attention from thinking about more serious problems and from active oppositionist work. But all the same, discontent and protest can ripen within such groups too, and the authorities watch them carefully.

IDEOLOGY AS A GUIDE TO ACTION

Communist society is also an ideological society in the further sense that in it ideology is a weapon which regulates not only people's consciousness but also their conscious *behaviour*. It forces people to develop a particular standard mode of thought and action, namely, a practical ideology, which is especially important for the government of society.

Under Communism man lives from the cradle to the grave in a powerful 'magnetic field' of ideological influence. He is a particle in it receiving a particular 'charge', position and orientation. Once created, this field renews and strengthens itself and becomes continually more professional and effective. The important thing about ideology is not what its statements mean but the way of thinking which it inculcates in people. It is an aggregate of models by reference to which the phenomena of reality can be understood. These models are chosen to train people to grasp things in a certain way and to coach them in a standard mode of understanding. When they have completed this training, all who need to understand new phenomena in the real world will respond in a similar manner: they will have developed a common intellectual reaction to their environment. Thus Soviet people, without entering into a conspiracy or being prompted by the government, usually react to events in a uniform way whether they happen at home or abroad. They react similarly to scientific discoveries or to natural events. Ideology doesn't only organize people's consciousness, it creates the social intellect of society as a whole and an intellectual stereotype for individual members of society.

In Communist society one should distinguish two functions of power which in real life are interrelated to such an extent that the authorities themselves distinguish them only in critical periods when attempts are being made to destroy the subordination of these functions: namely, the function of governing society as a whole, and the function of governing the activities of its component parts and subdivisions. The essential purpose of the first function is realized by the activity of the ruling class and organizations and of a good number of citizens involved in them by virtue of whose activities the ability of society to act uniformly is worked out and actualized. This is the government by ideology. What is usually called political rule under Communism is really ideological rule because there is in fact no political rule in Communist society. Ideological government as of right dominates economic and every other kind of government because it is the guarantor of the social organism's integrality.

Ideology, I repeat, has two aspects: the philosophical and the pragmatic. The philosophical aspect relates to its world view, i.e. its doctrine about the world, society, man, mode of cognition. Its pragmatic aspect concerns the practical issues of rules of thought and behaviour. It is in the second of these that we must look for the key to the understanding of the essential significance of ideology. The practical ideology of a society is an aggregate of special rules and behavioural skills which people apply in situations which are intrinsically important. Knowing this, one can predict how the average ideologically-conditioned Communist citizen will behave in such situations. Of course there are exceptions, but they are very rare. Let us say, for instance, that a meeting has to take place in a certain institution with the task of discussing a speech or a book by the Party leader. Before the meeting colleagues may make as many jokes as they like about the speech or the book and tell the most devastating anecdotes about the leader. But everyone knows perfectly well in advance that at the meeting the speech or book will be unanimously appraised as an outstanding contribution to science and literature. Critics of Soviet society usually regard such a phenomenon as an index of two-facedness and cynicism, but they are using moral concepts which are quite irrelevant. All that is happening is that people are acting in strict accordance with the rules of practical ideology and in so doing experience no second thoughts or pangs of conscience; unless, that is, they have some psychic derangement which would, I repeat, be something quite exceptional and can occur in any large agglomeration of people.

The importance which practical ideology has for the activities of the country's governing organs is very great because it contains a whole series of instructions concerning behaviour. In Stalin's time, when the essence of ideology was revealed in all its nakedness, it took on a clearly normative character. In the post-Stalinist period there has been a certain muddying of the ideological waters, which was of positive significance for the preservation of the ideology. At the same time it somewhat weakened the normative side and caused people temporarily to be at a loss. But despite the occasional vacillation and deviation ideology, from the very first days of Communist power, is a practical weapon as regards the general management of society. When the rulers of the Soviet Union say that they are acting in consonance with the teaching of Marxism-Leninism they are not being deceitful or hypocritical. It really is the case. For them Marxism really is 'not a dogma but a guide to action'; but not literally. It has to pass through a definite system of interpretation, which is the proper procedure with regard to ideological texts. Ideology sets before the rulers a general goal which, whether attainable or not, plays a huge organizational role and it indicates the main paths to that goal; or, to speak more exactly, the paths along which society should move in the direction of the goal. Ideology provides a general orientation for the process of social life and establishes a general framework and principles of action for the leadership. Ideology is the core of the whole directive system.

IDEOLOGICAL RESOURCES

Communist society works out its own system of ideological myths, cults, rituals and forms. These include the cult of the leader, the cult of self-sacrifice, the cult of overcoming difficulties, the cult of the enemy. It invents its rituals of punishing the guilty and of encouraging those who have distinguished themselves; rituals to do with every kind of assemblage and adoption of 'measures'. But the sense of all this is very much down-to-earth. For example, the cult of self-sacrifice makes it easier for the government to send young people off to the 'great construction-sites of Communism' and adulterates discontent about difficult living conditions. The cult of leadership strengthens (only to a certain degree, of course) the authority of the government. I will say something in more detail about the cult of the enemy.

One of the general principles of any government is this: the government never errs. All normal people know this principle, but a lot of effort goes into masking it. If a government can hide its mistakes with impunity, it will do so or interpret its behaviour as having been correct. A government recognizes mistakes only when it can't hide them and there are sufficiently large numbers of powerful people or groups of people who are longing to expose these mistakes. Moreover, those who expose the mistakes of government may survive and even gain from the exposure. This leadership principle acquires great strength in Communist society. Here are the chief factors which favour it. Opposition is either absent or minimal. Differences within the government never amount to a split in the government, and if there is a split, then one side is quickly defeated and saddled with the blame for the mistakes of the government in general. The government acts in the name of the laws of nature and society as they have pronounced them. Once that is so, mistakes are excluded in advance. But what is to be done if something in life isn't right? One can accuse the weather, for example, in the case of bad harvests. But one can't always do this, and therefore there is a need of an *enemy* upon whom the fault can be laid for the government's failures. Such an enemy can always be found, both inside the country and outside it. The enemy is selected, or created, in such a way that he can be generally recognized in his role of enemy by the broad masses of the population. The ideological apparatus systematically sets to work to condition the population to this end. Moreover, in this instance the government, consciously or unconsciously (whether from experience or spontaneously), acts in full accordance with the laws of mass psychology: the people themselves are looking for a scapegoat for their wretched conditions of existence. They cannot demonstrate their discontent directly to the government. Many don't understand that the reason for their wretched circumstances is the policy of their own rulers. Many feel there is something wrong with the whole system of life. Many are afraid of repression. Many derive advantage for themselves from the poverty of others. Many take part in government themselves. In short, there is a multitude of reasons why the discontent of the masses is directed into the channels which are most convenient for all: it is like water in a river, flowing where it can flow. And since the necessary channel is chosen cleverly and consistently, things turn out as I described above: an enemy is found whom everyone can identify. The discontent of the population with its conditions of life now has a focus. It can now come out into the open, which brings relief. Examples of this in Soviet history are well known. From the earliest days of Communist society in the Soviet Union the ideological Enemy No. 1 has been something called the West.

The enemy has various functions. Not only can he be blamed for the difficulties of life and be used to channel discontent in a false direction, he also serves as a focus for the ideological education of the nation and as an excuse to rid society of inconvenient individuals and a pretext for ritualistic demands on the population to economize. I have described all this in detail in my books, especially in *In the Ante-Chamber of Paradise*. Enemies are divided into internal and external ones. But usually the two are presumed and proclaimed to be identical. For example, the dissident movement in the Soviet Union is regarded as the consequence of the pernicious influence of the West and of its incursion into the country's internal affairs. The external enemy is inevitably transformed into the internal one and vice versa.

IDEOLOGY AND MORALITY

Communist society is not a moral society just as it is not a society under the rule of law. Moral norms do not actually operate here. The point is not that they have been broken, it is simply that there aren't any. I will explain in what sense I make this statement.

The word 'moral' is used in various senses. In the Soviet Union they talk about the moral cast of mind of Soviet man, about the moral code of the builders of Communism, about Communist morality. It is impossible to forbid this particular use of words. But we have the right to distinguish different phenomena described by the same words and to introduce some precision into their use. I shall distinguish between ideological morality (or pseudo-morality) and personal morality (or real morality or morality proper). Ideological morality is a part of ideology which preaches about what man in Communist society should be and exhorts people to follow this example. It is very like genuine, personal, morality, but in fact it is only morality to the same extent that Communist ideology is a new form of religion. Communist society tries to be moral in the sense of its ideology; i.e. it tries to be pseudo-moral and tries in every way it can to destroy the germ or the remains of personal morality, i.e. of morality in the true sense of the word.

When we speak about morality we must pay attention to

the following: 1) doctrine about what a moral person should be; the norms of moral behaviour and criteria for evaluating both the doctrine and the norms; 2) people's actions which are subject to moral evaluation; 3) people's qualities as influenced by moral ideas and norms and manifested in behaviour that is subject to moral evaluation. Not all teaching about how to become an ideal person is moral teaching. Not all behaviour is subject to moral evaluation. One and the same action in some circumstances is subject to moral evaluation, in others it isn't. Behaviour that is bad from one point of view is not necessarily immoral behaviour, nor is all good behaviour obviously moral. People often do good to other people when they intend to deceive them or to get some advantage for themselves, and they cause evil when they sincerely intend to do other people good. Someone who is *forced* to do good or who has no chance of doing evil *unharmed* is not someone who is acting according to norms of morality.

Man as a communal individual is the sort of being I have already described. And it is naïve to count on people's innate nobility. If people tell you that they are 'not the sort who would do a thing like that . . .', do not believe them. Either they are being hypocritical or they are deceiving themselves, mistaking for innate qualities those limitations on their own behaviour that are forced on them by circumstances, or which they willingly accept for one reason or another. A snake doesn't always bite you, but that doesn't mean that it secretes nectar and not poison. There are objective laws of nature which one cannot cheat. The communal individual is forced, alas, to behave as we have described above; that is neither a good thing nor a bad thing. Virtues only develop as a defence against evil or as one of the means of doing evil. Moreover, good and evil are relative terms if we look at them from the point of view of the individuals themselves who have to live life as it really is, and not from that of uninvolved, self-satisfied moralizers.

The basis of moral ideas, norms, criteria, behaviour and

qualities, is in fact a person's voluntary decision to limit the force of the laws of communality in his own behaviour towards others. I emphasize that the decision is 'voluntary', and not forced on him by juridical norms, by custom or by fear of punishment. Of course, the decision is not something totally disinterested. When a person takes such a decision he assumes that other people value his sacrifice and will follow his example in their relationships with him, and that as a result life in a certain milieu will become better in at least some respects. But that gain is of the same nature as the sacrifice itself. And at bottom sacrifice *is* the motive rather than profit. Any advantage is merely a consequence. Moreover, there isn't always an advantage and if there is it comes afterwards and not before. I would emphasize further that this is a self-imposed limitation on the laws of communality and not of anything else. Not *all* behaviour is committed because of communal laws. For example, soldiers going into the attack and killing enemy soldiers are not acting according to the laws of communality, and their behaviour in the given instance does not fall into a category subject to moral evaluation. The essence of moral self-limitation lies in not doing individual people harm, or else in doing them good even in those situations when you are forced to do them harm or abstain from doing them good by the rules of communal behaviour. People perform such moral actions despite communal forces and in opposition to them. Furthermore, these actions are actions which do not coincide with those of the country's authorities: authorities which have themselves evolved from, and have their basis in, communality. For this reason morality is directed not only against the communal forces at the base of society, but also against the powers in society that personify communality. Morality also is man's self-defence against Communist power.

The ideal man as described by Communist ideology is not a moral being. I repeat that what is moral is not necessarily good and the non-moral not necessarily bad. Here I am excluding subjective evaluations and speaking about real phenomena. Ideal Communist man, whatever he may be from other points of view, is not a moral being. I will adduce some arguments in support of this thesis that are sufficient for this essay. Firstly, Marxism presupposes that man is fully conditioned by the circumstances of his existence and his virtues are deemed to be the product of ideal conditions of life and not of his own free will. Secondly, a person is compelled to be what in theory he should be by the general forces of power, ideology and the collective. Thirdly it is only outwardly that a person is compelled to correspond with the ideal: in practice he is trained in his behaviour by the rules of communality. These last are limited by the collective, by the authorities and by ideology only for the purpose of preserving society which is itself based on communal laws.

In my books I have described the type of man who corresponds to the norms of ideological 'morality', and a good deal of material has been presented in this book as well. Here I will adduce only one hypothetical case which illustrates the difference between ideological 'morality' and morality. Suppose your best friend has committed an act that is officially considered reprehensible and punishable and you swore that you would not give him away. If you told the powers-that-be about his behaviour, you would be doing yourself some good; if you did not, you yourself would be punished should the offence be discovered. In terms of Communist 'morality' you should break your oath and denounce your friend who has put his trust in you. And your action in that case would be justified according to the principle that the interests of the collective are higher than the interests of the individual, although in actual fact you would have been acting according to the rules of communality which compel you to avoid danger and turn everything to your own advantage. Your behaviour would be moral only if you kept your promise – even under the threat of punishment.

Morality in my sense comes into conflict with ideological 'morality' and is persecuted in Communist society as a threat to its very foundations. People are brought up from birth under Communism in such a way that only a few people in their adulthood are capable of being moral beings and even then not all the time. Again I have described in considerable detail in my books the types of self-restraint which serve in Communist society as a source of morality. Here are a number of examples: do not coerce anyone and let nobody coerce you. Resist. Do not humble yourself. Do not be a lackey. Pay tribute to those who deserve it. Have nothing to do with bad people. Avoid their company. If there is no need to speak, be silent. Don't draw attention to yourself. Don't thrust your help on anyone. Refuse undeserved honours. Keep your word. Do not preach at people. Do not gloat over the misfortunes of others. Take no part in power and do not co-operate with it. These, of course, are somewhat literary recommendations. But they are adequate to explain the difference in general orientation between morality and ideology.

Ideological 'morality' has undeniable advantages over morality. It releases people from internal self-restraint. It justifies every crime committed by the country's government *vis-à-vis* the population and against other peoples. The government acts in the name of 'progress', the liberation of the workers 'from exploitation and colonialism'; in the name of building the most 'just' society; in general in the name of the most noble aims. And if in pursuit of these 'aims' there is need to wipe millions of people from the face of the earth, this will be done without hesitation and with a clear conscience, inasmuch as there is no such thing as conscience under Communism.

The lower levels of the population in their turn are compelled by truths and untruths (especially untruths) to adapt themselves to the conditions of life, repaying the torrent of lies and violence streaming down on them from above with lies, idleness, theft, drunkenness, hack-work, and other phenomena of this kind. Corruption, deceit and coercion penetrate the whole of society from top to bottom. In these conditions only occasional individuals, or people who somehow fall outside the general swim, can afford to follow the precepts of morality. For the rules of morality to play a noticeable role in social life, society must contain enough people interested in their observance; and there must be means of defending these rules that are socially recognized, such as publicity, religion and uncensored literature. There is nothing of the kind under Communism. The whole apparatus of ideological education and propaganda aims to teach people to live in an atmosphere of hypocrisy, deceit, coercion, meanness and corruption, and to live according to the laws of communality, which themselves are limited by means devised by communality itself for the purpose of its own self-preservation.

A habit has developed of dubbing Soviet people 'double-thinkers'. But in fact there is no such double-thinking. There is a surprising unanimity of thought, and adaptability to the conditions of life. For example, someone tells someone else what he thinks about the Soviet government and of his intention to 'do something'. He asks this person to keep the conversation confidential. The latter sincerely promises to keep the secret, but then the authorities ask the confidant to tell them about his meetings and conversations with the first person. Of course, they appear to be asking him to help them help this man who has fallen under a bad influence; and the confidant just as sincerely reveals the secret to them. He is not breaking his oath because his oath was purely verbal. He does not possess any self-restraining mechanisms. Besides, when the occasion arises he can always betray his friend without being asked to at all: at a meeting, during conversation at table, perhaps even from a wish to amuse visitors. This is what the overwhelming majority of people do. As a result people are in the habit of calculating the consequences of their behaviour from this angle in advance. People don't believe in the moral qualities of their neighbours and place no reliance on them. This in fact is the deepest source of immorality in society. Of course, there are exceptions, and it is not difficult to find instances of moral behaviour. But they do not determine the pattern of social life. Besides, often in such cases morality merely turns out to be apparent. Often people only pretend to be moral beings or they simply lack the opportunity and the need to present themselves as individuals conditioned by Communism.

The behaviour of the Soviet Union on the world stage as a collective individual is a classic example of immoral behaviour.

It would, of course, be wrong to think that ideology always excludes morality in the sense that we are talking about. It allows it and even encourages it to a certain degree, i.e. to the degree to which it presents no danger to society's foundations but rather supports them: morality, that is, which is secondary and subservient to ideology. For example, it is useful to careerists that there are people who willingly renounce any idea of a career. But if such people elevate their non-participation in power into a principle and begin to propagandize it, they become dangerous to the ideology and to careerists. There are various sorts of social group where people *are* open with each other, help each other and fulfil their promises. But in such cases these beginnings of morality do not burgeon into moral principles because when they are put to the test in serious situations they quickly evaporate by yielding to communal rules and 'morality' of the ideological type.

THE IDEOLOGICAL TYPE OF INTELLECT

The very form of people's lives in Communist society forces them to be flexible and resourceful in the struggle of their daily existence. The housewife who is compelled to keep the body and soul of her family together on a shoestring can sometimes calculate things so finely right down to the last kopek that, from a logical point of view, they exceed the professional intellectual rationalizations of the majority of professors and academicians. The petty official who is desperate to make his tiny little step in his miserable functional career plunges into such a web of cunning intrigue that he makes the machinations of Talleyrand look like the coarse work of an amateur. The ideological conditioning of the population teaches people to be just as flexible and calculating in their thoughts and judgements about the reality surrounding them. The most active segment of the population consequently develops a kind of ideological-dialectical type of intellect. This type of intellect closely resembles the dialectical method of reasoning, i.e. appears to be a scientific method for orientating oneself in the complex and ever-changing system of events in the day-to-day life of society. But in reality it isn't. It is the product of people's adaptation to circumstances, a process encouraged and cultivated by the ideology itself. It is part of ideology's practical mechanics embodied in the intellectual apparatus of individual people.

The mechanism includes lack of principle, the deliberate destruction of the laws of logic, double-think and other manifestations of intellectual prostitution. The dialectical method of reasoning as a *scientific* method is an aggregate of methods for the logical understanding of the world, but not a method of adaptation to social conditions. However, the ideological-dialectical type of intellect is nonetheless more robust than the ideological type of intellect of the ordinary man-in-the-street of Western society. I don't want to suggest that the average Communist citizen is more intelligent than his Western counterpart, but both theoretical considerations and comparative data give serious grounds for stating that the Communist is more flexible and calculating than the Westerner.

So in combination with an ability to live in more difficult conditions the Communist type of intellect creates a higher level of adaptability to circumstances, whatever anyone may feel about this type of adaptability. It isn't only something negative, by which I mean something that only occurs as a result of the disappearance of constraining factors such as the principles of religion, morality and consciousness of law. It is also something positive, something cultivated by the life-style of society and its ideology.

SOCIETY AS A WHOLE

The investigation of such a complex subject as society as a whole presents the researcher with both an analytical and a synthetic task. First he must isolate the components and aspects of the whole, and its special qualities and regularities. Then he has to explain in what way and with what consequences these separate rivulets of social life merge into one complex mainstream. The synthesizing process is not only a matter of incorporating the evidence obtained in the analysis into one text. It is also the searching out of ways of obtaining new evidence from the evidence already obtained analytically; evidence which to some degree or other will approximate to concrete reality. The result of the synthesis should be the discovery of a scientific theory with the help of which one can explain the observed facts of social life and predict the behaviour of the society in certain situations with a fair degree of confidence. But for that to be achieved, the analysis itself must from the beginning pay heed to the synthesis, i.e. the analysis itself must yield up such evidence on the subject as will give the desired result when the synthesizing process is carried out. The synthesis should provide a method of enumerating the characteristics of society as a whole together with explanations of its tendencies on the basis of some primary soundings and assumptions in the analysis.

If one leaves aside the quantitative aspect of the soundings, then the synthesis must be able to answer 'qualitative' questions: what may we expect from a given society, what is it pointless to expect from it, how will it behave in certain types of situation, in what direction will it evolve? For this purpose society must be understood as a great empirical system, with certain more or less constant characteristics; as a particular milieu in which the events which concern us will happen or are likely to happen. The knowledge of these characteristics should enable us to foresee the run of presupposed events in the milieu, the system's behaviour in response to them and its behaviour *vis-à-vis* its own environment. These characteristics are, for example, solidity, coherence, stability, inertia, dynamism, capacity for survival, combativeness and so on. These will be expressed in orders of magnitude or by evaluative concepts such as 'high', 'average' and 'low'. How one establishes the characteristics of the system which I have mentioned above is a question of scientific investigative technique. I shall give a short description below of the method by which I very often used to arrive at my own judgements, but without going into the detail of its logical nature. It is a special variant of systems analysis. Communist society is a particular case of a large empirical system, and should be regarded as such if it is our task to describe it as a single whole. Here are some of the principles of such an approach.

An empirical system is an aggregation of a large number of elementary bodies existing in a given space and time. Elementary bodies are regarded as being indivisible. Neither their spatial dimensions or forms, nor their length of existence need be taken account of. Certain norms are presupposed in their regard. But in the method itself size and length of existence do not play a role. For us the important thing is that the elementary bodies last long enough, renew themselves and possess the requirements without which they cannot be elements of the system. Since elementary bodies enter into frequent and varied 'contact' with each other, there is a process whereby any 'jagged edges' tend to be 'smoothed off', which means that they tend to look alike. This is an inevitable consequence of the huge size of the empirical system and of the compulsory collision of the bodies. In different systems there are different mechanisms of assimilation. From this point of view influence of mass society on the individual, for example, is like the influence of the waves of the sea on fragments of rock. The end result is an average, smoothed down individual, who is in principle interchangeable with any other individual within the same category. This gives us the right to regard elementary bodies as indistinguishable.

In view of the abstractions that we have established only those properties of elementary bodies are taken into account that are indispensable and sufficient for their existence as elements of a system. It is postulated that all of them have these properties in one way or another. People, for example, are able to know their environment, evaluate situations correctly, have wishes, set themselves goals, and act towards their fulfilment. For an elementary body to exist as an element in a system, it must perform certain actions in relation to the other elementary bodies of the system: in other words systemic actions. The elementary body must have the capacity to live in the system and demonstrate that fact regularly. These activities are not analysed: they are taken as given. The process of registering the actions of elementary bodies leads to the introduction of terms designating potential attributes or abilities, for instance, the capacity to speak, think and move about. All the capabilities of elementary bodies can be reduced to a finite number of primary capacities, i.e. of capacities that cannot be defined in terms of each other. The attempt to reduce them to a minimum is natural. Even if one allows that the number of these capacities is infinite, this fact doesn't have any importance in practice. Time is needed for even a single realization of a capacity, and since we presuppose that these capacities will be activated repeatedly, and regularly, the number of primary capabilities of the bodies is in practice very small. Primary capabilities are the regularly realizable capabilities of elementary bodies which are peculiar to all bodies. Deviations from the norm exist, of course, but these should not form part of our theoretical analysis. Elementary bodies are distinguished only by the magnitude of their primary capabilities. Here there are minimum and maximum limits beyond which the elementary body cannot survive. For example, people suffer and die not only from an excess of stupidity and dishonesty, but also from an excess of intelligence and honesty.

Complex bodies in the system are composed of two or more elementary bodies, groups, and groups of groups of different rank. A group seen as a whole has its own dimensions and position in space. From the point of view of the systemic approach the only important thing is the number of individuals or groups of which it is formed. This number is finite. The groups have certain minimum and maximum dimensions depending on the physical nature of the elementary bodies. If the dimensions are less than this minimum, then the links between bodies which would produce a regular systemic effect cannot be formed. If the dimensions exceed the maximum, then the group falls apart; it collapses into sub-groups or a part of it splits off as a normal group. From what has been said it must be clear that the bigger the number of individuals within a given system, the more ranks of groups there are in its hierarchy. Groups are regarded primarily according to the same criteria as elementary bodies. Moreover, phenomena appear within the group by virtue of the very fact of there being a conglomeration of a multitude of bodies in a single spatio-temporal sphere. The task of the systems-approach is to register these consequences of the mass of bodies and events, and indicate methods of calculating their magnitude as functions of the magnitudes characterizing the elementary bodies and groups of bodies of lower rank.

In principle all properties of objects are measurable. I will remark briefly on some of the particular features of measurement within systems. Certain magnitudes are attributed to the primary capacities of elementary bodies. They emerge from observations, from experiments and by agreement. Then, taking these as a starting point, a method is worked out for calculating the magnitude of secondary, derivative capacities. It must be one and the same for all the analogous magnitudes throughout the groups. One way of assigning magnitudes to the primary capabilities of elementary bodies is to use a points system.

Using a points system for estimating magnitudes is widely known: for instance in sport and in scholastic institutions. In the case I am considering we need one scale of measurement for all the phenomena of the system which are being measured on a points system. The number of points must be finite and small. A large number of points makes calculation difficult while adding absolutely nothing to the content or accuracy of knowledge. For instance, in the case of social systems, very often a three-point scale suffices: normal, below the norm and above the norm. What needs to be measured include the primary capabilities of the bodies in the system; the number of elementary bodies (in estimated magnitudes); the number of bodies they come in contact with; the dimensions of groups; the ranks of groups; the ranks of derivative bodies and derivative links, the duration of their influence. In brief, we must invent methods of measurement similar to those used in physics for the measurement of length, width, weight, temperature and other characteristics of bodies and methods of calculation of derivative magnitudes.

I would draw attention to the fact that, in a task of the kind we are considering, it is impossible to obtain a casual explanation of the phenomena generated by the system. Because of the huge number of mutually influential phenomena, it is practically impossible to trace relationships of cause and effect. At the same time the contradictory character of the consequences of one and the same causes, the similarity between the effects of opposite causes and the presence of situations in which some causes level out the effect of other causes, as well as other properties of the system, make a causal explanation impossible in principle. I will instance yet one more curious example of the effect of systems-analysis that works in the same direction.

In an empirical system bodies influence each other. The mechanics of exercising this influence take a certain amount of time and other forms of expenditure for its realization, with the result that there are losses in what is transferred from one body to another (in weight, energy and information). Among these losses there are some constants. If these constants are known then we can work out the number of intermediaries it will take before the

317

force of the influence is totally dissipated. For example, by the time an instruction issued by a director has passed through a number of intermediate bodies, its effect is reduced to zero and consequently is never enacted by the people to whom it was originally directed. This is not because of some chance defect in the institution concerned. It is a normal systemic effect.

The losses of influence in transfer which we spoke of do not conflict with the physical law of conservation, since an empirical system is not an isolated bit of the world but only a special network which is set up in real pieces of the world and partially organizes them. Something always falls out from and is lost to the system: these are inevitable outgoings of the system. But at the same time something enters it from the outside which then is subject to systemic conditioning. So in an empirical system we must allow for cases in which the source of influence of some bodies on others has no causal basis in the given system.

Some of the bodies have the immanent power of producing influence: they influence other bodies by transferring something to them but do not receive anything in return. Thus there are not only forces of influence which dissipate themselves but also sudden primary forces of influence which come from nowhere, as it were. An example of such an immanent entry into the system in the case of social systems is the intentions of the powers-that-be to carry out reforms that raise the level of the organization of society. In the framework of a social system such intentions have no sources or even explanations within the terms of the system. An examination of the system in its other aspects introduces a whole new series of circumstances which render a causal explanation of the behaviour of the authorities and attempts to predict their behaviour devoid of sense. In this instance only probabilistic explanations and predictions are appropriate, and even then they would have to be couched in preferential and evaluative terms. For example, 'relaxations are very improbable'; or 'a rise in prices is very possible'; or 'the authorities prefer repression'.

Explanation in terms of cause and effect in empirical systems is not the only problem. Only serious theoretical research, free from the prejudices not only of the philistine but also of the trained scientific thinker, is able to deal with the task of synthesis which we have been examining.

THE EFFECTS OF SYSTEMS-ANALYSIS

I will give some examples which illustrate the cognitive orientation of the systems-approach. Let us suppose that it has been calculated by certain methods that a harvest of a certain size may be expected in the Soviet Union during the current year. The question arises: how much bread will there really be in that year? Certainly not as much as the harvest. To indicate, and predict the real magnitude we must know some systems-coefficient which expresses the inevitable losses which are due entirely to the system itself. Then one can estimate that in reality the country will have considerably less bread than the academic projections presuppose. Quite apart from the weather and other phenomena, the systems-coefficient operates implacably, because it is itself a function of where people live and the actions they perform. Another example: it has been estimated that a certain amount of money must be spent on the construction of a building (e.g. housing, factory, aerodrome). If one knows the systems-coefficient one can say in advance that in reality it will cost much more . I should add that the authorities are familiar with these phenomena from their own experience and will sometimes take them into account in advance during the planning phase. True, other laws of the system prevent it from operating fully. Besides, a systems-effect of another sort comes into operation: systemic losses that are taken into account in advance do not all the same rid the system of some unforeseen losses.

The general dictum about the behaviour of Soviet people is well known: each individual is against, but everyone together is for. People view this trait on a purely moral plane, which is completely absurd. In reality it is a characteristic example of a systems-effect: each element of the system operates in virtue of its allotted role in the system, but the result of the sum total of their actions can even be opposed to their subjective wishes, because the result is not under their control. This systems-effect makes itself felt with pitiless force in all the links in the social system, at all levels of the hierarchy and in all groups including the higher reaches of government and those organizations which determine the behaviour of the country as a whole in relation to this or that task.

When Western politicians and philistines hope for changes in the behaviour of the Soviet Union as a consequence of changes in government and in the composition of the responsible organs of government, they display total ignorance of the strength of systems-effects. What is amusing here is that they themselves are the slaves of their own system, as is evident to the dispassionate observer. But they apprehend their bondage to their own system as freedom and regard the systems-slavery in other societies not as something different but as something analogous to their own system.

At the present time humanity is naturally disturbed by the question of a new world war. People console themselves with the thought that the Soviet leaders and the Soviet people themselves do not want war because they know that they also will suffer from it, perhaps to an apocalyptic extent. But, alas, this awareness plays no role. People don't start wars; wars start themselves. Relations in a system of government may be such that the outbreak of war will be the end result of individual people who are trying to prevent its happening. The Soviet Union has created an offensive army and conducts an aggressive foreign policy acting in the interests of self-defence. This isn't only propaganda. It is first and foremost a systems-effect that excessive defence turns into attack.

The peculiarity of the Communist system consists in this: it has very weak internal restraining forces and very weak self-control. The fateful consequences of the activities of the Communist system are terrible not because of their premeditation but because of the uncontrollability of the system. It is a gross error to think that everything under Communism is subjected to the central government and to its will. The laws of these relationships do not obey anyone.

The activity of the government organs of a Communist country presents a most striking example of a systems-effect. The members of these organs themselves really think that they are planning the events and behaviour of the country. To the superficial outside observer it seems that there are certain people and small groups in the government organs who are pursuing this or that policy and working out decisions and taking them. More than once I have heard people say that the operation in Afghanistan was carried through upon the insistence of the 'military' and that there is a struggle in the Soviet government between the 'doves' and the 'hawks'; that the 'economists' are in conflict with the 'ideologues' and other rubbish of this kind, all of which demonstrates that the speakers have no notion of systems-concepts when confronted with social phenomena.

In actual fact the government of Soviet society exemplifies a system in which phenomena are inexplicable by conventional concepts. For example, a man who is interested in a certain decision being taken may come out against the decision, knowing in advance that the decision will be taken all the same, that his position in the matter will be well known and that it will enhance his image. The decision-taking by the highest organ of power may be a pure formality, the rubber-stamping of a state of affairs which is independent of it and which itself has dictated the decision in question.

Conflicts between persons and groups about some exalted problem may be nothing other than a primitive struggle for posts. The point is not that there are no inter-personal and inter-group relations, no differences between people and no personal idiosyncrasies or things of that kind. All that does exist. The point is that if you had absolutely all the information about people's character, people's views, people's relations with each other and people's intentions you would, on the basis of this knowledge, still not be in a position to predict the possible behaviour of the country's government as a whole. In order to make more or less hopeful predictions on such subjects, you must throw away all this information as something superfluous and even as something that hinders the understanding of the matter. You should then adopt information about the Communist system of an entirely different kind as a basis for your judgements.

STABILITY, INTEGRALITY AND VITALITY

When I used to make declarations to the effect that Communist society was a stable society my numerous audiences and my conversational partners expressed dissatisfaction with my judgement. They, on the contrary, insisted on the instability of this society, indulging thereby in a totally unwarranted amount of wishful thinking. And yet this society is not only stable: it is in the highest degree stable.

But stability is not necessarily a positive feature of society. Stability may be the result of a low level of social organization, of backwardness, conservatism, destruction of the institutions of civilization or simply their absence. Instability may be the result of a dynamic style of existence, of a high level of organization, of the growth of civilization. This is precisely how it is with social systems.

Let us define the concept of 'stability' itself. The stability of a social system is its capacity to preserve its existing structure, which appears normal to it; the will and effort to preserve this structure and the ability to recreate the structure should there be need to deviate from it for a time. Any social system of a certain size has a tendency towards stability once it comes into existence. But it also produces phenomena that threaten this stability. In the process of the life of a society the two tendencies will be related in a very fluctuating manner. There are no absolutely stable and no absolutely unstable societies. But they differ in terms of the degree of their stability (or instability) and in their means of constitution (or destruction). So far history has given us few data for making categorical judgements about the stability of Communist society. I base my conclusions about its high degree of stability on an analysis of this society as an empirical system and on some principles belonging to systems of this kind.

Communist society is highly stable because of these attributes, among others: 1) the homogeneity of the structure, of all its parts, organs, fabric, strata and groups; 2) the standardization of the conditions of life of the population and of the system of government; 3) centralized government of all aspects of social life; 4) a mighty unified system of power which penetrates all cross-sections of society from top to bottom; 5) a single ideology and powerful conditioning of the population which results in uniformity of behaviour in important situations; 6) the ability of a huge number of people to occupy any government post and to act in a way demanded by the interests of the whole; 7) the absence of a serious opposition movement and the presence of a powerful network of organs to repress manifestations of discontent; 8) the ability to preserve the cohesion of society in face of great losses, i.e. a high degree of durability in difficult conditions; 9) the ability to impose a low living standard on the people for a long time without there being serious protests. If we were to trace how these and many other factors of the Communist system are woven into a single pattern, then the thesis formulated above would have a convincing ring, even without precise measurements being taken.

Communist society is stable to such a degree that forces serious enough to destroy it simply do not materialize within it. It is, therefore, senseless to hope that the internal requirements of Communist countries will give rise to radical changes in this society in the direction of Western countries. As regards stability in the sense of the cohesion of the country, Communist countries dispose of means of securing it unprecedented in history, such as powerful armies, systems of state security, control of frontiers, obstacles to external influences, and so on. Powerful armies are created in Communist countries not only for defence and for attacking other countries, but to preserve internal cohesion and social stability.

The cohesion of the system does not necessarily mean harmony among the elements of the system and its component parts. Within the whole there can be enmity and strife. Absence of conflict among the components does not necessarily strengthen the system, nor do enmities and conflicts necessarily weaken it. It is the proportions which count. And when we examine conflicts of various kinds in the system we must pay attention not only to what divides elements of the system but also to what unites them. In the West, for example, hopes are placed on national conflicts in the Soviet Union in ignorance of the fact that, despite everything, it is more advantageous to the different nationalities to remain components of the Soviet Union than to separate from it. Hopes are placed on conflicts within the government, although these conflicts in no way affect the general governmental line and only reflect a struggle between people for posts in government and never cross the point beyond which they might threaten serious damage to the cohesion of society as a whole. Even the dissident movement in no way threatens the cohesion of society. Indeed, to some extent it fulfils a positive role by informing the government about the situation in society.

Communist society is unusually robust in difficult situations. The Soviet Union has proved this by its own experience. It is possible to give a theoretical explanation of this phenomenon, but not at all in the spirit of Soviet propaganda. When it was preparing to go to war with the Soviet Union, Hitler's Germany gravely underestimated the vitality of the country, although there was plenty of factual information available. True, this mistake was inevitable for psychological reasons: it was wishful thinking. But that does not exclude the possibility that events might have gone differently if Germany's rulers had had at their disposal a trustworthy method of assessing the vitality of the Soviet Union. They would then have been able to establish in advance that the vitality of the Soviet Union as a Communist system was considerably greater than that of Germany as a state based on the capitalist system.

The degree of vitality or viability of a country is a function of many factors. In Communist countries it is high because the living standards of the population can, with impunity, be lowered beyond the limit tolerable in a Western country; because a serious opposition is impossible; because every part of the social organism is standardized, including the ideology; because the government is ready to make any sacrifices while the population is ready to *offer* them. All these elements of social life add up to a high coefficient of social vitality.

However, this quality is not absolutely positive. If the conditions of life in society are comparatively favourable, then a high degree of vitality is a serious obstacle to social progress. In particular, it prevents the growth of productivity. The Communist system was born as a means of overcoming a catastrophically difficult situation in the country; it took shape and stabilized in conditions of chronic difficulty with the result that both the production and the overcoming of difficulties became second nature to it.

At the same time existence on the verge of economic collapse is as normal a feature of Communist society as stability. This state of affairs is conditioned by the whole social order of the country and by the following factors among others. The government is forced to set tasks before the country, each of which seems feasible on its own but which in aggregate are beyond the country's strength. The country is forced to live according to a co-ordinated state plan, but the systems-effect inevitably leads to deviations from the plan, to its non-fulfilment and to unplanned and uncontrolled consequences. The planned economy, standardization, communality, the attitude to work and other elements of social organization bring about a tendency towards a lowering of economic growth and to stagnation. And this in turn heightens the ambition of the government as regards its plans, and the consequence of that is a discrepancy between the real state of the country and the government's perception of it. The ambitions of the top leadership and the self-interest of the ruling classes of the population are satisfied at the expense of damage to the country as a whole. Forces are absent which could restrain society in its movement in a direction that worsens the state of the country, and only the catastrophic results of this movement force the government to take restraining measures.

Thence develops the tendency to solve internal problems at the cost of a rapacious exploitation of natural resources and by the creation of a semi-war situation, by the exploitation of other countries, by deceit, blackmail and theft. It is no accident that the Soviet Union, which possesses a gigantic territory and a vast number of people engaged in agriculture, is compelled to acquire foodstuffs abroad. And who knows the extent of the theft of the West's scientific and technical achievements in relation to the progress of science and technology in the Soviet Union? In any case, progress via theft seems to be economically more advantageous than the development of its own internal forces. Some of the important characteristics of Communist society, the tendencies to stagnation and to economic crises, are weakened at the present time by making use of the Western countries and by colonialism. If the world were fully Communist, these tendencies could become fatally pronounced. So what Communism should fear most is not the coexistence of a competitive West, but its own world victory – not to speak of future military conflicts between Communist countries which will lead to wars entailing the total destruction of countries and peoples.

THE TENDENCY TOWARDS EXPANSION AND HEGEMONY

Everything that lives seeks to preserve itself. The laws of communality are the laws of human behaviour that express the urge to self-preservation. The urge to expand is one of the principle means of self-preservation and self-consolidation for social groups. There are many reasons for this, and I will mention the most important. An increase in the size of the group means an increase in its social significance, and that means an increase in the social significance of its rulers. A group that expands receives more means of existence and deals more easily with its affairs. People's wish to work as little as possible necessitates the performance of the same amount of work by more people. The general tendency of the governing class of the population to proliferate stimulates the creation and extension of governing groups in the least productive segment. The ruling classes have enough power to look after themselves. Innumerable posts are invented for oncoming generations of the *privilegentsia*. A direct consequence of the increasing complexity of the productive and business life of society is an increase in the complexity of the ruling apparatus and an expansion in the number of social groups in the form of new specialists and managers.

The tendency to expand is found not only in existing groups but manifests itself in another direction, via the formation of new spheres of activity and new groups within it. An enormous number of people exert pressure in this direction, all thirsting to improve their social position. This somewhat reduces the intensity of the usual social struggle and gives some hope to youth as regards its chances in life. The tendency to expand is strengthened by a whole series of other stimuli on the scale of the country as a whole, such as the drive to make surrounding areas homogeneous with and similar to oneself; the drive to destroy anything which allows a comparison between Communist life and other kinds of life; the drive to destroy the potential threat of being unmasked and discredited; the drive to subordinate other countries and to compel them to help hide the economic defects of one's own country (for example, by supplying food products). From all this follows the ceaseless attempt to penetrate and spread wherever and whenever it is possible. The ideology justifies this, saying that the most humane and progressive activity of the country is to free humanity from colonialism and exploitation. Over the years the apparatus created to realize this aim obtains such force within the governmental system that it becomes almost impossible to oppose it. No small part is played here by the vanity of the rulers, which is encouraged enormously by the ideology and by the ruling caste. Communist society has no restraining capacity to set against this tendency. It is only external constraints that can (*if* they can) stop the spread of the system throughout the whole world.

The Soviet Union is the first Communist country in history and the most powerful. Communism was installed in the other countries of the Soviet bloc by means of conquest during war: it was foisted on them by force. Therefore the role of the Soviet Union as leader of the bloc cannot be doubted as a historical fact. Its deeper social tendency towards hegemony remains veiled. But yet it is precisely that, plus the tendency to expand, which has determined the present situation in the Communist Imperium.

The tendency towards hegemony over other countries arises from the position of the leadership within the country. In its relationship to other countries it tries to behave as it does towards parts of its own country. The Soviet Union tries to behave in a´ similar way towards non-Communist countries: that is to say, it tries to include them in its own sphere of influence, to subordinate them and to force them into the desired form of behaviour (Finland is an example). A non-Communist country that finds itself in this situation has every chance of being swallowed up by the Soviet Union and recast in the Soviet mould, as in the case of Afghanistan.

The Soviet Union's tendency to hegemony over its own neighbours stems, I repeat, from its own nature as a society and from the nature of its government. The government has an obedient apparatus for this purpose, the army, and it has the experience. It knows how to do it. It is absurd to expect anything else of the Soviet government. The tendencies to expansion and hegemony form together a tendency to convert humanity into a super-society, into one social organism with one system of command: into world Communism. However, according to the laws of large empirical systems, these latter have critical dimensions. So even if Communism is victorious in every country in the world, a split of humanity into groups of Communist countries will inevitably follow, each with its own leader, and these groups will inevitably struggle for hegemony. The present relations between China and the Soviet Union are eloquent in this regard. So it is naïve to hope that the victory of Communism in all countries will lead to disarmament and eternal peace. On the contrary, wars between Communist blocs will exceed in horror all the wars of the past. Moreover, militarization is dictated by the country's internal needs, and of course the threat of war is the best means of settling internal social problems.

The tendency to expansion and hegemony naturally compels the Soviet Union to take full advantage of the West in its own interests; to achieve a noticeable military preponderance over the West; to create a dense network of spies and fifth columnists in the West as well as masses of potential and actual collaborators: in short to do everything possible to turn itself into the governing organ of a single world super-society. The attempt to rule over the whole world is a schizophrenic idea of vain Communist leaders only because the tendency to world-wide rule has an objective existence in the social organism itself. The Soviet Union has already acquired such a momentum of inertia in this direction that only a world catastrophe is capable of stopping it.

THE WAY OF LIFE

If we were to form judgements about life in Communist countries on the basis of the articles of Western journalists, of polemical literature, of the statements made by dissidents, and of the memories of émigrés, we should get the impression that it is impossible for the ordinary person to live in the Soviet Union. There is, it seems, nothing to eat there and nothing to wear, and nowhere to live. One cannot open one's mouth without risking arrest or compulsory treatment in a psychiatric hospital. One can't move about the country or read contemporary books. The impression is given that people do nothing but fight for civil rights, organize religious sects, resurrect Orthodoxy, get drunk and dream about the monarchy, wait for the collapse of the Soviet regime, and of course dream about going to the West. But in fact millions of people lead a normal life there, never even think about the West and are not planning to change their way of life at all. They are born, go to school and to university, fall in love, marry, work, rest, amuse themselves, eat and drink, laugh and cry. Many don't live badly at all and some very well indeed.

Communist apologists naturally give an utterly different picture of their society than the critics. But there is much that is just in this picture too, just as there is in the critics' picture. Where does the truth lie? Not somewhere in the middle, nor in a combination of the apologist's light and the critic's shade. Real life is sometimes colourful, sometimes monotonous, sometimes diffuse, sometimes clear and straightforward, sometimes stable, sometimes shifting. An accurate description of it requires, not the enumeration of all the possible observable facts, but the special methods of science and literature. The way of life of a country is a resultant of all the efforts of all the people in all the cross-sections of society in the course of generations. I have described all these component elements in a fair amount of detail in my books. Here I will merely confine myself to a discussion of some tendencies which exhibited themselves with implacable force in the first years after the war and which now appear as attributes of mature Communism.

The relevant characteristic of Communist life is its despondency, its greyness, its boredom. But all this is enveloped in official *bravura*, festivities and celebration. Everything is grey: the feast-days, the week-days, the speeches, the books, the films, the successes, the defeats, the crimes, the joys, love and hatred. Even the lying, which is meant to brighten life up, is grey. Even on those occasions when people, so it would seem, have something to be happy about, happiness is done to death like something alien to the system. As soon as there is anything to be happy about, the authorities put on a great educational campaign to show everybody the superiority of the Communist way of life. They arrange meetings and sessions, accept greetings, assume obligations, mount special intensified labour campaigns. The country's history consists of speeches, sessions, congresses, meetings, departures, visits, prize-givings, jubilees, anniversaries, plans, accountings, overcoming difficulties. Open any newspaper or journal, switch on the television or the radio. Always and everywhere it is the same, moreover of an amazing monotony and all predictable. Ordinary life is dispiritingly grey and eventless. It consists of the repetition of the same primitive operations, and in part of the slow movement up the service ladder, which slightly changes and colours the daily routine. And the content of the philistine consciousness is quite adequate to this life, it is just as depressed, grey and monotonous. Sometimes sparks of protest flash in people's souls, and it seems that they are about to break into flame. But the days and the months and the years go by. The sparks go out by themselves or friends diligently stamp them out, or neighbours, or colleagues, or bosses, or subordinates, or all together. What is the use of sparks? It's quieter without them. Do your job. Eat your food. Sleep. Give thanks to the government. Wait for things to get better, and don't make a fuss, you won't change anything.

Under Communism everything is made difficult: eating, living, recreation, entertainment, getting ahead, thinking, speaking. One has to fight for everything, by hook or by crook. People talk about temporary difficulties. But the 'temporariness' can last as long as you like because it is a means of society's self-preservation, a means of unity and of government. The individual who is bounded and enmeshed by difficulties is suited to manipulation in mass situations. In this respect the possibilities which the government has for the uncontrolled manipulation of the popular mass and of material resources are really unlimited. The government, in fact, supports and cultivates this way of life, and the kind of individual that suits it, with all the means at its disposal.

The prevalent tendency is a slide downwards. This is something stronger than the 'improvements' which I spoke of earlier. This doesn't mean that life gets constantly worse every day (although it may well do). At the very least it means that, on that downward slide, endemic in the whole of Communist life, those improvements that world-wide progress would normally bring are swept aside. Under Communism people are always aware of the threat of things getting worse. 'If only things don't get worse,' they say. 'If only we can survive.' This sort of mood is a permanent feature of popular psychology: the mass lives in fear of things getting worse – and expects them to do so.

Communist society does offer *some* guaranteed provision of the necessities of life and confidence in the future. So do all societies, including those in the West. But the character and the level of the guarantees are different: and so is the psychological type of confidence in the morrow. In Communist society one has to fight for one's guaranteed security at each and every level. The guaranteed minimum is so low that only people who are unfitted for the all-against-all struggles of communality are forced to be satisfied with it. But a higher standard of living requires the expenditure of all one's physical and spiritual forces. Even at the highest levels everything has to be paid for by a certain form of behaviour which itself engenders boredom. Confidence in the morrow can perfectly well be the bedfellow of continual fear of things getting worse and of catastrophic events. For although the creative force of the powers-that-be is comparatively small, people know that its negative potential is vast.

The standard of living and general way of life depend on the policy of the central government and on its intentions. People can actively improve their position, but only within the framework of a general level of style of life which doesn't depend on them personally. Even the level and way of life of the *privilegentsia* depend on the general state of affairs within the country. One can get a partial idea of this by noticing what the high-ups can have in their special shops. These days, for example, the ordinary shop in the West is far better stocked than the relatively well-stocked special hidden retail outlets in the Soviet Union. The tendency of society to take maniacal measures and the ability of the government to follow them, the general tendency towards grandiose unproductive expenditure, parasitism, adventurism, the setting up of fictitious enterprises on paper, all these and other phenomena I have described have one inescapable consequence: even in very good years a Communist country can have an extremely low living standard and for years on end the country as a whole may live on the edge of an economic catastrophe. The shining example of this has been life in the Soviet Union during the last decades. The population becomes aware that these are permanent features of the system from its own personal experience, and they become part of its own consciousness, its own psychology.

DISCONTENT

Communist society is a society of people who are discontented with their position in life. People accept their own form of life under Communism because it is their own product and the context in which they live. But they are not content with what they accept. Everyone is discontented from the small fry to the high and mighty, from bottom to top. Cleaning ladies are discontented because the workers behave like swine, don't wipe the mud off their feet and throw their empty bottles and cigarette stubs all over the place. The leaders are discontented because agriculture refuses to reach a new and higher level, despite their own wonderful directives to this end and because critics appear who have doubts about their good intentions and brilliance. The workers are discontented because of housing difficulties, the rising cost of goods, especially strong drink, shortages in the food supply, the difficulties they encounter when they try to get their children into higher education, queues and overcrowded public transport. In short, life for the majority of the population is so arranged that there is always a reason for discontent.

Moreover, even if there are no special reasons for discontent at a given moment, citizens are used to doing each other a bad turn just for fun, without any reason at all. A state of tension, discontent, suspicion, ill-will towards others and lack of generosity is the usual psychic condition of at least a considerable part of the population and certainly of the most active part of it. Amongst the causes of discontent the following are very real: the discrepancy between the actual standard of living and the promised one; between real life and life as it is portrayed in propaganda; internal economic discrepancies and injustices; information about the high living standards of the West; difficulties connected with work; the difficulty of changing one's place of residence and in general of moving about the country; the absence of civil rights; the arbitrariness of local authorities; the costly adventures of the top leadership in foreign policy.

I have already said enough about the manifestations and the results of discontent in the Soviet Union in my book *Without Illusions* and I see no special need to repeat it here. I will simply present a few general considerations on the subject of discontent. It takes various forms: direct and indirect, hidden and open, active and passive, legal and illegal. Broad strata of the population proclaim their discontent with their work position and with mass measures by discovering their own individual methods of compensation, through cunning, drunkenness, and other means that form part of their daily lives. Criticism of insufficiencies plays a substantial role at the level of the commune (especially in Party organizations), and in the official press there are countless complaints to the various organs of power.

One may mention among the active forms of expression of discontent those which come from the following categories of citizens: improvers, reformers, oppositionists. The improvers want slight improvements in living conditions in the country as a whole and large ones for themselves. These improvers are a bulwark of the regime. Usually they come from the *privilegentsia*, sometimes from the top leadership.

The reformers want real changes in the country, and also want to preserve the regime. But they want the kind of changes that even the improvers stand out against. For instance they talk about introducing a tenancy-system in agriculture, if only around the big towns, and about industrial self-management. In his time Khrushchev wanted to solve all the country's difficulties by means of maize. The authorities themselves are inclined towards reforms of this type but usually their wish is a vain one. Usually all of it degenerates into idiocies or propaganda sound-effects.

The characteristic criticism brought by oppositionists concerns the foundations of the social order and their manifestations in the lives of people. The composition of the opposition is always heterogeneous and inconstant. Individual members of the *privilegentsia* turn up in it: academicians, professors and writers, and even a few Party officials and generals, and from the lower orders there are workmen and students. However, the opposition is mostly drawn from people in the middle and lower ranks of officialdom, employed in the cultural, artistic or scientific sectors. Sometimes oppositionists advance ideas about deep social transformations in the country, even to the point of advocating the removal of Communism and the transformation of the country on the basis of a nonexistent orthodoxy. But these ideas do not serve as a guide to action; they have no success with the population and are more an object of scorn. The most important thing about the opposition is the very fact that it exists. A great part of it is formed by people who are trying to drag the country back into the past. Such, for instance, are the religious sects, and it is only the fact that they protest against the regime that is persecuting them that makes them something of a positive phenomenon.

In spite of the fact that many people in the West talk and write a lot about opposition in the Soviet Union, its role within the country is fairly pitiful and futureless. The point is that the scale and fate of the opposition depend on the conditions of life within the country and on the extent to which it expresses the interests of this or that group; on the realism of its aims; on the relationship of the population and of the authorities to it. If we take account of these circumstances, we shall surely conclude that conditions in Communist countries are extremely unfavourable to an opposition. If the citizen tries to engage in oppositionist activity as a member of a primary commune, he will encounter in the first instance the pressure of the commune-collective itself. If he does not desist, he will be expelled from it. It is very hard to live without regular wages or a regular salary. Besides, the powers-that-be will immediately prosecute such a citizen as a 'parasite' and force him to attach himself to some commune, but one in a worse place and with worse conditions. This will put an end to his opposition. The population is disinclined to support oppositionists at any cost to itself or to help them, because ordinary citizens simply do not have the means to support them, and it is, moreover, not without risk. If oppositionists unite in a group this is stopped by the authorities on legal grounds. The means at the disposal of oppositionists to influence the population are very limited, and the powers-that-be have the force and the legal right to reduce them practically to nothing.

But the most important reason for the weakness of an opposition within Communist society is the social structure itself and a person's position in society. It is practically impossible to originate a serious programme of reform such as would hold the attention of broad strata of the population deeply or for a sufficiently long period. People are condemned to fight for their own individual livelihoods by their own methods, or through their primary collectives. A whole historical epoch and huge sacrifices are needed to solve the problems which cause opposition in Communist society. That society is still at the beginning of its historic journey. But people want improvements for themselves now or at least for their children and not for remote posterity. The real needs of the majority of the population are such that only the official powers-that-be can represent its interests. These needs are the usual commodities of life: food, housing, clothing, leisure, education, entertainment. The opposition is compelled to divert attention to problems which affect separate groups of the population and to the excesses of the regime. So the problem of democratic freedom seems a vitally important question for only a tiny part of the population. For the reasons we have shown the tendency to suppress discontent and opposition is the prevalent one. The apparatus of repression can deal with this task fairly easily because it has the support of the population itself, or if not, the most it has to face is very weak opposition.

It does not follow from what has been said that one can eradicate the opposition in this society once and for all. Once it has arisen the opposition becomes a constant factor in social life. The birth of opposition is just as much an inescapable consequence of the whole form of social life as is its repression. It is a normal phenomenon in any large conglomerate of people. One can calculate *a priori* all possible variants of the manifestations of discontent and all the actions that the powers-that-be could take to cut it off. But for the time being one has no grounds for hoping that the opposition will play a discernible role in the country's social structure. For the time being the position is that the population of a Communist country is on balance inclined to fight for its unfreedom against those who wish to free it.

THE SOURCES OF PROGRESS

Communist society contains a strong tendency towards stagnation, but it would be a big mistake to think that it is incapable of making any progress. Here I do not have in mind any substantive changes in the social structure and its principles, but an improvement in the living conditions of certain groups of the population and of the country as a whole. The sources of this improvement are scientific and technical progress, the general growth of culture and the rationalization of communal activity, the organs of government and different departments of the Communist system.

Moreover the functions of carrying out reform and ensuring progress belong to the government. Here progress mainly comes not from below (which is usually the source of stagnation) but from above. This is the case because of the position, role and resources of government in Communist society. Government does not merely take the functions of ensuring progress into its own hands. It is forced to do so by the whole organization and activity of the people. All significant reforms are carried out as decisions of those at the top. The population and the communes are conditioned to receive every improvement and deterioration as a gift from above. The government fulfils its progressive function not out of a love of progress nor from a wish to make humanity happier, but in accordance with what is best for its self-preservation and the preservation of a stable, cohesive society.

The point is that in this society the government must provide some improvement merely to preserve the status quo, otherwise society will start to go downhill. That is why progress takes the form of compulsory reform and orders from above. Besides, the government has to over-come the inertia and the opposition of the popular mass. This partly explains the irritation of the authorities at oppositionists who criticize shortcomings and demand quick reforms. The representatives of the ruling circles know by experience that even a small step in the direction called for by the critics needs effort and time, while most of the critics' demands are in practice not realizable at all, or, if they were, would cause even greater shortcomings.

The position of the central government in society and its real possibilities of initiating reform are such that, even if the government wished to bring about the progress which people desire, nothing would come of it. For instance, the abolition of the system of residence permits (i.e. the limita-tions on the choice of residence and the attachment of the citizen to his place of residence), or the introduction of unlimited access to higher educational establishments to all final-year students, or a decision not to bind people to primary collectives, i.e. not force people to be members of communes and other such 'progressive' measures, would lead to such catastrophic consequences for society that the country would find itself in a state of emergency. The Communist system is stable only on condition that the limitations I have mentioned are religiously observed. All sorts of experiments have been tried in the Soviet Union in order to improve this or that aspect of the life of the country. But in the majority of cases they have ended in failure, and only those reforms survived which helped to establish the most natural state of affairs; and that is what exists now.

THE IRREVERSIBILITY OF SOCIAL EVOLUTION

There are people in the world who hope that the Soviet Union and other Communist countries will return to their pre-Communist state. These hopes are vain. Communism is not a temporary historical zigzag. It is an epoch. It is not a political regime which can be discarded and replaced by another while the country's social order is preserved. Communism itself is a profound social order on which everything else is based. One can remove and replace 'everything else', but not that which forms its basis. Communism amounts to such a revolution in social organization that its reversal via an evolutionary return journey is logically excluded. In reality only two roads are possible. The first is the physical destruction of the Communist bloc. One cannot confidently predict what would grow out of its ruins. Most likely a society of the same kind but with even crueller regimes. The second road is via the struggle for the blessings of civilization on the basis of Communism itself. But this will require time and sacrifices. The destiny of civilization depends on people's ability to make sacrifices and to find the means of self-defence. Nothing is absolutely predetermined. Communism is only the beginning of a new cycle of history, not the end of human suffering.

Communism, like any other type of society, brings with it its own forms of inequality, injustice and the exploitation of some people by others. But it also brings something much more serious: a 'natural selection' of the most adaptable individuals reinforced by a systematic ideological conditioning of the population. This system inevitably sets the socio-biological evolution of mankind in a certain direction. Society produces the citizens that suit it; i.e. people who are only able to live in society of the Communist type and who in turn preserve the cohesion of that society in their own way of life. Mankind's switch to Communism is not just a new play in a theatre performed by the same old actors. The actors themselves have changed and they will have to act out the old plays in a new style and to invent new ones of their own.

Well, now, Homo sapiens, what happens from now on is up to you alone! Show what you are good for, O Highest Form of Life!

Literature in Paladin Books

Fear and Loathing in Las Vegas   £2.50   □
Hunter S Thompson
As knights of old sought the Holy Grail so Hunter Thompson entered
Las Vegas armed with a veritable magus's arsenal of 'heinous chemi-
cals' in his search for the American Dream. 'The whole book boils
down to a kind of mad, corrosive poetry that picks up where Norman
Mailer's *An American Dream* left off and explores what Tom Wolfe
left out.' *New York Times*.

Marx's Grundrisse   £1.95   □
David McLellan
A substantial set of extracts from the classic work in which Marx
develops an account of the process of alienation, analyses the nature
of work, and develops a vision of the fully automated society in
which social wealth could be devoted to the all-round development
of the faculties of each individual. Edited by one of Britain's leading
Marxist scholars.

The Stranger in Shakespeare   £2.50   □
Leslie A Fiedler
A complete radical analysis of Shakespeare's work which illuminates
the sub-surface psychological tensions.

Confessions of a Knife   £1.95   □
Richard Selzer
In this riveting book Richard Selzer seeks meaning in the ritual of
surgery, a ritual 'at once murderous, painful, healing, and full of
love'. In the careening, passionate language of a poet he speaks of
mortality and medicine, of flesh and fever, and reveals something of
the surgeon's thoughts and fears as he delves into the secret linings of
our bodies. 'I was awed and strangely exalted.' Bernard Crick, *The
Guardian*.

Notes from Overground   £2.50   □
'Tiresias'
Man is born free, and is everywhere in trains. More than a commu-
ter's lament, *Notes from Overground* is a witty, wide-ranging medita-
tion on a horribly familiar form of travel.

To order direct from the publisher just tick the titles you want
and fill in the order form.   PAL8082

Politics in Paladin Books

Aneurin Bevan (Vols 1 & 2) £2.95 ☐
Michael Foot each
The classic political biography of post-war politics.

Karl Marx: His Life and Thought £3.95 ☐
David McLellan
A major biography by Britain's leading Marxist historian. Marx is shown in his private and family life as well as in his political contexts.

The Strange Death of Liberal England £2.95 ☐
George Dangerfield
This brilliant and persuasive book examines the forces responsible for the breakdown of Liberal Society in England. At once an exposition of the causes for the dissolution of a great period in English history and a reluctant threnody for the age of purpose and order. 'A brilliant analysis.' *The Times*.

War Plan UK £2.95 ☐
Duncan Campbell
The secret truth about Britain's civil defence. The result of more than five years' research, the book reveals the incredible history of how one government after another has planned to protect itself and survive. 'An unprecedented break in the secrecy surrounding civil defence planning.' *The Observer*. Fully illustrated.

The Plutonium Business £2.95 ☐
Walter C. Patterson
Concerned by the rarity of uranium at the dawn of the nuclear age, physicists came up with a compelling concept – the fast breeder reactor. But uranium is no longer scarce and a great vision has gone sour. In this searching analysis, Patterson argues that the plutonium people must be stopped – for the sake of all humanity.

To order direct from the publisher just tick the titles you want and fill in the order form. PAL7482

Biography in Paladin Books

Mussolini £2.95 ☐
Denis Mack Smith
'Will be remembered . . . for the exceptional clarity and brilliance of the writing. His portrait of Mussolini the man is the best we have.'
Times Literary Supplement.

Karl Marx: His Life and Thought £3.95 ☐
David McLellan
A major biography by Britain's leading Marxist historian. Marx is shown in his private and family life as well as in his political contexts.

Miles Davis £3.95 ☐
Ian Carr
'For more than a quarter-century Miles Davis has personified the modern jazz artist. Mr Carr's biography is in a class by itself. He knows his music and his Miles' *New York Times Book Review*

The Life of William Blake £1.95 ☐
Mona Wilson
Poet, printer, prophet, philosopher – the importance and influence of William Blake's extraordinary vision continue to grow. Originally published in 1927, this is still the most authoritative biography available.

Freud: The Man and the Cause £3.95 ☐
Ronald W Clark
With great objectivity, Ronald Clark provides a new, human and revealing portrait of the physician who changed man's image of himself. He also gives a clear and balanced account of the medical world of Freud's early professional years; the conception of psychoanalysis; Freud's struggle for recognition; and how his achievement can be viewed in the light of contemporary knowledge. Illustrated.

To order direct from the publisher just tick the titles you want
and fill in the order form. PAL4182

All these books are available at your local bookshop or newsagent, or can be ordered direct from the publisher.

To order direct from the publishers just tick the titles you want and fill in the form below.

Name _____

Address _____

_____

Send to:
Paladin Cash Sales
PO Box 11, Falmouth, Cornwall TR10 9EN.

Please enclose remittance to the value of the cover price plus:

UK 45p for the first book, 20p for the second book plus 14p per copy for each additional book ordered to a maximum charge of £1.63.

BFPO and Eire 45p for the first book, 20p for the second book plus 14p per copy for the next 7 books, thereafter 8p per book.

Overseas 75p for the first book and 21p for each additional book.

Paladin Books reserve the right to show new retail prices on covers, which may differ from those previously advertised in the text or elsewhere.